Evelyn S. (Evelyn Shirley) Shuckburgh

A History of Rome for Beginners

From the Foundation of the City to the Death of Augustus

Evelyn S. (Evelyn Shirley) Shuckburgh

A History of Rome for Beginners
From the Foundation of the City to the Death of Augustus

ISBN/EAN: 9783744766524

Printed in Europe, USA, Canada, Australia, Japan

Cover: Foto ©ninafisch / pixelio.de

More available books at **www.hansebooks.com**

A History of Rome

For Beginners

*From the Foundation of the City to the
Death of Augustus*

By
Evelyn S. Shuckburgh, M.A.
Late Fellow of Emmanuel College, Cambridge

With Illustrations & Maps

London
Macmillan and Co., Limited
New York: The Macmillan Company
1897

All rights reserved

PREFACE.

THIS book is not a mere abbreviation of my larger history. It has been written for the most part entirely afresh, and is intended to put the main events of Roman history, both in regard to political development and imperial extension, as simply and briefly as seemed possible. Military events, as such, are given with a minimum of detail, and the effects of campaigns have been dwelt upon rather than their nature and circumstances. Whether I have succeeded in hitting the mean between a Primer and an advanced History I must leave to the judgment of my readers: but that has been my aim. The book, such as it is, owes a great deal to the kind criticisms and suggestions of my friend and former colleague at Eton, Mr. C. H. EVERARD, formerly Fellow of King's College, Cambridge, whose patience in reading the proofs I am glad to acknowledge with gratitude.

E. S. SHUCKBURGH.

June, 1897.

MAPS AND ILLUSTRATIONS.

	PAGE
GREAT DIVISIONS OF ITALY,	3
LATIUM,	6
TOGA AS WORN AT SACRIFICES,	9
PLAN OF ROME,	14
AGGER OF SERVIUS,	15
CLOACA MAXIMA,	17
TEMPLES OF VESTA AND CASTOR RESTORED,	24
AUGUR WITH LITUUS,	27
GROTTA CAMPANA AT VEII,	33
SHRINE OF THE PALLADIUM,	42
SAMNITE WARRIOR,	48
APPIAN WAY,	51
MAP OF COLONIES IN ITALY,	56
TOMB OF SCIPIO,	58
MAGNA GRAECIA,	62
ROMAN SOLDIERS,	69
SELLA CURULIS AND FASCES,	72
SICILY,	78
TOGA,	85
ROMAN COUNTRY HOUSE,	91
SPAIN,	94
GALLIA CISALPINA,	99
ROMAN STANDARD BEARER AND SOLDIER,	103

MAPS AND ILLUSTRATIONS.

	PAGE
BUST OF SCIPIO,	111
As WITH PROW OF SHIP,	115
ROUND DINING COUCH,	132
RUINS OF CARTHAGE,	136
TRICLINIUM,	140
As WITH HEAD OF JANUS,	154
REMAINS OF CAPITOLIUM,	173
ASIA MINOR,	177
MITHRIDATES EUPATOR,	178
GLADIATORS FIGHTING,	199
STATUE OF POMPEY,	211
BUST OF CICERO,	229
TESTUDO,	245
BUST OF CAESAR,	246
CENTRAL ITALY,	256
HARBOUR OF BRUNDISIUM,	258
MAP OF N. GREECE FOR CIVIL WAR,	263
NORTH AFRICA,	272
COIN OF IULIUS CAESAR AND AUGUSTUS,	273
COIN OF ANTONY AND CLEOPATRA,	302
ROMAN EMPIRE IN TIME OF AUGUSTUS,	308
M. VIPSANIUS AGRIPPA,	315
ROSTRA OF IULIUS,	326

CHRONOLOGICAL TABLE OF PRINCIPAL EVENTS.

I.

Regal Period, B.C. 753–509.

Institutions traditionally assigned to each reign.

CHAPTERS I.-II., pp. 1-27.

(1) ROMULUS.
   Roman Senate of 200. Three Patrician Tribes—Ramnes, Tities, Luceres. Thirty wards or *curiae*, hence *Comitia Curiata*. Clients.

(2) NUMA POMPILIUS.
   Religious Institutions—Pontifices, Augures, Vestal Virgins, Salii.

(3) TULLUS HOSTILIUS.
   Destruction of Alba Longa. Plebs. Legend of Horatii and Curiatii.

(4) ANCUS MARCIUS.
   Pons sublicius. Conquest of Latin Towns. Mamertine Prison. Settlement of Plebs on the Aventine.

(5) LUCIUS TARQUINIUS PRISCUS.
   Farther conquest of Latium. Public works; cloacae, Circus Maximus. 100 new members of Senate *(patres minorum gentium)*.

(6) SERVIUS TULLIUS.
   Five classes according to census of income, subdivided into *centuriae*, hence *Comitia Centuriata*. He includes the Quirinal, Viminal, and Esquiline hills within the walls. Four city and seventeen country tribes, whence afterwards the *Comitia Tributa*.

(7) LUCIUS TARQUINIUS SUPERBUS.
   Conquest of Gabii. Great temple of the Capitol. Expulsion of the Tarquins.

II.

Early Republic. Struggles of Plebeians for Political and Social Equality with Patricians, B.C. 509–286. Parallel with the gradual subjugation of Italy by Rome, B.C. 509–266.

CHAPTERS III.–V., pp. 28-66.

CONSTITUTIONAL HISTORY—
STRUGGLES OF THE PLEBEIANS.
B.C.

509. Two consuls first appointed. *Lex Valeria de provocatione.*

507.

496.

495.

493. First secession of the Plebs. Five Tribuni Plebis and two Aediles.

488.

486. Agrarian law. Spurius Cassius put to death.

485-479. Seven consecutive consulships of the Fabii.

479.

472. *Lex Publilia.* Tribunes and Aediles to be elected by *Comitia Tributa.*

458.

457. Ten Tribunes instead of five.

451. First Decemvirate. Ten tables.

450. Second Decemvirate. Two new tables (Appius Claudius).

449. Second secession of the Plebs. Valerian and Horatian laws. *Comitia Tributa* of equal authority with the *Comitia Centuriata*; persons of the Plebeian magistrates sacred.

445. *Lex Canuleia. Conubium.*

ROMAN CONQUEST OF ITALY.

Defection of Prisci Latini.
First treaty with Carthage.

Rome besieged by Etruscans (Porsena).

Latin war. Battle of Lake Regillus.
Wars with Volscians, Sabines, and Aurunci.

League with 30 Latin towns (Spurius Cassius).

War with Aequians and Volscians (Coriolanus).

War with Aequians and Veientines.

Legend of Fabii at the Cremera.

War with Aequians and Sabines. Two battles of Mount Algidus. Cincinnatus Dictator.

[Frequent border warfare with Volscians and Aequians.]

PRINCIPAL EVENTS. xiii

CONSTITUTIONAL HISTORY—
STRUGGLES OF THE PLEBEIANS.   ROMAN CONQUEST OF ITALY.
B.C.
444. *Tribuni militares consulari
potestate*, to which Plebeians were eligible, instead
of Consuls.
Censorship.
439. Spurius Maelius killed.
434. Censorship restricted to 18
months.
421. Plebeians admitted to the
Quaestorship.
405-396. Pay first given to soldiers.   Siege of Veii—taken by Camillus
                                          as Dictator (396).
390. People much impoverished.   Battle of the Allia. Destruction of
                                          Rome by Gauls.
389-8. The restoration of the City   Latins, Hernicans, Aequians, Etrus-
    carried out unskilfully.   cans in arms.
    Commons much burdened
    with debt.
387.   *Four new tribes* (25).
384. Manlius executed for treason,   Gauls conquered by Camillus near
    owing to his support of   Alba.
    debtors.
376. Licinian rogations proposed
    —(1) Relief of debtors;
    (2) Regulation of the *Ager
    publicus*; (3) One Consul
    to be Plebeian.
367. Licinian rogations passed.
366. First Plebeian Consul. Praetor
    appointed, a patrician.
365-345. Death of Camillus.   Wars with Faliscans, Tarquinii,
                                          Etruscans, Cisalpine Gauls.
                                          Stories of Curtius, T. Manlius
                                          Torquatus, M. Valerius Corvus.
                                          Treaty with Carthage.
358.   *Two new tribes* (27).
351. First Plebeian Censor.
343-340.   First Samnite war: battles, Mt.
                                          Gaurus, Suessula.
339. *Leges Publiliae*—(1) *Plebis-
    cita* to bind all citizens,
    and to be confirmed before-
    hand by the Senate; (2)
    One Censor to be Plebeian.
340-338.   Latin war: battles, Veseris, Tifer-
                                          num. Latin League dissolved.
334. First Plebeian Praetor.
332.   *Two new tribes* (29).

CONSTITUTIONAL HISTORY—
STRUGGLES OF THE PLEBEIANS.
B.C.
327-304.

326. Abolition of *nexum* by *Lex Poetilia*.

312-308. Censorship of Appius Claudius Caecus.

302.

296. Plebeians admitted to the sacred colleges by *Lex Ogulnia*.

298-290.

286. Third secession of Plebs. *Lex Hortensia*. The *auctoritas* of the Senate not required for laws passed by *Comitia Tributa*, which thus becomes a sovereign legislature.

283.

281-275.

275-266. Plebeian Aediles and Tribunes obtain the *entrée* of the Senate.

[The only political distinction between the orders remaining is now in favour of the Plebeians, who alone are eligible to the Tribunate.]

ROMAN CONQUEST OF ITALY.

Second Samnite war: battles, Caudine Forks, Cinna, Bovianum.

Aequians subjected.

Third Samnite war. Samnites joined by Gauls, Umbrians, and Etruscans: battles, Sentinum in Umbria (295), P. Decius Mus and Q. Fabius; Aquilonia (293). C. Pontius is at length defeated and captured by Q. Fabius.

Quarrel with Tarentum.
War with Pyrrhus: battles, Pandosia or Heraclea (280), Asculum (279), Beneventum (275).

Capture of Rhegium and Tarentum. Gradual reduction of Samnium, Lucania, Bruttium, and their security by a system of *civitates foederatae* and *coloniae*.

[All Italy south of the Rubicon subject to Rome.]

III.

Contest with the Gauls, Carthage, and Macedonia. Formation of Empire beyond Italy, B.C. 264-133.

CHAPTERS VI.-X., pp. 67-140.

FOREIGN WARS.
B.C.
269. FIRST PUNIC WAR, to help the Mamertines of Messana against Hiero and Carthage.

PRINCIPAL EVENTS.

FOREIGN WARS.	PROVINCES.
B.C.	
269. Victory of Claudius in Sicily. Storm of Agrigentum. Romans build a Fleet. Victory of Duilius at Mylae, B.C. 260 Of Regulus at Ecnomus, B.C. 256, who is defeated and captured in B.C. 255. Victory at Panormus over Hasdrubal. Defeat of Claudius at Drepanum, B.C. 249. Victory of Lutatius off the Aegates insulae, B.C. 241.	
241. Peace with Carthage. Carthaginians evacuate Sicily.	Sicily made a Roman Province. (1) *Six new tribes* (35).
238. Carthage exhausted by three years' war with her mercenaries. Romans demand from Carthage the cession of Corsica and Sardinia.	
235-225. Hamilcar in Spain. Hannibal's oath.	Corsica and Sardinia made a Roman Province. (2)
228. War with Illyrians under Queen Teuta.	
224-222. Defeat of Gauls near Telamon in Etruria, and at Clastidium (Marcellus).	
221. Hannibal succeeds Hasdrubal in Spain.	
219. Hannibal takes Saguntum.	
218-202. SECOND PUNIC WAR.	
First Period. Roman Disasters.	
218. Ticinus, Trebia.	
217. Trasimenus Lacus (Flaminius).	
216. Cannae (Varro).	
216-212. Revolt of Capua, Lucania, Bruttium, Greek towns in Italy and Sicily (Q. Fabius Maximus Cunctator). Hannibal takes Tarentum.	
[213-205. War with Philip of Macedon.]	
Second Period. Roman Successes.	
212. Marcellus takes Leontini and Syracuse. Fall of Publius and Cn. Scipio in Spain.	

CHRONOLOGICAL TABLE OF

FOREIGN WARS.	PROVINCES.
B.C.	
211. Recovery of Capua.	
209. Recovery of Tarentum by Fabius.	
208. Fall of Marcellus.	
207. Hasdrubal defeated on the Metaurus (Claudius Nero, M. Livius Salinator).	
210-205. In Spain Publius Cornelius Scipio gradually expels Carthaginians, and conquers the whole country.	
Laevinus reduces Sicily.	
Hannibal retires to Bruttium.	
204. Scipio goes to Africa: blockades Utica.	
203. Hannibal recalled to Carthage.	
202. Battle of Zama. End of the war.	
200-197. Second Macedonian war.	
Battle of Cynoscephalae (T. Quinctius Flamininus).	
Proclamation of the freedom of Greek cities from Macedonia.	
200-191. War with Insubrian and Boian Gauls.	Gallia Cisalpina a Roman Province. (3)
197.	Two Provinces in Spain. (5)
190. War with Antiochus, K. of Syria.	
Battle of Magnesia (L. Cornelius Scipio Asiaticus).	
183. Death of Hannibal and Scipio.	
171-168. Third Macedonian war.	
Battle of Pydna (Aemilius Paulus).	
155-150. Spanish war (Marcellus and Lucullus).	
149-146. War against pseudo-Philip of Macedonia and against the Achaeans. Corinth destroyed (Mummius).	Macedonia made a Roman Province. (6) Illyricum made a Roman Province. (7)
149-146. THIRD PUNIC WAR. Destruction of Carthage.	Africa made a Roman Province. (8)

FOREIGN WARS.	PROVINCES.
B.C.	
146-140. War against Viriathus in Spain.	Achaia (Peloponnesus) attached for certain purposes to the province of Macedonia.
143-133. Numantine war (Scipio Africanus the Younger).	

IV.

Period of Civil Strife in Italy, and of Foreign Wars, ending in Revolution, B.C. 134–30.

CHAPTERS XI.-XX., pp. 141-302.

ITALY.	THE PROVINCES.
B.C.	
134-132. Servile war in Sicily.	
133.	The royal property and rights in Pergamus bequeathed to Rome by Attalus III.
133-131. Measures of Tiberius Gracchus as to the *Ager Publicus*.	
129.	Asia made a Roman Province. (9)
121. Reforms of Gaius Gracchus	The Province of Transalpine Gaul first formed about this time. (10)
113-101. Cimbrian war.	
Aquae Sextiae, B.C. 102.	
Vercellae, B.C. 101.	
111-106. Iugurthine war (Marius).	
90-88. Social war. Battle of Asculum.	
Admission of Italians to citizenship.	
88. Flight of Marius.	
87-84. First Mithridatic war (Sulla).	
87. Return of Marius, and massacres in Rome.	
86. Death of Marius.	
83-72. War with Sertorius in Spain.	
82. Sulla appointed Dictator.	
80.	Cilicia made a Roman Province. (11)
79. Sulla abdicates.	
78. Death of Sulla. Attempted revolution of Lepidus.	
74.	Bithynia made a Roman Province. (12)
73-71. War with Spartacus and his gladiators (Crassus and Pompey).	

b

CHRONOLOGICAL TABLE OF

| ITALY. | THE PROVINCES. |

B.C.
70. Pompey and Crassus Consuls.
68-67. Pompey conquers the Pirates.
63. Cicero Consul. Catiline's conspiracy crushed. Birth of Augustus.

Syria made a Roman Province. (13) Crete and Cyrenaica made a Roman Province, though not fully organized till B.C. 27. (14)

61. Caesar pro-praetor in Spain.
60. First Triumvirate, informal agreement between Gn. Pompeius, C. Iulius Caesar, M. Licinius Crassus.
59. Caesar's Consulship.
58-51. Caesar's victories in Gaul.
56. Conference at Lucca.
53. Defeat and death of Crassus at Carrhae.

The rest of Gaul added to the Province.

52. Pompey sole Consul for six months.
49. Caesar crosses the Rubicon. Civil war. Pompey crosses to Epirus.
48. Caesar defeated near Apollonia, Pompey at Pharsalia. Murder of Pompey in Egypt.
46. Defeat of Pompeians at Thapsus, Africa.

Caesar, perpetual Dictator and Imperator, Consul for ten years.

45. Battle of Munda, Spain. Defeat of Gnaeus and Sextus Pompeius.

Transalpine Gaul administered as three Provinces—Narbonensis, Belgica, Celtica. (16)

44. Assassination of Caesar.
44-43. Octavian takes the field against Antony at Mutina.
43. Defeat of Antony at Forum Gallorum near Mutina (13th April). Death of the Consuls C. Vibius Pansa and A. Hirtius. Formal appointment of Octavian (now called Gaius Iulius Caesar Octavianus), Antony, and Lepidus as *triumviri reipublicae constituendae.*
42. Battles of Philippi. Death of C. Cassius and M. Brutus.

PRINCIPAL EVENTS. xix

ITALY.	THE PROVINCES.
B.C.	
41-40. Perusian War. L. Antonius and Fulvia against Octavian and Agrippa.	
40. Peace of Brundisium between Octavian and Antony.	
39. Treaty of Misenum with Sextus Pompeius.	
38. Hostilities with Sext. Pompeius recommence.	
Marriage of Octavian with Livia.	
36. Sextus Pompeius defeated at Naulochus by Agrippa.	
Lepidus expelled from the Triumvirate.	
Antony meets with disasters in the Parthian war.	
35. Sextus Pompeius killed in Asia.	
33. Antony returns to Greece from unsuccessful Parthian war.	Mauretania made a Roman Province. (17)
31. Battle of Actium.	
30. Death of Antony and Cleopatra.	

V.

Reign of Augustus.

CHAPTER XXI., pp. 303-326.

THE REIGN.	THE PROVINCES.
B.C.	
30. *Tribunicia potestas* and other honours voted to Caesar Octavianus (Augustus).	Egypt made a Province with special regulations. (18)
29. Three triumphs 'over Illyricum,' 'for the battle at Actium,' 'over Cleopatra.' The temple of Ianus closed.	
27. Division of Provinces between the Imperator and the Senate.	
The title of AUGUSTUS bestowed on Caesar.	
26. Augustus conducts a campaign against the Cantabri.	

THE REIGN.	THE PROVINCES.
B.C.	
25. The temple of Ianus again closed.	Galatia and Lycaonia made a Roman Province, but Mauretania restored to its king. (19)
24. Expedition of Aelius Gallus in Arabia.	
23. The *tribunicia potestas* for life, *proconsulare imperium* for five years (always renewed) secured to Augustus. Death of Marcellus, nephew of Augustus.	
21. Agrippa marries Iulia, daughter of Augustus.	
20. Return of the standards and prisoners from Parthia. Birth of Gaius Caesar, son of Agrippa and Iulia.	
19. Cantabri subdued by Agrippa. Death of Vergil.	
18. Campaign of Drusus against the Rhaeti.	
17. Birth of Lucius Caesar, son of Agrippa and Iulia.	
16. Defeat of M. Lollius by the Sicambri.	
16-14. Augustus in Gaul.	Cisalpine Gaul organized as four Provinces—Narbonensis, Aquitania, Lugdunensis, Belgica (with Germania, Superior and Inferior); and later two Alpine Provinces— Alpes Maritimae and Alpes Cottiae. (22)
13-12. German wars of Drusus, step-son of Augustus, against the Frisii and Chauci. Death of Lepidus.	
12. Death of Agrippa.	
11-10. Campaigns of Drusus in Germany against the Cherusci and Chatti, and of Tiberius in Dalmatia.	District between Rhine and Elbe occupied.
9. Death of Drusus.	Moesia made a Roman Province about this time. (23)
8. Successes of Tiberius in Germany. Death of Maecenas and Horace.	
7. Association of Tiberius in the *tribunicia potestas*.	
A.D.	
2. Death of Lucius Caesar.	

PRINCIPAL EVENTS.

	THE REIGN.	THE PROVINCES.
A.D.		
4.	Death of Gaius Caesar. Tiberius adopted by Augustus, receives *tribunicia potestas* for ten years.	
5-6.	Campaigns of Tiberius in Germany.	
7-8.	Wars in Pannonia and Dalmatia.	
9.	Campaigns of Tiberius in Dalmatia. Defeat and death of Varus in Germany.	Roman frontier pushed back to the Rhine.
11.	Tiberius crosses the Rhine, but fights no battle.	
14.	Death of Augustus (19th August).	

FAMILY OF AUGUSTUS.

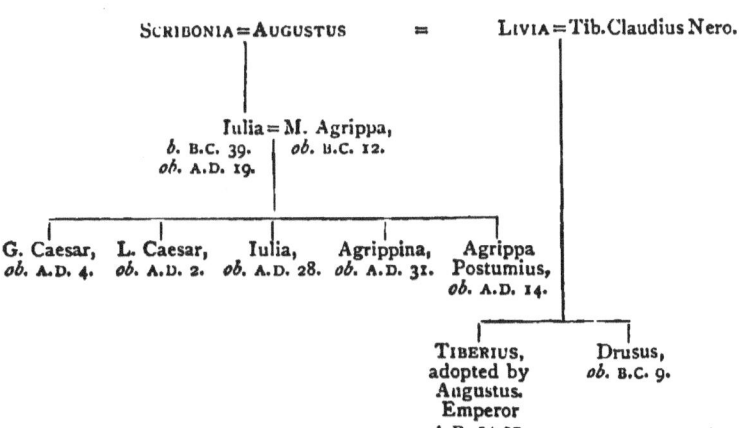

A HISTORY OF ROME FOR BEGINNERS

HISTORY OF ROME FOR BEGINNERS.

CHAPTER I.

1. *The nature and importance of Roman History; the influence of Rome in consolidating Europe.* 2. **Italy** *at the time of the foundation of Rome; the different extensions of the name; the inhabitants of the Peninsula—the* **Etrusci,** *the* **Umbrii** ; *the* **Sabellians,** Lucani, Apuli, Bruttii, Sabines, Samnites ; *the Greeks in Italy.* 3. **Latium** ; *the* prisci Latini ; *the surrounding tribes*—Aequi, Hernici, Volsci, Aurunci ; *the larger* **Latium** *and its division from* Campania. 4. *Beginnings of Rome ; Trojan legend and Alba Longa ; the excellent site of Rome ; the colony from Alba on the Palatine.* 5. **Roma Quadrata**—*its foundation on the Palatine ; meaning of the term ; other villages on neighbouring heights ; date of foundation ; the Romans' view of their own origin.* 6. *Extension of Roma Quadrata to* **Rome of the seven hills** *during the reigns of the kings* —(1) *Romulus,* (2) *Numa Pompilius,* (3) *Tullus Hostilius,* (4) *Ancus Marcius,* (5) *Tarquinius Priscus,* (6) *Servius Tullius,* (7) *Tarquinius Superbus ; Colonies during the Regal period.* 7. *Summary of the position of Rome in* 509 B.C.

1. **What Roman History is.** The history of Rome is the history of one city in a district of Italy called Latium, which, beginning as a small settlement of a pastoral folk, with a territory round it stretching scarcely five miles in any direction, gradually absorbed under its rule not only all Italy, but all Spain, Gaul, Sicily, and other islands, Illyricum and the provinces on the Danube, Greece

and Macedonia, Northern Africa and Egypt, Asia Minor and Syria. Some of the countries thus conquered had already an ancient civilization superior to her own; but some were still rude and barbarous. The former retained after their conquest much of their old civilization and principles of internal government; and largely modified the Roman character and habits by the introduction of their own. So that Greece, for instance, was said to have 'captured her captor.' In less civilized countries the Romans impressed their ways of thought, and their methods of government more completely. But in all alike they made changes. They enforced obedience to law; they opened up the countries by making roads, building bridges, and establishing some sort of control over robbery and disorder; and, when they became a naval power, and by the conquest of the great mercantile city of Carthage gained the chief control of the Mediterranean Sea, their generals after a time drove away the pirates which infested it, and forced them to allow peaceful merchants to carry on their trade safely. The general result was that in a large part of Europe the nations began to be acquainted with each other, to live in something of the same way, and to recognize something of the same principles of law and government. And this effect has never quite died away, though the great Empire of Rome has been from various causes broken up into separate countries. This is a great thing to have done, and it makes the history of Rome of very great importance in the history of the world.

2. **Italy at the time that Rome began.** The name *Italia* was not originally applied to the whole of the peninsula which we call Italy. During the time of the Republic it strictly only meant that part of it which was south of the river Rubicon on the east and the river Macra on the west, with the intervening range of the Apennines. The district between this line and the Alps

was called Gallia Cisalpina, and that between the Maritime

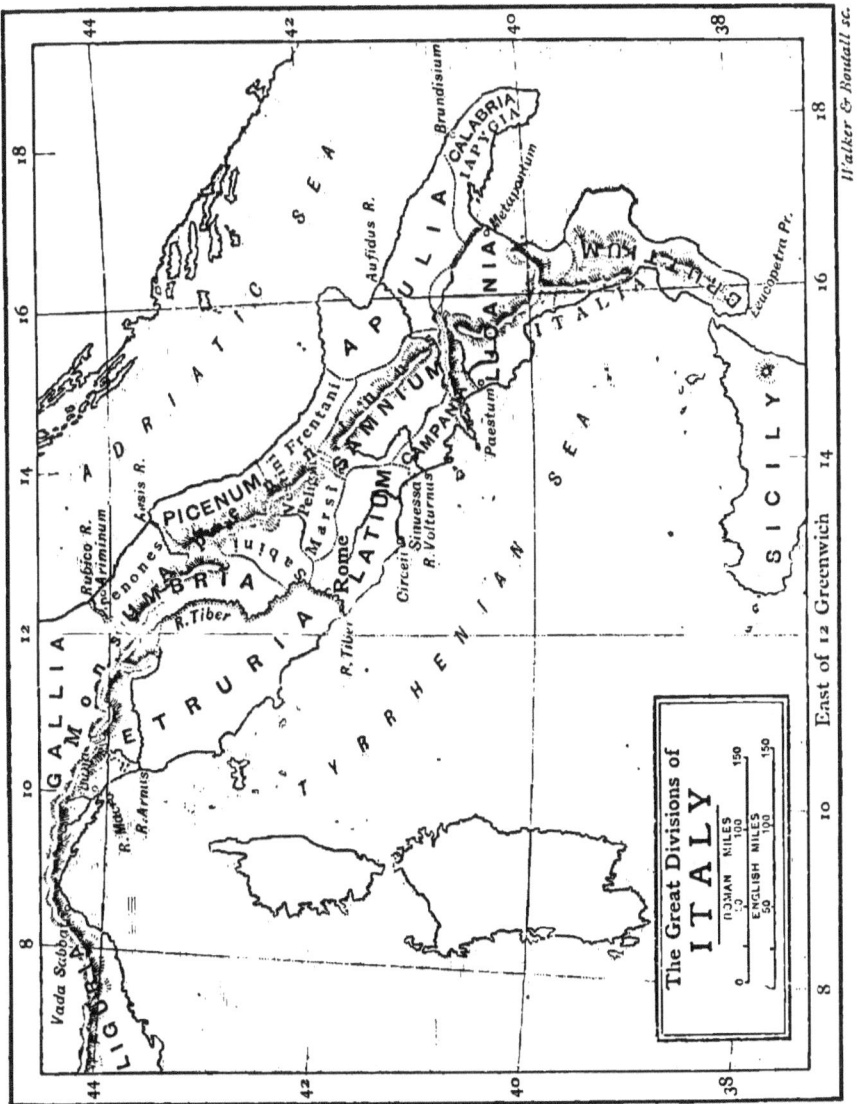

Alps and the sea was called Liguria. But even the rest of the peninsula south of the Rubicon had not always been called Italia. This name (derived by some from *vitulus*, a steer, but which the Romans as usual traced to a king Italus) was once confined to the south-western extremity or toe of Italy, taking in the two districts of Lucania and Bruttium, south of a line drawn from Metapontum to Paestum. As late as the third century B.C. the word Italy was not generally used for more than this. The districts were each called by their separate names. Between the Tiber and the Apennines lived the **Etruscans**, who were a very ancient race, supposed to have come from Asia, though we know nothing for certain about their origin. They had once lived beyond the Apennines in the valley of the Po, but had been driven southward by the Gauls. They were a very powerful and enterprising people, famous for their works in bronze and iron, and for their activity at sea. They had some settlements farther south, in Campania, and in the early times of Rome they were trying to get the mastery of still greater portions of Italy. We must notice them particularly, for they had a great influence on Rome at the beginning of her history; and many Roman customs, especially as to the worship of the gods and the taking of omens and auguries, were derived from them. East of the Upper Tiber a great people called **Umbrians** had settled, and given their name to the district of *Umbria*. They were akin to the Latins, of whom we shall have to speak by and bye. But though they were a brave and hardy people, who long retained their independence, they never became a real nation, and were afterwards absorbed by Rome. A number of other tribes, sometimes classed under the common title of **Sabellians**, had settled in the central mountain district, and spread out into various districts. Thus the *Lucani*, *Apuli*, and *Bruttii*, who gave their names to the southern districts of Italy, were off-shoots from them, as well as some smaller tribes in the east and centre.[1]

[1] Peligni, Picentes, Marsi, Marrucini, and Vestini.

But the members of this stock, which are of most consequence to note in relation to Rome, are (1) the **Sabines**, who occupied the country on the right bank of the Tiber, bounded on the north by its tributary the Nar. It is a hilly district, and the Sabines were a hardy simple folk, who, as we shall find, had a considerable share in creating Rome. (2) The **Samnites**, who, occupying the mountainous district of Central Italy, and spreading westward into Campania, held out against Rome longer than almost any people in Italy. Lastly, round the southern, south-western, and south-eastern shores of Italy there were so many Greek colonies that the whole district was sometimes called Magna Graecia; and though these towns were all at last conquered by Rome, they had great influence on the habits, literature, and religion of the Romans.

3. **Latium when Rome began.** The Latins, who seem to have been kinsmen of the Umbrians, occupied a small district south of the Tiber, as far down the coast as Antium, and up the Tiber, on its left bank, as far as about Crustumerium, where the Sabines begin. This is what is meant by *Vetus Latium*, 'Old Latium.' Round them were a number of other tribes, who were apparently of what is called the Oscan race, branches of the *Osci* or *Opici*, who had inhabited the country before the Latins came, though they were originally of a kindred stock. The chief of these were the *Aequi*, *Hernici*, *Volsci*, and *Aurunci*. The early history of Rome is much concerned with these peoples. The Romans are always fighting with them, especially with the Aequi and Volsci. And naturally so: for when Rome was first established, she was looked upon as a dangerous intruder even in *Vetus Latium*, and the towns of the Latin League were glad of the help of these tribes in attacking her; and when she became mistress of *Vetus Latium*, these same tribes hindered her extension southwards and eastwards into Campania and Samnium, and, being on her frontiers, were

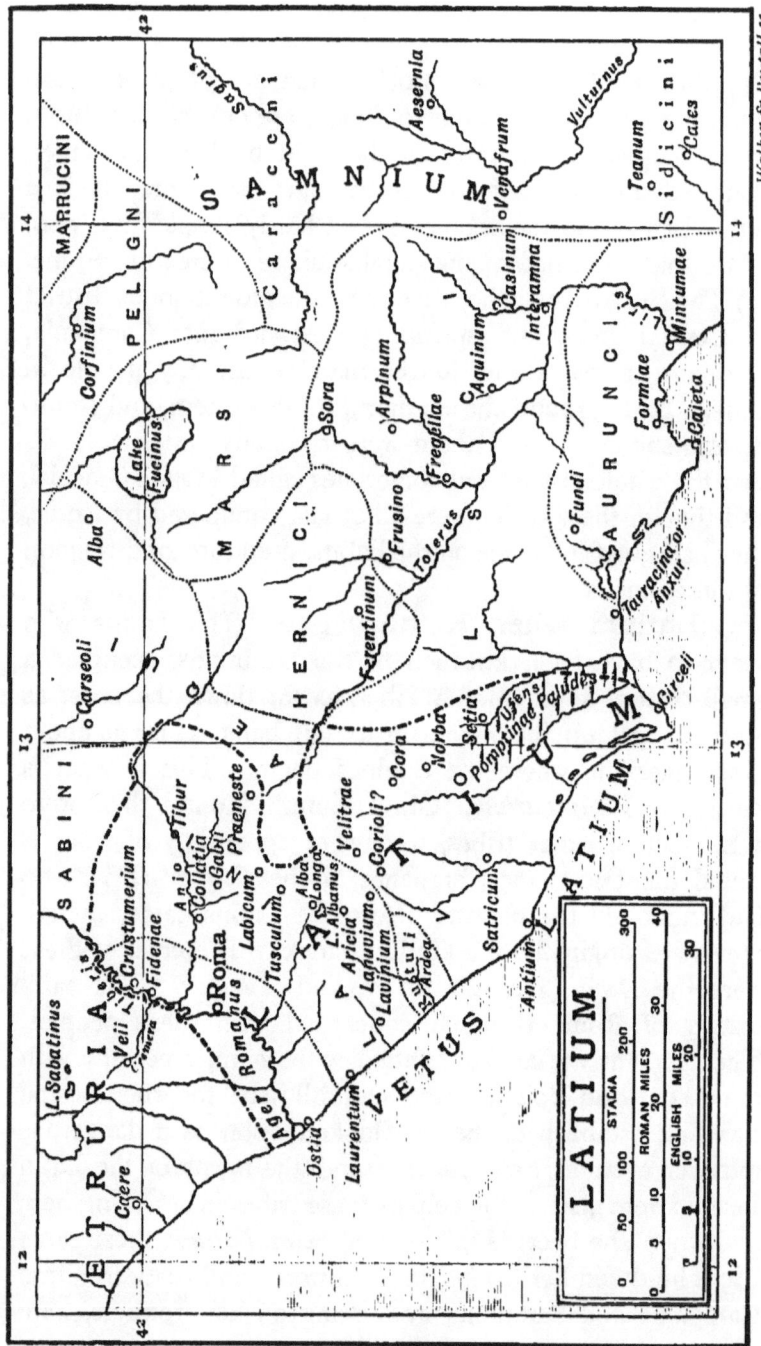

constantly quarrelling about mutual raids and robberies. When Rome had conquered them, the name of Latium was extended to the river Liris, the boundary between it and Campania, and to the mountains on the East, where the *Marsi* still shut them off from Samnium.

4. **The Beginnings of Rome.** So great was the popularity and influence of the poems of Homer, that wherever Greek was known we find legends of the foundation of towns by one or other of the heroes mentioned in the *Iliad*. Thus the native legends as to the beginning of Rome were soon embellished with Greek stories. The Trojan Aeneas was said to have escaped from the burning city, and with his companions, after many years of wandering, landed in Latium, married the daughter of king Latinus, and established a new kingdom at Lavinium, which his son Ascanius transferred to Alba Longa. Many generations afterwards, Romulus and Remus, sons of Ilia by Mars, being exposed by their usurping uncle, Amulius, as infants to perish on the river side, where afterwards Rome was built, and suckled by a she-wolf, were brought up by a shepherd. Eventually they restored their grandfather Numitor to his kingdom at Alba Longa, and founded a new city for themselves on the Palatine Hill, where, according to another legend, there had already been a Greek settlement made by an Arcadian named Evander. The site of Rome was a good one for a city in early days for many reasons. There was a hill suitable for a citadel, which was important among hostile neighbours; the Tiber formed a convenient highway to the sea, which was yet far enough off (about 18 miles) to prevent the town from being exposed to sudden attacks of pirates; and there were several hills of moderate elevation close by, where others of the shepherd folk could fix their dwellings, which were eventually to be enclosed within one wall and form a single city. It is very likely that there is thus much truth in the

legend of Romulus, that those who first settled on the Palatine came from Alba Longa, either attracted by the greater convenience of the site, or driven away by earthquakes and volcanic eruptions, to which the natural features of Alba show that at one time it has been subject. Alba Longa was the head of the League of 30 Latin towns, or at any rate the temple on the top of the Alban Mount (now called *Monte Cavo*) was the place of joint worship for the League. But soon after the rise of Rome Alba Longa was destroyed; and if many of its inhabitants had already migrated to Rome, and it had also suffered from volcanic eruptions, this destruction would not be difficult.

5. **Roma Quadrata.** A new city, then, was begun upon the *Mons Palatinus*, a hill just west of a bend of the Tiber, rising now 166 feet above the level of the sea, and then considerably more. Perhaps it was only a village at first: but fortifications would soon be needed, and the fortification of old Italian towns was begun with certain solemn rites, which were probably taught by the priests of the Etruscans. A day having been selected when the omens were favourable (*auspicato*) a hole was dug, into which corn and other necessaries of life were thrown. If the new inhabitants came from different lands, they brought clods of earth from these to throw in also. The hole was then filled up, an altar erected on the spot, and an offering made upon it. This was called a *Mundus*, and was to be the central hearth (*focus*) of the new city. Then the founder, with his toga girt in what was called the 'Gabine fashion' (*cinctu Gabino*), *i.e.* with one end covering his head, traced the line of the new walls with a plough drawn by a white ox and white cow, lifting the share at the spots where the gates were to be. In some such way, no doubt, the city on the Palatine was founded, and called Rome. The term *Roma Quadrata*, 'Square Rome,' is properly applied only to the *mundus* made in its centre; but

was used afterwards to describe this old original Rome, which, as far as it can be traced, was of rectangular shape, including the Palatine, part of the low ground between it and the river, the *Vallis Murcia* on the west (where was

THE TOGA AS WORN AT SACRIFICES.

the *Circus Maximus*), the valley on the south between the Palatine and Mons Coelius, and part of the depression to the south-east where was afterwards the forum. There were perhaps villages on the other hills, and tradition tells us of Saturnia on the Mons Capitolinus, as well as of a town of some sort on the Ianiculum across the river; but this fortified village on the Palatine was always regarded as the nucleus of the future Rome, and the date of its foundation as that of the foundation of Rome. The Roman antiquaries of a later time calculated this to be the **third year of the Sixth Olympiad**, answering to B.C. 753, and the day to be the 21st of April, the first day of the pastoral festival called Palilia. There is this historical importance in the story of the new foundation from Alba, and the foreign origin of Alba itself, that though Rome was avowedly made up by a mixture of inhabitants, some Sabine and some Latin, the Romans proper always regarded themselves as something distinct in origin and race, and the *nomen Latinum*, that is, the inhabitants of the cities in *Vetus Latium*, as belonging to a people originally different, though eventually absorbed by the stronger stock.

6. Extension of Rome during the Kingly Period to B.C. 510. At first this new city was governed by kings; and during their reigns Rome was not only extended so as to embrace the seven hills within a wider ring of walls, but for a time at least extended her power beyond the *ager Romanus* (originally, as I said, not more than five miles in any direction from the walls) over some of the other towns of Latium. We will trace this gradual extension of city and territory through the periods traditionally assigned to the seven kings (though these dates have no historical value), leaving for another chapter the account of the people and their institutions.

(1) **Romulus** (? 753-716). To Romulus, the name-hero and first king of the new city, is ascribed its first extension, so as to embrace six other minor villages, not apparently included within the wall, but joined on to it by trenches or embankments, so that a national festival called *Septimontium* was instituted to commemorate the

union. He is said also to have attracted settlers to his new town by opening an *asylum*, a place of refuge for those who were obliged to fly from their own towns, on the eastern slope of the Mons Capitolinus, over which therefore he must have had control. He also obtained wives for his new citizens by the famous device of inviting the neighbouring peoples, Latins and Sabines, to a great festival, and detaining their unmarried women; the result of which was that the people of Antemnae, Caenina, and Crustumerium, when they attempted to avenge their wrong, were conquered and subjected to Rome; while the king of the Sabines took the Mons Capitolinus, but eventually agreed to unite with Romulus, and jointly rule an extended city. These legends accounted for the undoubted fact that there was a large Sabine element in the inhabitants of Rome (illustrated by the name of *Quirites*, used to late times for 'citizens,' from the Sabine *quiris*, 'a spear'), and that in very early times the Mons Capitolinus was united with the Palatine as one city. But to Romulus still further extensions were attributed. He conquered Fidenae, secured a district on the right bank of the Tiber, repelling attacks from the Etruscan Veii, fortified the Capitol and the Aventine, and included in the limits of the city, though not of the walls, the Caelian and Quirinal hills.

(2) **Numa Pompilius** (? 715-672). The next reign was said to have been a peaceful one. Numa Pompilius came from the Sabine town Cures, and introduced various religious institutions and ceremonies, and, above all, was believed to have taught a truer mode of calculating the seasons. Though no extension of Rome or its territory is directly attributed to him, yet, as one thing said of him is that he introduced the habit of dividing lands of conquered towns among citizens, the annalist seems to conceive of his reign as one of increased dominion.

(3) **Tullus Hostilius** (? 672-640). The next king, Tullus Hostilius, conquered and destroyed Alba Longa, removing its inhabitants to Rome, and settling them on the Mons Coelius, thus doubling the number of the inhabitants. He also warred with the Sabines to protect Roman traders engaged at the fair at the temple of Feronia, near Mount Soracte. The removal of the Albans to Rome, and the control of the Alban mount by the Romans, with its temples (which were left intact) as the central meeting ground of the League of Latin cities, was a direct bid on the part of Rome, not only for admission to the Latin League, but also for supremacy in it. It is the first step therefore of Roman expansion in the direction of Latium.

(4) **Ancus Marcius** (? 640-616). The result of the taking of Alba Longa was hostility on the part of the Latins. Ancus Marcius, the next king, was thought to be unwarlike, and the Latins at once invaded the Roman territory. But not only was the attack repelled, but some of the Latin towns were taken by him, and their inhabitants transferred to Rome. This required a still farther increase of the area of the city, protected by some kind of defence. Accordingly to Ancus Marcius was attributed a trench called the *fossa Quiritium*, which perhaps formed a loop including the Aventine, and joining some entrenchments already existing on the Coelian hill with the Tiber. To him is also attributed the construction of the 'Bridge of Piles,' the *Pons Sublicius*, the first bridge over the Tiber at Rome, which appears to indicate that the Romans were now strong enough to keep possession of the right bank of the Tiber, in spite of the Etruscans. Lastly, he founded the harbour town of Ostia, which shows that the commerce of Rome was becoming important.

(5) **L. Tarquinius Priscus** (? 616-578). With the reign of the elder Tarquinius we begin to have some

clearer indications of history; and many of the things attributed to this family are at any rate to be assigned to this period. He was an Etruscan from Tarquinii, and as the Etruscans were at this time very powerful it may be that an Etruscan dynasty at Rome means that for a time at least Etruscan influence was paramount there too. However this may be, he proved an able sovereign, and did much to extend Roman power. He fought with the Sabines, took Collatia, and gradually reduced most of the Latin towns to own the supremacy of Rome. As a sign of this supremacy he planned and began a great temple of Jupiter on the Capitol, to be the central place of worship for all those who were ruled by Rome. The enlargement of the ground now considered to be within the city of Rome is also shown by the laying out of the Circus Maximus for races in the valley between the Palatine and Aventine, and the construction of *cloacae* or sewers to drain the valleys between the hills, and the wide meadow (300 acres) called the *Campus Martius*. These *cloacae*, many of them of astonishing size and structure, formed a network of drainage over the whole site of the enlarged Rome, and one especially, the *Cloaca Maxima*, was always believed to have been the work of Tarquinius Priscus. A considerable part of it still remains, and justifies the description of Pliny that it was 'large enough for a cart loaded with hay to pass up.'

(6) **Servius Tullius** (?578-534). The work of the next king was to recognize and perpetuate this extension and importance of the city. His constitutional changes will be discussed in the next chapter; but here the chief thing to notice is that in his time Rome had so outgrown its old limits that it became necessary to plan a far greater wall to enclose all that needed protection. This is said to have been actually begun by Tarquin, but its completion is always assigned to Servius Tullius. It enclosed the

seven hills—the Mons Capitolinus, Palatinus, Aventinus, Coelius, Esquilinus, and the Colles Viminalis and Quirinalis —in a circuit of about five miles, with nineteen gates, and remained the boundary of the city for nearly seven hundred years; one part of this fortification, from the Porta Collina to the Porta Esquilina, was formed by cutting through the

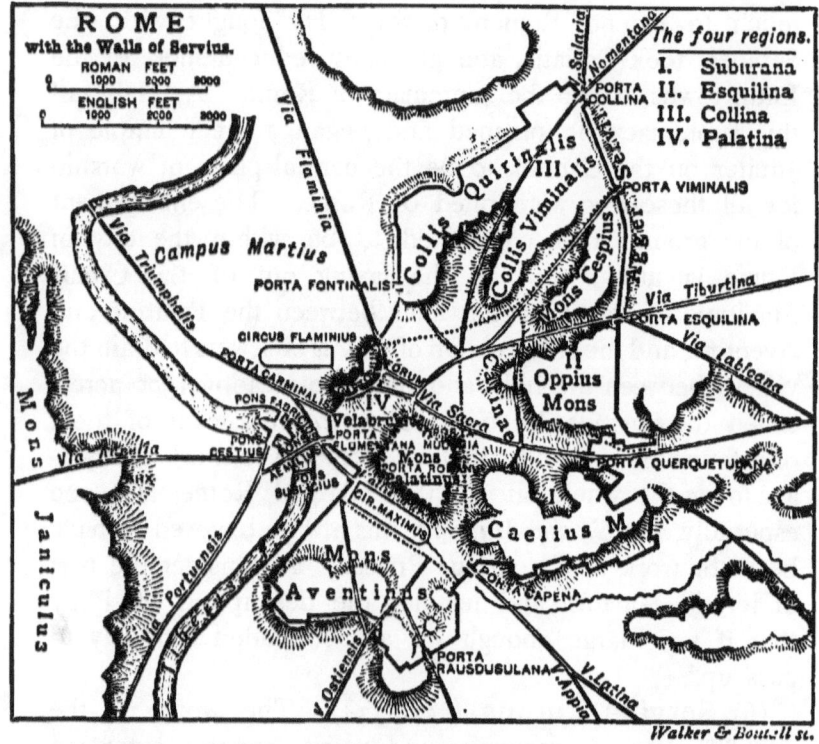

spurs of the Quirinal, Viminal, and Esquiline hills with a ditch, and piling up the earth into a lofty platform, which was called the *Agger Servii*. Thus Rome, as we shall have to think of it for the whole period of its history contained in this book, was formed. The supremacy which she was now exercising in *Vetus Latium* Servius maintained more by diplomacy than wars; he induced the Latin cities to

THE DITCH OF THE AGGER OF SERVIUS.

join in building a temple of Diana at Rome to be a common place of worship, and did something to confirm peaceful relations with the Sabines.

(7) **L. Tarquinius Superbus** (? 534-510). The next king, though his tyrannical rule brought an end to royalty at Rome, and roused opposition in Latium, yet did something while in power to maintain and extend the prosperity of the city. One of the grievances against him was that he compelled the people to work at his great public buildings, which shows that he was beautifying or improving Rome. The great temple of Capitoline Jove, begun by his father, was all but completed when he was driven out; many of the *cloacae* are attributed to him; and he forced the Latin towns to submit to his orders, and the Latin youths to enlist in his armies. He even began to push the Roman arms beyond the limits of *Vetus Latium*, and was the first to fight the Volscians, and to prevent by negotiations the raids of the Aequians upon Latium. Colonists now also were sent out to form outposts of defence at Signia, near the borders of the Hernici, to Suessa Pometia, on the borders of the Pomptine Marshes, and to Circeii, on a promontory in the territory of the Volscians. To all towns which showed signs of disliking the Roman yoke he was ruthless, and he was besieging Ardea of the Rutulians when the revolution occurred which expelled him from Rome.

7. **Rome at the beginning of the Republic,** B.C. 509. Thus at the beginning of the Republic we take up the history of Rome with a city as wide in extent as it was to the last day of the Republic and the first two centuries of the Empire. Its *ager* or territory indeed was quite insignificant; but it had already asserted itself as a predominant member of the Latin League, and was beginning to push its aims beyond and to found colonies. Moreover, however small its territory, the wealth and activity of its

people was shown by the vast public works which had been constructed; and this wealth could only have come from foreign traffic, the importance of which is proved by the rise of the harbour town of Ostia, conveniently situated (as its name denotes) at the mouth of the Tiber.

THE "CLOACA MAXIMA" IN ITS PRESENT STATE.

CHAPTER II.

THE PEOPLE OF ROME.
THEIR GOVERNMENT AND RELIGION.

1. *The origin of the name of* **Rome.** 2. *The original settlers in Rome shown to be a pastoral people by legends and their earliest festivals, the Lupercalia and Palilia; they early became also a mercantile and warlike people.* 3. *The* **Populus Romanus,** *the gentes, the three tribes, thirty curiae, and* Comitia Curiata. 4. *The kingship not hereditary; the king supreme; he forms and consults the senate; is judge and lawgiver; the interregnum; the earliest example of the administration of justice by a king.* 5. *The Roman* **Plebs**; *its probable origin; its inferior position; the reform of Servius Tullius recognizes it as part of the populus.* 6. *Abolition of the life kingship and substitution of two yearly officers.* 7. *The religion of Rome; ceremonies introduced from Etruria; the country gods; amalgamation with Greek divinities.*

1. **The Name of Rome.** It was a common practice among historians in ancient times to assume the name of a city to be derived from that of its founder. This may sometimes have been the case; but where no exact information existed it was at least as possible that the name given to the founder was invented from that of the city. We can never be certain which of these two things happened in regard to Rome. Some have regarded the name as derived from 'Ρώμη, 'strength,' others from an Italic word *rumon*, 'a river,' as though the Alban settlers coming from their city among the hills thought of it

chiefly as the 'river town.' To the ordinary Roman it was the town of *Romulus*.

2. **The Earliest Inhabitants.** There is good reason for believing that the earliest settlers on the Palatine and other hills were a pastoral people. The most ancient festivals were connected with pastoral life,—the *Lupercalia* on the Palatine were in honour of the Wolf-ward god; the *Palilia* in honour of Pales, a god or goddess of shepherds, celebrated on the 21st April, the day traditionally assigned to the foundation of the city. Moreover, the *forum Boarium*, 'the cattle market,' was one of the most ancient sites marked off for a special purpose, and near it was the altar of Hercules, who, before he was confused with the Greek Herakles, was himself perhaps a Latin god of the sheep-fold. That the Romans very soon became a mercantile people also was owing chiefly to the conveniency of the river. Thus the earliest settlement outside Rome was said to be Ostia, at the mouth of the Tiber, attributed to Ancus Marcius; and that Roman trade before long became important is shown by the fact that immediately after the fall of the kings a treaty was made with the great commercial people of Carthage. That the Romans became a nation of soldiers was again the result of their position in the midst of hostile tribes. For a long time there was no regular army; all citizens were liable to be enrolled when a fighting-force was required, and were disbanded when the need was over, returning to their farms and shops, from which they had been summoned. At first then we must think of the Romans as mainly a nation of farmers and shepherds, gradually adding to those employments that of merchants and soldiers.

3. **The Populus Romanus.** Of course, as soon as a regular community was formed there must have been some plan of conducting its business and regulating the conduct of its members. The *populus Romanus* consisted

of the members of certain *gentes* or families who formed the early settlers, and had perhaps certain definite portions of land which they held in common. Attached to them in very early times were certain *clients* or dependants, the protection of whom was the concern of the heads of the gentes. The earliest division of the *populus* of which we hear is into three tribes—Ramnes, Titii, and Luceres —who may perhaps have formed separate villages which afterwards combined. But we know nothing for certain about them; only that all the early divisions are by threes,—whence the name 'tribe,' afterwards used of any division. The first division of which we can give any account is that into thirty *curiae* or wards, including both the members of the gentes and their clients (*gentiles* and *gentilicii*). When the people had to meet for any purpose, such as the election of a king, the trial of a citizen, the making of a law, or the proclaiming peace or war, they voted according to these curiae, and the meeting was called *Comitia Curiata*.

4. **The King and the Interreges.** The existence of a king is assumed in the early legends of Roman history. But there is no trace in the earliest of these legends of an hereditary monarchy. Romulus is naturally the king of his own city. He calls on the heads of the 100 gentes to furnish him with a council or *senate* with which he may consult; but it cannot control him by its advice, and he alone can summon either it or the people to a meeting; he alone acts as supreme judge and lawgiver. On his death, however, there is no question of a son (if he had one) to succeed him, and still less any question of doing without a king. The only way of getting a king was for the people to elect one, and until they have done so the Senate appointed an *interrex* to hold office for five days, and then give place to another. The time which elapsed between the two reigns was called an *interregnum*. The

king was elected for life, and had absolute power; acted as judge, commanded armies, declared war, made peace. A story is told of the third king (Tullus Hostilius) which shows us the most primitive way in which the king administered justice. In a war with the Albans it was agreed that three champions on either side, the Horatii for the Romans, the Curiatii for the Albans, should decide the dispute. Two Horatii and two Curiatii fell, and the surviving Horatius killed the last Curiatius. But as Horatius was being conducted home, bearing the spoils amidst a rejoicing people, he saw his sister weeping, for she had been betrothed to one of the Curiatii. In a passion of resentment he struck her dead. The king summoned the curiae and named two men (*duoviri*) to pronounce sentence on him. They sentenced him to be flogged and beheaded. Then he 'appealed' to the people, and the appeal was allowed by the people on condition of certain rites of purification being performed by him. This is the earliest specimen of trial for what was called *perduellio*, 'act of war' or 'treason.' The king does not appoint men to try the case: he decides on the guilt himself; they are only to pronounce the sentence according to the laws or customs existing. Here, too, we have the 'people' acting as a body, and voting by their curiae, and above all we have the principle, which was of great value afterwards, that against the sentence of a magistrate there was an appeal to the people. Of these things we shall hear again. The earliest known institutions therefore are, as often, illustrated by a story or legend.

5. **The Roman Plebs.** We said that the Roman *populus* consisted of the members of the gentes and their clients. But there were other people living in Rome who were neither of these. They had come there as settlers, or traders, or perhaps sometimes as captives, who, though forced to remain, were not made slaves. These people seem

to have had no civil rights or duties. They did not vote in the curiae, or serve in the army. They could not hold any office or marry among the citizens. They could however trade, and perhaps farm the land under the citizens; and gradually came to look upon themselves as citizens with a claim to fuller rights. They were called the Plebs or multitude. Now in the reign of the sixth king, Servius Tullius, according to general tradition, a change was made which recognized these Plebeians as part of the Roman people, and imposed fresh duties upon them, though it did not do much at first towards putting them on an equality. First of all he divided all the people, that is, the members of the old gentes (who now began to be called Patricians) and the Plebeians alike, into twenty-one tribes, according to where they lived,—four being city tribes, seventeen country tribes, in order that a census might be taken of their property. Then the whole people were again divided into five 'classes,' according to the amount of property which they possessed. All who possessed property valued at 100,000 *asses* were in the first class, 75,000 *asses* in the second, 50,000 *asses* in the third, 25,000 *asses* in the fourth, 12,500 *asses* in the fifth. Of course the members of the first class were much smaller in number than those in the other classes, and yet the first class was subdivided into eighty centuries, as they were called, while the second, third, and fourth were arranged in forty each, and the fifth in thirty-two.[1] This division into classes and centuries was originally for military purposes, and at the head of the whole list were eighteen centuries of knights or cavalry, which had always been the most important part of the Roman army. All who had less than 12,500 asses were grouped in one century and

[1] *Classis* probably means a 'summoning'; *Centuria*, properly a group of one hundred, afterwards used for a 'division' of any number. The *as* originally a pound of copper, but eventually reduced to half an ounce.

were called *capite censi*, 'numbered by the head.' When the army was called out, only those were summoned who were in the five classes. Thus the whole people were in a way recognized and organized, and were now all 'citizens,' though not with equal rights; and if it was necessary for them to meet to vote on peace or war, or to make laws, they voted in these centuries, the majority of each century determining the vote of that century, and the majority of centuries determining the whole vote. Such a meeting was called *Comitia Centuriata*. We are not told of any such meetings during the kingship; but directly the kings were expelled we begin to hear of them. Notice that this manner of voting gave a great advantage to rich men. For the first class had eighty centuries, and the equites or knights had eighteen, and the two together made up more than half of the whole number (193), though they must have contained much fewer individuals than the other centuries. Again, though the whole people soon began to vote in this assembly, the old distinction between the members of the original gentes, now called Patricians, and the rest of the multitude, or *Plebs*, was still maintained; for the former only were thought capable of holding offices, of making valid marriages, or taking the auspices. The old *Comitia Curiata* still existed for certain purposes, conferring *imperium* on magistrates, and recording wills and adoptions, but had none but formal powers.

6. **The Kingship is abolished, and two yearly Magistrates elected in its place**, B.C. 510. Thus there was a Roman people, though with a wide division of ranks. Presently they had reason to wish for a new form of government. The seventh king, Tarquinius, called the Proud, proved to be a tyrant. He neglected or insulted the Senate and oppressed the people by imposing heavy labour upon them in his buildings and other works, while members of his family began to show the vices

TEMPLES OF VESTA AND CASTOR. ANERS'S RECONSTRUCTION.

and licence which generally accompanied regal power. Therefore for the time both classes of citizens were united in a resolve to get rid of him. While he was encamped opposite Ardea, which he was besieging, a party of discontented nobles got possession of the city, and were able to repel his efforts to regain it. The army which he had with him at Ardea declared against him also; and he was obliged to seek safety in exile. Popular indignation is said to have been specially roused at the time by the wrong done by the king's son Sextus Tarquinius to Lucretia, the wife of Collatinus, and it was decided by a vote of the people that they would never more elect a king for life, or call any man king again; but would, in his place, elect every year two magistrates to do the duties which the king had been accustomed to perform. These magistrates seem at first to have been called *Praetores* or 'leaders,' but later on they were called *Consules* or 'colleagues.' This took place in B.C. 510, and the first consuls were elected for the year beginning in March B.C. 509. In times of danger, however, when the rule of one man was necessary, the kingly power was revived temporarily under another name, by the consul naming a *dictator* who, while in office, had absolute power over all citizens and over the consuls themselves.

7. **The Religion of the Romans.** The Romans were a very religious people, and were very particular as to the proper manner of worshipping the gods. Early in their history we hear of a great change in this matter. Many religious ceremonies, the right way of learning the will of the gods by observing the flight of birds, by the flash of the lightning, by the feeding of sacred fowls, or by inspecting the entrails of victims at sacrifices, were introduced from Etruria. But before this there was a religion existing among them, traces of which remained both in the city and country, and especially in the country. The

chief feature of this religion was that it personified and tried to appease the various forces of nature which affected the cultivation of the land and the safety or destruction of crops and cattle. The chief deities were *Saturnus*, the god of sowing; *Iovis*, the sky-god; *Ianus*, the two-headed sun-god, facing east and west; *Tellus*, the earth-goddess, mother of all living things; *Lupercus*, 'the wolf-ward'; *Flora*, the goddess of flowers; *Minerva*, guardian of olives; *Ceres* and *Liber*, goddess of corn, and god of wine; *Lympha*, the source of water; and *Bonus Eventus*, the Good Luck, on which the farmer depended for the reward of his labours. These were all beneficent deities. But the powers of evil were also propitiated: *Mavers*, the god of destruction and murrain, and *Robigus*, god of blight. The worship of these gods mostly took the form of cheerful village festivals along with offerings of the first-fruits of field and fold. Very early, however (from the south or through Etruria), Greek theology found its way into Rome. New deities were worshipped, or the old Latin deities were identified with the Greek: Iovis with Zeus; Liber with Bacchus; Ceres with Demeter; Minerva with Pallas Athene; Diana (Iana or Luna) with Artemis; Mavers (or Marmar) with Ares; and a temple to Apollo, the sun-god, was very early built in Rome. Whatever gods were worshipped, it was thought so important that the worship should be conducted in the right way, that a college of pontiffs, the head of which was called Pontifex Maximus, was appointed to superintend all matters connected with religious observances; and another college, of Augurs, to preserve and carry out the rules which ought to be obeyed in taking auspices and interpreting omens. It was the fear of doing anything wrong in religious worship also that caused the appointment of the *rex sacrificulus*, 'sacrificial king'; for there were some sacrifices that, according to tradition, could only be offered by a 'king.' So when the life-kings were abol-

II. THE PRIESTS AND THE VESTAL VIRGINS.

ished it was thought right that there should be some one with the title to perform them. Three of the chief deities had priests specially attached to their service. Such a priest was called a *flamen*. There was a *flamen Dialis* (of Jupiter), a *flamen Quirinalis* (of Romulus or Quirinus), a *flamen Martialis* (of Mars); and originally each Curia had a separate priest of its own called the *flamen Curialis*, or sometimes simply *Curio*. As in each house near the hearth was a shrine of the Lares, or deified spirits of the departed, and of the Penates, the special gods of the family, so the most sacred place in Rome was the temple of Vesta, the altar in which was to the whole city what the hearth was to each house, the centre of its life and worship. Six Vestal virgins had the care of it, whose duty it was to keep the sacred fire ever alight, and to preserve the Palladium and other sacred objects on which the safety of the city was believed to depend. On occasions of public danger the Sibylline verses,—a collection of Greek oracles said to have been given to King Tarquin by a wise woman from Cumae,—were solemnly consulted. No public business was begun without previous religious ceremonies,—prayer or sacrifice, or taking of omens,—and this was strictly maintained all through the time of the Republic and far into that of the Empire, even when a large proportion of the people had learnt to disbelieve or doubt their religion.

AUGUR WITH LITUUS.

CHAPTER III.

FROM THE EXPULSION OF THE KINGS TO THE CAPTURE OF THE CITY BY THE GAULS.

B.C. 509–B.C. 389.

1. *On the fall of the kings Rome loses its high position in the Latin League.* 2. *The Etruscans, under Lars* **Porsena**, *attack Rome, but do not restore the Tarquins; story of Horatius Cocles.* 3. *Stories of Brutus, Caius Mucius, and Cloelia.* 4. *Rome again admitted to the Latin League, after the battle of the Lake Regillus* (B.C. 498); *the policy of* **Spurius Cassius**; *a colony sent to Signia.* 5. *Wars with the Volscians, Aequians, and Sabines; Roman power expanding in Latium, and colonies sent to five towns.* 6. *The Wars with* **Veii**, *and its capture by Camillus; pay given to soldiers; extension of Roman power in Etruria.* 7. *The struggles of the Plebs for equality; harsh laws of debt; first secession and appointment of* **Tribunes** (B.C. 492); *growth of the* Comitia Tributa. 8. *Death of Spurius Cassius; the Plebeians obtain the right of electing Tribunes in the* Comitia Tributa. 9. *The* **Decemvirs**; *the Laws of the Twelve Tables* (B.C. 451-450); *the Plebeians obtain conubium* (B.C. 455); *Tribuni militares consulari potestate; the Censorship; the right of making laws in Comitia Tributa* (B.C. 449); *death of Spurius Moelius.* 10. *The capture and burning of Rome by the Gauls* B.C. 390.

1. **The Latin League.** We have seen that, by the time the Roman people had become strong enough to change its form of government, the city had also risen to a high position among its neighbours. It had not only been admitted as a member of the League of thirty Latin

towns, but had held a kind of commanding position in the League. The last three kings, if they were oppressive at home, had been powerful abroad. But the fall of the kings was followed by the loss of this position. Rome was again isolated, and reduced to its immediate territory, or *ager Romanus*. The chief cause of this seems to have been that the expulsion of the Etruscan dynasty brought upon her the enmity of the Etruscans; and thus, becoming an object of attack on the north, she became a danger rather than a protection to the Latin towns on the south. The banished Tarquins may have helped to stir up this feeling in Etruria; but, though the Etruscans conquered Rome, they did not restore them.

2. **The War with Veii and with Lars Porsena**, B.C. 507. No sooner, however, had Tarquin gone into exile at Caere, than attacks upon Rome by Etruscan cities began. At first these came from Veii, a town about sixteen miles north of Rome, which had long been its rival for the command of the right bank of the Tiber. But presently Lars Porsena of Clusium, led an army drawn from the several cities which formed the Etruscan League against Rome. He seized the heights of Ianiculum, and was only prevented from entering the city by the cutting of the wooden bridge, the *pons Sublicius*. This is the occasion of the famous story of Horatius Cocles, who, with two comrades, defended the northern end of it until the Roman troops that had been beaten on the Ianiculum got across and the bridge had been cut. He then sprang into the river, and swam safely to shore. But though Porsena did not actually take Rome, he forced the Romans to submit to humiliating terms, to give up all arms, to use no iron except for ploughing, to give hostages, and by a present of an ivory throne and sceptre to himself to acknowledge his supremacy. But he did not restore the Tarquins or in any way harm the city.

3. **Stories connected with the Etruscan War.** The Romans cherished more than one tradition connected with these early struggles. One of the consuls elected in the first year of the Republic was M. Iunius Brutus, who had led the revolt against the Tarquins. In that year a conspiracy among the partizans of the fallen king was discovered, and among the conspirators were two sons of Brutus. The father not only pronounced sentence upon them, but witnessed their punishment and execution. Thus the Romans represented their belief that duty to the State was above all other ties. Again, when Porsena was besieging Rome, a young man named Caius Mucius is said to have made his way to the Etruscan camp with a dagger concealed in the folds of his dress. He killed a man clad in purple, whom he believed to be Porsena, but who was only his secretary or judge. He was arrested and hurried before the king, and when threatened with torture by fire if he would not betray the names of his confederates, he thrust his hand into the flame, and allowed it to be consumed, to prove how little could be wrung from him by pain. But he warned the king that three hundred youths had sworn like himself to risk all dangers in order to slay him. A third story is told of the heroic girl Cloelia, who, being given among the hostages to Porsena, escaped her guards, and, plunging into the Tiber, swam back to Rome. The people, however, kept faith with Porsena, and returned the hostages; and this honourable conduct, among other things, induced Porsena to grant better terms to the city when at length he resolved to break up his camp on the Ianiculum and return home, leaving his son Aruns to attack some of the other Latin towns.

4. **Rome once more enters the Latin League**, B.C. 496. For about twelve years after the Etruscan invasion the Romans were engaged in frequent wars with the Sabines

III. EARLIEST ENEMIES OF THE REPUBLIC. 31

or the Latins, till at length the latter are said to have been defeated at the battle of the Lake Regillus (15th July, B.C. 498), when the Romans were commanded by the Dictator Aulus Postumius Albus, and legends say that they were assisted by the great twin brethren, Castor and Pollux, who charged at the head of the Roman cavalry; in celebration of which a solemn procession of Roman knights was held every 15th of July, from the temple of Mars outside the wall to that of Castor and Pollux, which was erected after the battle by Aulus. After this, chiefly by the influence of Spurius Cassius Viscellinus, Rome once more became a leading member in the Latin League, and showed that she was increasing in power and numbers by again sending colonists to Signia, and by raising the number of the rural tribes from seventeen to twenty-one.

5. **The Volscians, Aequians, and Sabines.** But Rome now, as head of the Latin League, had continually to guard against the attacks of two new enemies, the Volscians and Aequians, as well as against those of the Sabines in the north. Most of this warfare consisted of border raids. The smoke from burning homesteads and the flight of rustics gave notice that the enemies were on the march, and the citizens were hastily called to arms, and having repulsed the foe returned to their business or pleasure. If we had been living on the Scotch or Welsh border four or five hundred years ago we should have had a very clear idea of what such warfare was like. Every now and then some battle rose in importance above the rest, and some successful commander celebrated a triumph: that is, he rode on a high chariot drawn by four horses through the forum and up to the Capitol, along what was called the 'Sacred Way,' followed or preceded by men bearing the spoil he had secured, and by the captives whom he had taken. Thus two battles were fought near Mt. Algidus, a little north of Alba, in B.C. 458 and 428; in the former

of which the famous Cincinnatus, who was appointed Dictator whilst working on his farm, conquered the Aequians. With the Volscians they were constantly engaged in a struggle for the possession of Antium, on the Volscian coast, which, with Circeii and Terracina, had in the later kingly period been in some way under the supremacy of Rome. The upshot was that Rome was steadily growing, sending out colonists (really advanced guards of her dominions) to neighbouring towns, such as Velitrae, Norba, Ardea, Labicum, and Circeii. If you will look at a map you will see that this means that Rome is gradually pushing her rule beyond the limits of the old Latium, taking in pieces of the larger Latium, and securing herself against enemies on her borders. It was in the war at Antium that the story is told of Coriolanus, who having won great glory as a soldier, was yet forced to leave Rome because he was hated by the Plebs. He joined the Volscians, and was only deterred from taking Rome by the tears of his mother.

6. **The Fall of Veii**, B.C. 395. But having thus secured herself toward the south, Rome had next to fight for the full and undisturbed command of the right bank of the Tiber. Veii, about sixteen miles north of Rome, was the nearest Etruscan city of any importance, and struggles between the two towns for the possession of the intervening territory were the natural result of their situation. Veii, while supported by the rest of the Etruscan League, could hold its own: and for a long while it had that support, because the Etruscans had settlements in Campania, and wished to keep the road open to them. For some years, however, the Veientines had been quiet. But in B.C. 482 they began again making raids on Roman territory: and finally a great disaster occurred to the Roman arms. An attempt was made to occupy permanently a strong post on the Cremĕra, the river on which Veii stood. The force was composed of the clan of the Fabii, and their dependents, headed by Kaeso

THE GROTTA CAMPANA AT VEII.

Fabius, consul in B.C. 479, who, according to the story, offered to maintain this post without calling out the usual levy. After some months, however, the Veientines tempted them down into the plain, by letting cattle loose in it, lying in ambush themselves to take them at a disadvantage. Nearly the whole clan of the Fabii are said to have been cut off in this affair; and it so encouraged the Veientines that they ventured farther and farther into Roman territory, even occupying Ianiculum, and threatening the city. Throughout the remaining part of the century the war went on, sometimes at long intervals, sometimes year after year; sometimes the Veientines acting alone, sometimes with the assistance of other Etrurian towns, sometimes in alliance with the Sabines. In one of these wars (B.C. 437), in which the Veientines were in alliance with Fidenae, a certain Cornelius Cossus won the *Spolia Opima*, by killing and stripping of his armour the Veientine king or leader, Lar Tolumnius. At length after a truce of twenty years (B.C. 425-450) the quarrel broke out afresh, apparently on the old score of border raiding; and the Romans, now grown stronger from successful warfare with the Aequians and Volscians, determined to put an end to the trouble by the destruction of Veii. The siege lasted nine years, to B.C. 395, and was at length brought to an end by M. Furius Camillus, who is said to have restored discipline to the Roman armies engaged in it so long, and at last to have taken the town by assault, when by means of a mine or tunnel the citadel had been entered and secured. The length to which the siege was protracted may perhaps be accounted for by the Romans having at the same time to resist fresh raids of the Volscians, and to divide their forces in attacks upon other Etruscan towns, such as Falerii and Capena, which were giving help to Veii. But whatever the cause, it had one important effect on the Romans. For the first time Roman soldiers remained in camp throughout the winter, not returning as heretofore at the end of the summer campaign to their homes and their work. This was a step in the direction of making soldiership a profession, instead of an occasional duty falling on all citizens in their turn; and this change was still farther promoted when the soldiers began to receive pay for their services. This last change had been begun, it seems, just before the siege of Veii: but during the nine years' siege it must first have become important, both from the length of time during which some had been receiving pay, and from the burden it must have imposed on the exchequer, which depended principally on the *tributum*, or property tax, paid by the citizens. Then again, the paying of the men made it possible to enlist in the legions those whose property was under the standard of the fifth class, and thus a fresh claim was established on the part of the poorest citizens for equality of rights. The immediate effect of the fall of Veii, however, was the removal of a long-standing danger to Rome. The inhabitants who survived were sold into slavery, and, though the town was not destroyed, it stood a long time empty, and eventually fell into total decay, its building materials being carted off for use elsewhere. It also brought with it a great extension of Roman power in South Etruria, for the capture of Falerii, Volsinii, and Sutrium, which followed it, made the Romans masters of all Etruria south of the Ciminian forest, and as at the same time Gauls coming over the Alps were pressing the Etruscans on the north, Rome had nothing to fear from them for a long time.

7. **The Struggles of the Plebeians for Equality and the Appointment of Tribunes,** B.C. 492. But while the Romans had been engaged in these external wars and in pushing their power farther north and south, there had been going on inside Rome itself another struggle, which was often much influenced by the fact of there being peace or war at the time. When there were dangerous wars on foot then generally the civil dissensions

were suspended: when the wars were ended then the civil dissensions broke out afresh. But sometimes the need for soldiers gave the Plebeians just the opportunity they needed to enforce their rights. The grievances under which the people laboured were twofold: first, poverty, and second, civil disabilities. As to the first, the Romans were still mainly a nation of farmers, and the constant raids of enemies reduced a great many of them to poverty, partly by the actual loss inflicted when the enemy burnt farmsteads and crops, or drove off cattle, and partly by having themselves to quit their holdings to serve in arms against the invader. They were often therefore heavily in debt, and the law of debt made the defaulter practically the property of his creditor. He became at once 'bound' or 'nexus': his creditor might arrest and load him with chains, and after a certain period of time sell him as a slave. Then, again, when Rome took a town a certain amount of its territory was retained as public land (*ager publicus*), which the State let out for a rent or kept open as public pasture. But the rich men managed to monopolize this, either by paying a small rent to the State and then treating it as their own, or by feeding more than their fair proportion of cattle and sheep on the pastures. Many poor citizens, therefore, who had no land of their own, or not enough to support them, thought that this public land ought to be divided among those who had now little or none, or at any rate that the rich men should be restrained from using it unfairly. These were the two material grievances. But, as a rule, the richest men were the Patricians: the bulk of the land still belonged to them: therefore this division of rich and poor answered roughly to the division between the privileged and unprivileged; and the Plebeians thought that if this distinction was done away they would get better terms as to the division of lands and the burden of debt. Thus for the first hundred years of the

III. SECESSION TO THE SACRED MOUNT.

Republic there were constant struggles between the two orders. It began with resistance to the cruel treatment of the *nexi*, or debtors. The only remedy in the hands of the Plebeians was to refuse to give in their names when the levy was needed in the Volscian and Aequian wars. But this was a dangerous measure, for it might expose the city to destruction; and in B.C. 495, when they had done so, they gave way on the promise of relief for the debtors. But when they found themselves more than once deceived as to this promise, the whole armed force, instead of returning to their homes at the end of the campaign, marched in good order to a hill beyond the Anio, afterwards called the Sacred Mount, and there encamped. They 'seceded' and refused to return to the service of the State. The Patricians were alarmed, because being surrounded by enemies they could not afford to be without these men. As a compromise it was agreed that certain Plebeian officers, called **Tribunes**, should be elected, whose duty it should be to protect men from unrighteous or harsh sentences of the consuls; and a law was passed making their persons sacred, and placing those who violated them under a curse. At first there were five and after B.C. 457 ten. They were not magistrates with a fixed sphere of duty. Their primary business was to give aid (*auxilium*) to all citizens who appealed for it against the magistrates; and in order that this aid might always be at hand, they were bound to keep the doors of their houses open and not to be more than one day absent from Rome during their year of office. Gradually they got more extensive powers, but at first their chief function was negative: by their *veto* they could stay proceedings, and prevent a magistrate's sentence being carried out or a law being passed. They must be Plebeians, though at first they seem to have been elected by the *Comitia Curiata*. At the same time new officers called *Aediles* were elected to take cognizance of legal matters which concerned only the Plebs.

8. The Plebeians obtain other Privileges (B.C. 492-391). After the appointment of tribunes the Plebeians gained step by step their civil rights. The points which were in dispute were: (1) That a Plebeian could not marry with a Patrician *(ius conubii)*; (2) that a Plebeian could not hold any magistracy, quaestorship or consulship *(ius honorum)*. The struggles of the Plebs to abolish these disabilities were often mixed up with those caused by poverty. Thus Spurius Cassius, of whose services we have heard before in obtaining the readmission of Rome to the Latin League, being consul in B.C. 486, wished to relieve the poverty of some of the citizens by allotting land taken from the Hernici among poor Romans and Latins, as well as to distribute free some corn that had been sent by Gelo, tyrant of Syracuse. But the Patricians raised a cry that he was attempting to obtain kingly power, and when he ceased to be consul he was condemned and executed. Still the Plebeians did gradually obtain fuller rights. In B.C. 471 a law was passed allowing them to elect the tribunes in their own assembly, which up to this time had been an informal meeting for consultation *(concilium Plebis)*, but from henceforth is called *Comitia Tributa*, because they voted by tribes and not by centuries.[1]

9. The Decemvirs and the Laws of the Twelve Tables (B.C. 451-0). The next advantage gained was that the laws should be engraved on stone or bronze, and exposed in some public place, so that all should know what they had to obey, and what were the limits to the power of the magistrates. This was only gained after a long contention.

---

[1] The Patricians were of course members of the tribes and so could vote if they chose; but they were numerically much inferior, and would have little effect on the result, and they seem for a long time at any rate to have abstained from voting.

Commissioners having been sent to examine codes of law at Athens and other places, in B.C. 451 ten men *(decemviri)* were appointed for a year to draw up the laws, and meanwhile to conduct the government without consuls or tribunes. At the end of the year the work was not done, and a new board of decemvirs was appointed, some of whom had been in the board of the year before. The most influential of them was Appius Claudius, and their government in their second year is said to have been so harsh and bad that they were forced to abdicate, and the Senate having named interreges, the consuls and other magistrates were elected for the next year. But whatever they may have done as magistrates, as legislators they produced a code of laws on twelve tables or slabs, which was the foundation of all Roman law in the future.

Military Tribunes with Consular Power (B.C. 445). The laws of the twelve tables, however, did not alter the relative position of Patricians and Plebeians. They, for instance, confirmed the disability of the Plebeians to marry with Patricians, and in regard to debt were no less harsh than the customs hitherto prevailing. It was definiteness that was gained by a written code, not relief. This relief had to be got by new laws. In B.C. 445 a tribune named C. Canuleius carried a law granting *conubium* or right of intermarriage to the Plebeians; and as a compromise to the demand of the Plebeians to be allowed to stand for the consulship, it was arranged that instead of consuls there should be Military Tribunes appointed each year with consular power, the number varying from three to six. To this office Plebeians might be elected, although no certain instance of one being so elected occurs till B.C. 400. At the same time, however, one important function of the consuls, that of taking the census, and making up the list of the Senate, was transferred to two new Patrician officers called *Censors*, who were to be elected every fifth year for this special purpose and were to hold office for eighteen months. In B.C. 449 again a law was passed recognizing the Plebeian Assembly as having power to pass rules *(plebiscita)* binding on the whole *populus*, though as yet they were in some respects of inferior authority to laws. In B.C. 421 the number of quaestors was doubled and the office was thrown open to the Plebeians. The Plebeians had gained something; but the Patricians had managed to retain a good deal, and Patrician magistrates still ventured to regard advocates of popular rights as traitors. Thus in B.C. 440, during a time of scarcity, a rich knight named Spurius Maelius purchased corn and distributed it to the people. The cry was at once raised that he was aiming at kingly power; and L. Quintius Cincinnatus was named Dictator, with C. Servilius Ahala as Master of the Horse. Ahala was sent to summon Sp. Maelius to the judgment-seat of the Dictator, and when Spurius tried to avoid obedience Ahala struck him dead.

10. **The Burning of Rome by the Gauls** (B.C. 390). But now a great disaster befel Rome. Gauls from beyond the Alps had for many generations been settling in Northern Italy. The earliest immigrants dwelt on the upper parts of the valley of the Po. The latest to arrive were the Senŏnes, who occupied a district on the shore of the Adriatic, between the two streams Utens and Aesis. This district was narrow (for the mountains there come close down to the sea) and not very fertile. They therefore presently tried to get better lands in Etruria. In B.C. 391 they had marched down the valley of the Clanis, and were besieging Clusium, situated on an olive-crowned eminence at the southern extremity of the valley. The people of Clusium had in previous years made some terms of friendship with Rome, and now sent to ask for help. The Romans sent envoys to warn the Gauls 'not to attack allies and friends of the Roman people.' But the

III. BATTLE OF THE ALLIA AND BURNING OF ROME. 41

Gauls answered haughtily; and when a battle took place the Roman envoys took part in it, and one of them slew and spoiled a Gaul. The Gauls sent to Rome demanding that these men should be surrendered to them for this breach of the law of nations. This was refused, and the envoys were even elected consular tribunes. The Senones, reinforced by another tribe, the Lingones, next year marched upon Rome, plundering the country as they went, but not stopping to besiege walled towns. They defeated a hastily enrolled Roman army on the Allia (18th July, B.C. 390), about eleven miles from Rome; and, after halting for two days, entered the city itself. The inhabitants had had time to escape, for the most part, to the empty city of Veii, and the Vestals saved the Palladium by burying it underground. But the army had retired to the Capitol, which was fortified strongly enough to resist an assault; and the Gauls, having plundered and partly burnt the city, sat down to besiege the Capitol. But after some weeks the Capitol still held out under M. Manlius, though once nearly surprised by a scaling party, who found the guards asleep. The cackling of the sacred geese in the temple of Juno, however, roused Manlius, who hurled back the leading Gaul, and saved the Capitol. The Gauls were never good at besieging strong places. They were impatient of the labour and hardship, and now their provisions were running short, and their plundering parties in the surrounding territory were sometimes cut off by Camillus, who was living in voluntary exile at Ardea, having been impeached in the matter of the division of the Veientine spoils in the previous year; the season was unhealthy, and they were suffering from pestilence; finally, news reached them that the Veněti were invading their territories at home. They therefore made terms, received a sum of gold, and departed. The Romans afterwards liked to believe that Camillus, who had been summoned home by the citizens at Veii, and named Dictator, arrived in time to prevent the gold being paid to the Gauls, and defeated and drove them away. But the most that can have happened is that he harassed their rear as they retired. At any rate they went away, and the citizens returned to Rome, elected the magistrates for the next year, and set about restoring the houses and temples which had been burnt. They did not follow any fixed plan in the restoration; and the streets were therefore irregular, and the old sewers often built over, which did not add to the healthiness of Rome, where pestilences were of frequent occurrence. The burning of the city had involved the loss of many historical records, so that the early history of Rome was rendered more uncertain than ever; but otherwise this disaster made little difference in the political situation. The poverty of the farmers, whose homesteads had been burnt or plundered, made them more inclined eventually to agitate for their rights; but no formal change was made at once. The weakness caused by the disaster induced some of their hostile neighbours—Etruscans, Volscians, and Aequians—to attack Rome, and, as usual, when there was war political disturbances stopped.

FOUNDATION OF THE SHRINE IN WHICH THE PALLADIUM WAS KEPT.

CHAPTER IV.

FROM THE CAPTURE OF ROME BY THE GAULS TO THE END OF THE SAMNITE WARS.

B.C. 389–B.C. 290.

1. *Roman conquests in Italy secured by Colonies; struggles with Etruscans, Volscians, and Aequians.* 2. *Intermittent war with the Gauls.* 3. *The Samnites in Central Italy.* 4. *First Samnite War* (B.C. 343-341). 5. *The end of the Latin League* (B.C. 340-338). 6. *Stories of Manlius and Decius.* 7. *The Second Samnite War* (B.C. 326-304.) 8. *The Third Samnite War* (B.C. 298-290). 9. *Civil history from* B.C. *390 to* B.C. *286; abolition of* nexum; *the Licinian rogations; the increasing power of the Plebs; the Censorship of Appius Claudius* (B.C. 312); *Gn. Flavius publishes legal formulae and the fasti.*

1. **Conquests from Etruscans, Volscians, and Aequians secured by Colonies.** The next century saw great changes in Rome, and a great extension of her power in Italy. This dominion, as it was bit by bit obtained, she everywhere secured by planting colonies, that is, by sending a number of citizens to live in the towns which she took or on their territories. To induce them to go, a third of the land belonging to the town was taken from its owners and given to the new settlers. Sometimes the colonists retained their full rights as Roman citizens, and then the colony was called a 'Roman Colony.' Sometimes they only retained some of those rights,—such as the right of intermarriage and trading,—but could not

vote at Rome or hold Roman magistracies; and then the colony was called a 'Latin Colony,' because it had the same rights as certain of the Latin towns, which were very early admitted to this partial citizenship. The government of the colonies was modelled on that of Rome. There were in each yearly magistrates elected and a senate,[1] and they became as it were bits of Rome settled in different parts of Italy, spreading Roman ideas and maintaining Roman authority. They were liable to military service, and formed outposts of the Roman dominions. By observing where they were placed and when they were formed, we may best see how the Roman power in Italy was gradually expanding. This expansion was not effected easily or all at once. The Etruscans tried to turn the Romans out of Etruria south of the Ciminian Forest; the Volscians and Aequians struggled to expel them from towns along the coast of Latium. There was pretty constant fighting for the thirty years following the sack of Rome by the Gauls. But about B.C. 352 the difficulties with these peoples seem mostly to have been overcome. The Roman territory was permanently increased. Six rural tribes were added to the twenty-one already existing, and Roman or Latin colonies were planted at various points of importance to the control of Latium and South Etruria.[2] The two most formidable of the hostile cities of Etruria were Tarquinii and Falerii, but they were about this time (B.C. 351) reduced to accept a forty years' truce; and Caere was deprived of half of its lands, and forced to join Rome with very inferior rights of citizenship.

2. **The Gauls.** Besides these enemies nearer home Rome was much troubled during this period by frequently recurring attacks of the tribes in Cisalpine Gaul,

[1] The two yearly magistrates were called *duoviri*, the senators *decuriones*.
[2] See Appendix to this chapter and map.

who were always restless and looking about for better lands and new chances of plunder. In these wars M. Furius Camillus gained still greater fame, and after his death, in B.C. 365, his son Lucius also won victories over the Gauls. Memorials of these struggles remained to late times in the names borne by certain noble families. Thus Titus Manlius was said to have earned the cognomen of Torquatus by killing a gigantic Gaul, and stripping off his gold bracelet or *torques*; and M. Valerius was called Corvus, because, when fighting in single combat with a Gaul he was helped by a crow, which lighted on his helmet, and attacked his adversary's face and eyes with beak and claw. But as Rome grew stronger and tightened her hold upon Etruria and Umbria, these Gallic raids ceased. From about B.C. 335, for nearly sixty years, we hear no more of them.

3. **The Samnites.** Now as the Romans became powerful in Campania, they found their progress southward hindered by an enemy more difficult to fight than any they had yet encountered. These were the Samnites, who lived in the highlands of Central and Southern Italy. Some of them, seeking better lands, had forced their way into Campania, and, having driven out the Etruscan settlers, had partly amalgamated with the original Oscans. This mixed race called themselves Campani, and their chief city was Capua. Those who remained in the highlands of Samnium presently quarrelled with their kinsfolk in Campania, and tried to wrest from them the Campanian lands and cities. In B.C. 343 they were besieging Teanum, on the borders of Latium and Campania, belonging to an independent tribe called Sidicini, who, failing to get effectual help from the Campanians, sent envoys to Rome. Nine years before the Romans had made some sort of an alliance with the Samnites at their own request; but they were afraid to allow them to possess a town so near

the borders of Latium as Teanum, or to occupy Capua and thus control Campania. They did not, however, go to war at once. They first tried to save the Campanians by sending an embassy to the Samnites, but when that was treated by them with contempt they determined to have recourse to arms.

4. **First Samnite War**, B.C. 343-341. The war lasted nearly three years, and began with victories at Mount Gaurus, Suessula, and Saticula. We know little of its details; but when peace was concluded in B.C. 341 the general result was that Roman instead of Samnite influence prevailed in Campania; and from this forward step the Romans never receded. The constant fighting rendered the army more important, and in the course of this war we are told of a mutiny, in which the soldiers claimed greater equality in the distribution of booty and a fairer law as to the holding of military offices.

5. **The End of the Latin League**, B.C. 340-338. The Campanians were dissatisfied at the result of the Samnite war. They did not feel that it protected them from their enemies, and they resolved, with the help of the Latins, to go on fighting. The Romans held that their supremacy in Campania entitled them to forbid this breach with the Samnites on the part of the Campanians, but that their connexion with the Latin League did not give them the same authority as to the Latins. These last looked on this as a sign of weakness, and resolved to assert their claim either to complete independence or to a full share in the Roman citizenship, demanding that one consul and half of the Senate should be Latin, and that Latium and Rome should form one Republic. The war that arose from this quarrel lasted three years, and in it battles were fought at Veseris and Tifernum (B.C. 341), Pedum and Astura (B.C. 338); and when the last stronghold of Pedum fell the Latins were forced to submit. The

Latin League ceased to exist as a political body, and Rome made what terms she pleased with each city. Some of them were allowed to have a partial citizenship, called the Caerite, from its having been first given to Caere, in Etruria; in other words, they were compelled to join the Roman system and bear the burden of military service, without getting full civil rights. Some towns, however, received better treatment, and were allowed full citizenship. Some were mulcted of territory, but were not otherwise disturbed; but the senators at Velitrae were deprived of their lands and obliged to live beyond the Tiber. All alike had to furnish men to the army. Much the same variety of treatment was meted out to the Campanians who had helped the Latins. In these towns only the 'knights,' or upper class of Samnite descent, were allowed the Latin franchise; while other towns had it for all their citizens. The net result was that in Latium and Campania there were a number of *municipia*, or towns which owed services (military and fiscal) to the State, but had only a limited share in civil privileges. But the confiscation of part of their lands caused a large number of Roman citizens to settle in them, till many of them, in course of time, became almost an integral part of Rome.

6. **Stories of Manlius and Decius.** To this campaign two famous stories belong. The first is the execution of Titus Manlius, son of the consul, for leaving the ranks contrary to orders, to fight the Tusculan Germinius, who challenged the Roman knights to send a champion against him. Manlius conquered and killed Germinius, and carried the spoils to his father. The stern answer, condemning his victorious son to death for a breach of military discipline, rendered the *Manliana imperia* a proverb of terrible import for ever. The other is the story of the devotion of Publius Decius Mus. He and his colleague dreamed the same dream. A man of

superhuman size and dignity warned them that on one side the leader, on the other the army itself, must perish. They offered sacrifice, and the inspection of entrails pointed out Decius as the man. Thereupon in solemn form he devoted himself to the "Manes and to Earth," and, mounting his horse, rode into the midst of the enemy, and was killed. A similar story is told of his son in B.C. 295, and even, it appears, of his grandson.

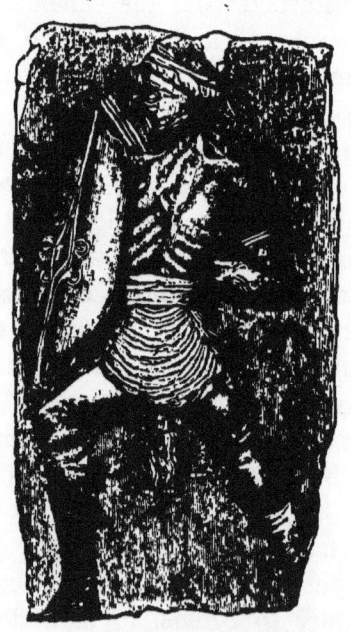

SAMNITE WARRIOR. Relief from Durazzo.

7. **The Second Samnite War**, B.C. 326-304. For eleven years there was peace. Then the Romans once more found themselves confronted by the Samnites, who still stood in the way of the extension of their power to the south. The war began from a quarrel with a Greek town, Palaeopolis, standing near the modern Naples. The

inhabitants had, it was said, harried the lands of Roman settlers in Campania, refused restitution, and were assisted by a garrison of Samnites whose help they had asked. Nor would the Samnites give in when Roman envoys remonstrated with them for helping enemies of Rome in spite of their treaty. So the Romans proclaimed war against both the people of Palaepolis and the Samnites. The former soon gave in and surrendered; and the New Town, or Neapolis, which took its place, made very favourable terms with Rome as a *civitas foederata*, that is, a town which, keeping its internal freedom, was joined with Rome on certain fixed terms (*foedus*). But the Samnites, secure in their mountain fastnesses, held out for many years, and inflicted more than one disaster on the Romans. The most famous was when Caius Pontius compelled a whole Roman army to surrender in a pass called the Caudine Forks (B.C. 321). The Roman commander, Postumius, attempting to march to the relief of Luceria, in Apulia, had to pass through a narrow valley. But Pontius had anticipated the movement, and had blocked up the pass out of the defile, and had men in ambush ready to block up the other end in their rear. When the Romans therefore attempted to return they found themselves again stopped. They could get no provisions; their attempt to force the passage failed, and there was nothing for it but to surrender. Pontius is represented as deliberating whether he should put them all to the sword, or allow them to depart unharmed. He eventually adopted a middle course. The consul agreed to a treaty, whereby the Romans were to withdraw from Samnite territory, and remove two colonies founded in the disputed border lands, Fregellae and Cales, and make a peace with the Samnites, leaving them independent. But the whole army was to go under the 'yoke,' as it was called. Two spears were fixed in the ground, with a third laid across, and the men had to march underneath without their arms. This was the last disgrace to soldiers, and they did not value lives granted on these terms. The Roman government refused to ratify the convention, and the war went on. The chief hero on the Roman side was Papirius Cursor, a rough and cruel soldier, but a great general; and the struggle took two forms. When the Romans were most successful, they attacked towns in Apulia. When the Samnites were getting the upper hand, they seized towns on or over the Latin border. But though there were these variations, and though the Romans were on several occasions worsted in the field, on the whole they made great progress. They secured a firm hold on Campania by occupying Nola and Calatia; they made a great military road (the *via Appia*) from Rome to Capua (B.C. 312); established colonies at various cities in Apulia (B.C. 312); and were able to advance into the heart of Samnium, and attack Bovianum; and, though in B.C. 311 the war was complicated by a union between the Etruscans, Umbrians, and Samnites—Rome being thus threatened from the north and south at once—and though more disasters were sustained, the energy and perseverance of the Romans in the end proved too much for her enemies. The Etruscans were defeated with great slaughter at the Vadimonian lake (B.C. 309), and again, in union with the Umbrians, at Mevania (B.C. 306); and in B.C. 304 the Samnites were content to renew their old treaty, which left the Romans in possession of the disputed colonies, supreme in Campania and Southern Etruria, and holding a kind of protectorate in Apulia and Lucania, while the Samnites only retained their own independence.

8. **Third Samnite War**, B.C. 298-290. The Samnites however were not conquered; nor, it seems, were the Etruscans content that the Romans should continue masters in Etruria. The Samnites were a nation

THE APPIAN WAY.

of plunderers, and their neighbours were always suffering from their raids. This brought on the next collision: for the Lucanians complained to Rome, and the Romans were glad of a pretext for once more making an effort to master these dangerous highlanders. Such persistence is the secret of Roman success. It was just in the same way that they afterwards subdued the Ligurians in the north. Year after year armies were sent out; disasters were repaired; small successes patiently improved; now this point and now that was lost or won. In details they at times went back, but on the whole they steadily progressed towards ultimate success. So it was in the wars with the Samnites and Etruscans. Though there was again a coalition of Senonian Gauls, Umbrians and Etruscans, in aid of the Samnites, and though more than one disaster was sustained by the Roman arms, the coalition was in the end broken up by a decisive victory of the Romans at Sentinum (B.C. 295), and the Samnites left to themselves had to bear invasions year after year. In the end, after being defeated more than once by Curius Dentatus, they sought and obtained peace. Of this Curius it is told that the Samnite leaders tried to bribe him with gold. They found him on his poor farm, cooking his own vegetables; but he repulsed them, declaring that he did not value gold but the ruling of those who had it. The history of this war has for the most part been lost; but if we remember the conditions in which it was fought we can imagine it almost as well as though we were told of this or that battle. War with a race of mountaineers must always be somewhat of the same type. They know the country better than their assailants; seize opportunities of waylaying and defeating them; go from fastness to fastness; sally out of strongholds; make raids and drive off cattle. But persistent civilization gets the better of them in the end; and military discipline and training finally triumph over wild warfare. At any rate, the result was that the Romans established their position of paramount influence in Campania, Apulia, and Lucania. The Greek cities round the coasts of those districts were still free. But the next movement in South Italy was to put them also under the authority of Rome.

9. **Civil History from B.C. 390 to 286.** But there is another side to Roman history during this period. The Roman State was increasing in vigour and numbers; and its constitution was developing. We find indeed the old quarrel of rich and poor going on, and the old jealousy of the Patricians active against those who promoted measures of relief, as though they were trying to secure undue influence for themselves. Thus, in B.C. 384, M. Manlius, the defender of the Capitol, who championed enslaved debtors, was declared guilty of treason and hurled from the Tarpeian rock. But this martyr's death was not without good fruit, and after many years of similar struggles the unfair institution of the *nexum*, whereby a debtor passed at once into the hands of his creditor, was abolished. There was also persistent attempts to obtain fair arrangements as to the *ager publicus*, and for the admission of Plebeians to the consulship. After ten years of agitation the *Licinian Rogations* (that is, bills proposed by C. Licinius Stolo and L. Sextius) became law in B.C. 367. By these laws (1) the debtors, who owed money on mortgages, were relieved by being allowed to deduct the interests already paid from the capital. (2) No one was to hold more than 500 *jugera* (about 300 acres) of public land. (3) Consuls were again to be elected instead of consular tribunes, but one of them was to be a Plebeian. The effect of the first was necessarily only temporary; the second was soon evaded in various ways. But the third was at once carried out. Only, as a compromise, the judicial business of the consuls was transferred to a third magistrate, who was to be called

Praetor, and was to be a Patrician; in alternate years the aediles were to be elected from the Patricians, and were Curule aediles, as opposed to the others, who were now called Plebeian aediles. In return, of the ten commissioners who had control of certain sacred objects and rites (*decemviri sacrorum*), five were to be henceforth Plebeians. This was valuable as, among other things, it gave the control of the Sibylline oracles, which were often used for political purposes. Moreover, the Plebeian assembly (*Comitia Tributa*) became more and more important, and votes passed in them (*plebiscita*) came gradually to have the force of laws binding the whole State. Next the censorship was opened to the Plebeians (B.C. 339); then the praetorship (B.C. 336); then the colleges of Sacerdotes and Augures (B.C. 296). And when by a law of the Dictator Hortensius (B.C. 286), the rule as to the binding nature of *plebiscita* was confirmed and made more distinct, all inequality between the orders was done away. Yet the distinction continued to exist; for the tribunes were still obliged to be Plebeians, and if any Patrician wished to be tribune he could only do so by being adopted into a Plebeian gens. The social distinction also remained, and the word *plebs* was long used for all under the degree of knight. It was about this time also that Appius Claudius Caecus, who as censor in B.C. 312-308 made the great Appian Way, tried to render the constitution of the Senate more popular by admitting men of low birth. Moreover by allowing people living in the city to be enrolled if they chose in country tribes he gave the populace of the city much more influence in the *Comitia Tributa*: for they were on the spot and always ready to vote, while the farmers were often unwilling to come to the city; and thus they determined the votes of many more tribes. These innovations however were soon cancelled; but Cn. Flavius (who had been his secretary) having become aedile (B.C. 304) took a step of which the effects were more lasting. He published the *formulae*, or forms of pleadings in law suits, and posted up the calendar in the Forum, showing which days were *fasti*, *i.e.* days on which business might be done. These things had been kept as a kind of mystery or secret by the sacerdotes and magistrates, and their being made public gave ordinary people an advantage in conducting their business, and deprived the official class of a great hold which they had had over them.

APPENDIX TO CHAPTER IV.

COLONIES in Italy before and after the two first Punic Wars, in chronological order. Compare this list with the map, and see how in most cases they command important districts, roads, or harbours, and follow the course of the Roman conquest of Italy. Those which had the full Roman franchise are marked (R). The rest had only the Latin franchise.

Colony	Region	Date
Ostia (R),	Latium,	⎫
Signia,	,,	⎬ Before
Circeii,	,,	⎭ B.C. 510
Suessa Pometia and Cosa, ,.		
Velitrae,	Latium,	,, 494
Norba,	,,	,, 492
Antium,	,,	,, 467
Ardea,	,,	,, 442
Satricum,	,,	,, 385
Sutrium,	Etruria,	⎫ ,, 383
Nepete,	,,	⎭
Setia,	Latium,	,, 382
Antium (R),	made a Roman Colony,	,, 338
Cales,	Etruria,	,, 334
Anxur (R),	Latium,	,, 329
Fregellae,	,,	,, 328
Luceria,	Apulia,	,, 314
Saticula,	Campania,	⎫
Suessa Aurunca,	Latium,	⎬ ,, 313
Pontiae,	off coast of Latium,	⎭
Casinum (R),	Latium,	⎫ ,, 312
Interamna Lirinas,	,,	⎭

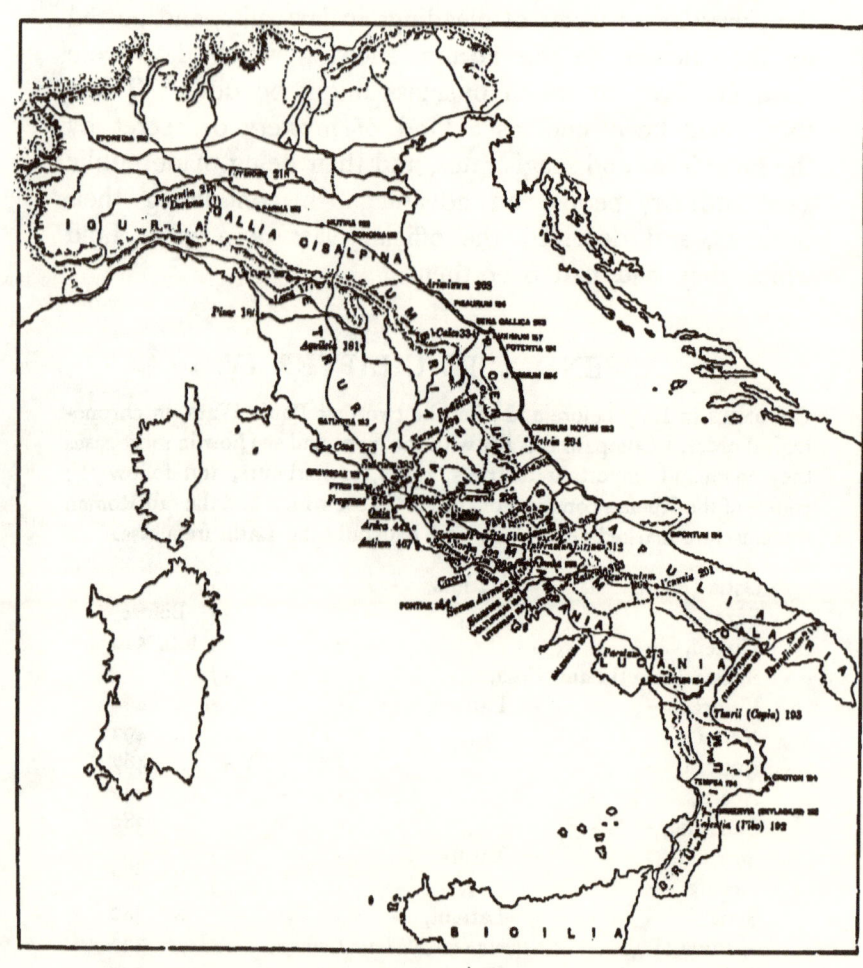

Names underlined are those of Colonies founded before B.C. 510.
Names of "Roman Colonies" are printed in capitals.
Names of "Latin Colonies" are in small type.

COLONIES.

Sora, - -	Latium, - - -	⎫ B.C. 303
Alba Fucentia, - -	,, - - -	⎭
Narnia, - -	Umbria, - - -	,, 299
Carseoli, - -	Latium, - - -	,, 298
Minturnae (R), -	Campania, - -	⎫ ,, 296
Sinuessa (R), - -	,, - - -	⎭
Venusia, - -	Apulia, - - -	,, 291
Hadria, - -	Picenum, - - -	,, 289
Castrum Novum (R),	Picenum, - - -	⎫ ,, 283
Sena Gallica (R), -	Umbria, - - -	⎭ (*circ.*)
Cosa, - -	Etruria, - -	⎫ ,, 273
Paestum, - -	Lucania, - -	⎭
Ariminum, -	Umbria, - -	⎫ ,, 268
Beneventum, -	Samnium, - -	⎭
Firmum, - -	Picenum, - - -	,, 264
Aesernia, - -	Samnium, - -	,, 263
Aesium (R), -	Umbria, - -	⎫ ,, 247
Alsium (R), -	Etruria, - -	⎭
Fregenae (R), - -	,, - - -	,, 245

AFTER THE FIRST PUNIC WAR.

Brundisium, -	Calabria, - - -	,, 244
Spoletium, -	Umbria, - - -	,, 241
Cremona, - -	Gallia Cisalpina, -	⎫ ,, 218
Placentia, - . -	,, - -	⎭

AFTER THE SECOND PUNIC WAR.

Puteoli (R), -	Campania, - -	⎫
Volternum (R), -	,, - -	
Liternum (R), -	,, - -	
Salernum (R), -	,, - -	
Buxentum (R), -	Lucania, - -	⎬ ,, 194
Sipontum (R), -	Apulia, - -	
Tempsa (R), -	Bruttium, - -	
Croton (R), - -	,, - -	⎭
Thurii (Copia), -	Apulia, - - -	,, 193
Valentia (Vibo), -	Bruttium, - -	,, 192
Pyrgi (R), - -	Etruria, - - -	,, 191
Bononia, - -	Gallia Cisalpina, -	,, 189
Potentia (R), -	Picenum, - -	⎫ ,, 184
Pisaurum (R), -	Umbria, - -	⎭

Saturnia (R),	Etruria,	⎫
Parma (R),	Gallia Cisalpina,	⎬ B.C. 183
Mutina (R),	,,	⎭
Graviscae (R),	Etruria,	⎫ ,, 181
Aquileia,	Gallia Cisalpina,	⎭
Luna (R),	Etruria,	⎫ ,, 180
Pisae,	,,	⎭
Luca (R),	,,	,, 177
Luna (R),	,,	,, 177
Auximum (R),	Picenum,	,, 157
Fabrateria,	Latium,	,, 124
Minervia[Skylacium](R),	Bruttium,	⎫ ,, 122
Neptunia[Tarentum](R),	Calabria,	⎭
Dertona (R),	Liguria,	,, ?
Eporedia (R),	Gallia Cisalpina,	,, 100

SARCOPHAGUS OF SCIPIO BARBATUS IN THE VATICAN.

CHAPTER V.

THE CONQUEST OF ITALY COMPLETED.
B.C. 289-271.

1. *Magna Graecia; the pretensions of Tarentum, and origin of its quarrel with Rome.* 2. *The invasion by* **Pyrrhus** *and battles of* **Heraclea** *and* **Asculum.** 3. *Pyrrhus in Sicily.* 4. *Return of Pyrrhus to Italy and his defeat at* **Beneventum.** 5. *Means taken to secure Southern Italy.*

1. **Magna Graecia.** After the end of the third Samnite war Rome still had some troubles to contend with in Etruria, and with some of the Gallic tribes in the north, especially with the Senones, whom they eventually cut to pieces, expelling the survivors from their territories; and with the Boii, who invaded Etruria, and with whom more than one desperate fight was fought. But it was in the south that the events occurred which had now the most important results on the extension of Roman sway. The Greek towns that fringed the southern coasts had not yet become subject to Rome, but they were so situated with regard to each other and the surrounding peoples that they were certain to become so, and already we find a party in most of them who looked for support from Rome. They were often threatened with attacks from the Lucanians and Apulians or the Samnites; and they were so jealous of each other that they could seldom combine to resist these attacks. The Tarentines tried to establish a kind of supremacy

among them, and the policy which was favoured by Tarentum was to get help from Greece or Sicily. For this purpose Alexander, king of the Molossi in Epirus, Agathocles, tyrant of Syracuse, Cleonymus of Sparta, had on various occasions come to South Italy. But these princes had done little good. They had their own purposes to serve, and the Tarentines were soon as anxious to get rid of them as they had been to bring them in. When Rome by her wars with the Samnites began to be the most notable power in Southern, as she already was in Central Italy, many of these towns began to look to her for protection. Tarentum, on the other hand, aimed at holding a kind of primacy among them, and was jealous of the interference of Rome. In the course of the second Samnite war the Romans had found it advisable to concede something to this jealousy of the Tarentines. They had made a treaty with them engaging not to sail in ships of war round the Lacinian promontory into the Gulf of Tarentum. But in B.C. 282 the Romans sent help to the Greek town Thurii, which was being attacked by the Lucani, and among other things ten ships were despatched under the command of L. Valerius. These ships, in spite of the treaty, visited several Greek towns on the coast, and eventually appeared in the harbour of Tarentum itself. There was an outburst of excitement among the Tarentines; they put to sea in some of their war vessels, sunk four of the Roman ships, and killed L. Valerius. Ambassadors were sent from Rome to demand reparation, but they were insulted in the assembly, and all compensation was refused. The Romans thereupon declared war, and the anti-Roman party at Tarentum determined to invite the help of Pyrrhus, king of Epirus.

2. **The Invasion of Pyrrhus**, B.C. 280-274. Pyrrhus was king of Epirus, cousin and successor to the Alexander who had, in former days, been also invited into Italy by the Tarentines. The dynasty at first only ruled the Molossi,

a tribe in Epirus, but Alexander had called himself king of Epirus upon extending his dominions beyond the lands of the Molossi. Pyrrhus had at times been driven from his kingdom, and at times been king of the larger realm of Macedonia. He had led an adventurous life, fighting in all directions and most often in other people's battles. He was therefore an experienced soldier, and indeed had studied tactics carefully, and even written a book on the subject. Especially he is said to have introduced improvements in the method of laying out and fortifying camps, from which the Romans themselves took some hints. Moreover, in character he was generous and placable, and the Romans always remembered their struggle with him without rancour. They were fond of contrasting him with Hannibal, to whom they attributed every kind of treachery and cruelty.

He arrived at Tarentum early in B.C. 280 with a large army and a troop of elephants, whose use he had learnt in Africa, and which the Romans had never encountered before. He endeavoured first of all to train and discipline the idle luxurious Tarentines and to collect forces from towns in Lucania, and from the Samnites. These contingents did not come in as quickly as he hoped; for a Roman army under P. Valerius Laevinus, one of the consuls, was already in Lucania, wasting the country, and often preventing aid being sent to Pyrrhus. However, he did get an army together and faced the Romans near **Heraclēa**, on the river Siris. He won the battle, though with such heavy loss that he declared that another such victory would be his ruin. The victory, however, brought him large reinforcements from Lucania and Samnium, and he determined to advance on Rome itself. But he failed to take Capua or Naples, and when he got to Praeneste, only twenty-three miles from Rome, taking Fregellae and Anagnia on his way, he found none of the towns willing to yield to him; and, as the Roman armies were dogging his foot-

steps wherever he went, he was in the end obliged to retire and go into winter quarters at Tarentum. Negotiations also were tried in vain. He sent his friend Cineas to Rome to offer the Senate peace on the condition of their leaving the Greek cities free, and restoring all they had taken from the Lucanians, Bruttians, and Samnites. But the Senate stood firm (greatly, it was said, owing to the spirited speech of the aged Appius Claudius Caecus), and would entertain no terms as long as Pyrrhus remained in Italy. Nor when Fabricius was sent in the winter to negotiate a return of Roman prisoners could the king get from him any hint of concession. The war therefore went on next year and Pyrrhus won another battle at **Asculum** (B.C. 279), but was himself wounded and unable to follow up his victory. He had to wait for reinforcements from Epirus, and in the next spring (B.C. 278) he was unable to do anything against the new consuls, C. Fabricius Luscinus, and Q. Aemilius Papus.

3. **Pyrrhus goes to Sicily** (B.C. 278). This inaction caused great discontent at Tarentum and defections among his Italian allies. He was glad, therefore, to accept an invitation from Syracuse and other Sicilian towns to come to Sicily to relieve them of their tyrants, and drive back the Carthaginians, who, having settlements in the west of the island, were always trying to extend their power in the east also. This was an expedition something like that on which he was engaged in Italy. For Sicily, too, was fringed with Greek colonies, often at variance with each other, and all of them the object of Carthaginian attacks. There were other reasons for the Sicilian towns wanting a deliverer from outside. They had mostly, from internal dissensions, fallen into the hands of military tyrants, who were at once oppressive and incompetent; and a few years before one of the towns (Messana) had been captured by some mercenaries from

Campania who called themselves Mamertini (sons of Mamers or Mars), and these men not only destroyed the ancient inhabitants of Messana, but made themselves a terror to the other Sicilians by raids and expeditions in search of plunder. Pyrrhus had a special tie with Syracuse, for he had married a daughter of its last great sovereign, Agathocles. He was to go to Sicily, therefore, to put down the tyrants, to suppress the Mamertines, and to drive back the Carthaginians. He stayed there nearly two years, and was at first very successful, and seemed likely to gratify his utmost ambition. If he were lord of Sicily, he would next pass over to Africa to subdue the Carthaginians, and then return to Italy with irresistible forces. But the same thing happened as in Italy. As soon as his tide of success turned, he found himself losing popularity: and late in B.C. 276 he resolved to return to Italy, where the Tarentines and Samnites were once more in great alarm at the progress of the Roman arms, which were carrying all before them in the lower parts of Samnium and in Lucania.

4. Pyrrhus returns to Italy (B.C. 276). His return was not easy, for the Romans had made common cause with the Carthaginians against one who was a danger to both, and the Carthaginian fleets were on the watch for him. Still he did land with the greater part of his men, and his return checked the tide of the Roman successes. The terror of him was so great that the consuls had some difficulty in getting men to give in their names for the legions. However, the consul M'. Curius Dentatus got his legion ready in time, and intrenched himself near what was then called Maleventum, but afterwards Beneventum (B.C. 275). It commanded the road into Campania, and if Pyrrhus was to do anything of importance against Rome he must first beat Dentatus. But Pyrrhus was no longer in such good case as he had been at Heraclea. His army had now too great an admixture of Italians; his elephants proved a weakness to him as they often did, for they fell into disorder and did him more harm than good; he failed in an attempt to surprise Dentatus by a night attack; and he found his enemy posted on rough ground unsuitable for manoeuvring his phalanx, that is, men in long line massed many deep. At any rate he was decisively beaten; and had to escape with a few cavalry back to Tarentum, whence he crossed again to Epirus and never returned (B.C. 274). He left a garrison in Tarentum under one of his officers, which, however, was forced to surrender little more than a year afterwards, being blockaded by the Carthaginian fleet and besieged by the Roman consul, L. Papirius Cursor (B.C. 272).

5. **How the Romans secured Southern Italy**, B.C. 274-267. The fruits of the defeat of Pyrrhus, and of the several campaigns carried on by the Romans during his absence in Sicily, were now to be secured. After the fall of Tarentum (B.C. 272) the Romans had first to capture Rhegium, not because Rhegium had rebelled, but because a garrison of Campanian soldiers, whom they had themselves placed there, had mutinied, seized the town, made alliance with the Mamertines, and expelled Roman garrisons from neighbouring towns. These men resisted desperately, because they knew they had no mercy to expect. But at last they were beaten, fighting savagely to the last, and about 300 survivors were carried off to Rome and executed. There was now nobody to dispute their supremacy, and the Romans set about securing their conquest. The method pursued was this. In the first place, 'Latin' colonies[1] were settled at various important places: in Samnium at Beneventum and Aesernia; in Lucania at Posidonia (Paestum); at Firmum in Picenum. The same policy was extended in the north also, Cosa being established about the same time in Etruria, and Ariminum in

[1] See Appendix to Chapter IV. and Map.

the *ager Gallicus*. In the second place, a number of cities with their territory, though not burdened by colonies, were joined to Rome on special terms, which always included military or naval service in some form or other; these were called *civitates foederatae*. We have already heard of Naples being thus treated in B.C. 326, and earlier still some towns in Latium had been placed in the same position. Certain cities in Campania, Lucania, and Bruttium had in the course of the last few years been added to this category, and in central Italy the entire tribes of Picentes, Marrucini, Marsi, Peligni, and Frentani were placed in the like condition. These peoples were in fact subject to Rome, but their internal government was left mostly to themselves, and their obligations to the State were regulated according to the particular *foedus* made in each case. In one sense a general term applied to them all—*municipium*, *i.e.* a town which had duties without full privileges. Later on we shall find them striking for admission to the full citizenship, and trying in default of that to found an Italian as opposed to a Roman State. Tarentum itself was not, it seems, deprived of freedom or admitted to the Roman military league. But a legion was kept there permanently in garrison, which occupied the citadel; and its prosperity gradually dwindled away. Those of the Samnites who were not included in this arrangement were for the present cowed into acquiescence, and the general result of it all was that from that time Rome was paramount from the Rubicon to the extreme South of Italy.

CHAPTER VI.

THE CONSTITUTION AND FORCES OF ROME AND CARTHAGE IN THE THIRD CENTURY B.C.

1. *Rivalry with Carthage takes Roman arms beyond the sea.* 2. *Rome as a military power.* 3. *Rome as a naval power.* 4. *The nature of the Roman government.* 5. *The Curule Magistrates.* 6. *The other Magistrates.* 7. *The Senate.* 8. *Carthage: her origin and greatness.* 9. *The Constitution of Carthage.* 10. *Rome and Carthage compared.*

1. **Rome extending her Power beyond Italy.** We have now seen how Rome, from being a single weak city, with a small territory, rose to be mistress of Latium, and then of all Italy. The next stage in her progress will be when she begins to stretch her hands upon lands beyond the sea, and becomes the chief power in the Mediterranean. This was begun by her rivalry with the great commercial city of Carthage, which for many years had been supreme as a naval and mercantile power. Let us stop for a short time to see what the two peoples were like in resources and government when they thus began a duel for power and dominion.

2. **Rome as a Military Power.** We must remember that the Roman government, however widely extended, was the government of a city. The magistrates and Senate must be citizens of Rome; the legions must consist also of citizens. The number of these of military age, according

to the census of B.C. 265, was 292,224. In ordinary times four legions were raised each year, two for each consul, which required (infantry and cavalry together) about 22,000 men. A'ter the conquest of Tarentum another legion seems yearly to have been raised to garrison it. But not only could the other citizens be called upon in an emergency, but d rectly Rome had begun the system of colonies and *municipia*, she drew troops also from them, which served with the legions, though officered and drawn up separately; and when the conquest of all Italy south of the Rubicon had been accomplished, the number thus available was about 350 000. Each town had to make out a list of its citizens fit for military service; and in time of need *conquisitores*, or recruiting officers, were sent round to see that the lists were correct and the men forthcoming. When it was necessary to enrol a legion, the consul having given notice of the day, all citizens liable to serve[1] had to attend to answer to their names. First six military tribunes for each legion were appointed—partly by nomination of the consul, partly by election—and these took turns in selecting suitable men. The recruits were then divided, according to age and wealth, into *hastati*, *principes*, *triarii*, and *rorarii*. The first three were armed with long shield, breastplate, helmet, and greaves,[2] and all had a short straight sword made for cutting or thrusting (*gladius*). The two first—the *hastati* and *principes*—had two *pila*, stout javelins with long iron head, which were thrown before charging. The third rank—*triarii*—had instead of this a pike or spear (*hasta*), though afterwards all alike had the *pilum*. The *Rorarii* were light-armed troops, who had a smaller shield (*parma*) and a helmet without plume, with the sword and light lance.

[1] That is, men between 17 and 46 who had not already served twenty years in the infantry or ten in the cavalry.
[2] Scutum, lorica, galea, ocreae.

ROMAN MILITARY FORCES.

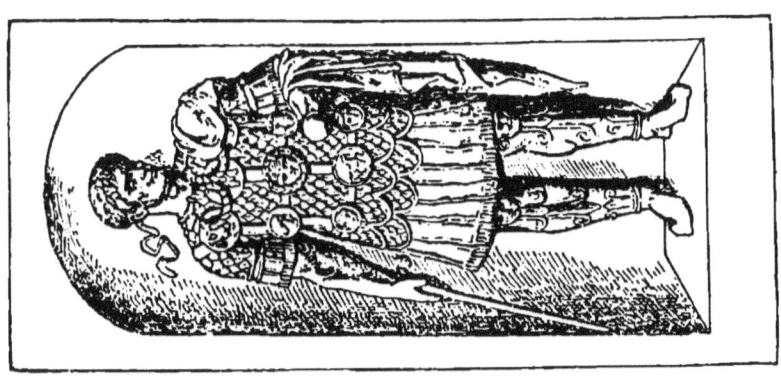

CIPPUS OF Q. SARTORIUS, A CENTURION. VERONA.

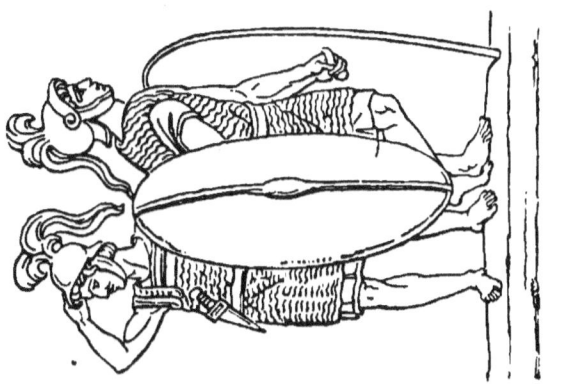

SOLDIERS WITH THE SCUTUM. RELIEF IN LOUVRE.

3. **Rome as a Naval Power.** The discipline and organization of her army, combined with the will and faculty for governing, had made Rome the mistress of Italy, but as yet she had done little towards the possession of a navy. From very early times she seems to have used the Tiber for merchant vessels; and the colony of Ostia, made during the period of the kings, was for the purpose of supporting the sea traffic. But it was on the capture of Antium (B C. 338) that she seems first to have possessed war vessels, when the whole fleet of Antium was removed to Ostia, though the ships seem to have been left there in neglect. But about B.C. 314, when a colony was being sent to the islands called Pontiae, it seems that the Romans first began to feel the need of having vessels, capable of defending themselves, for the transport of troops. In B.C. 312 *duoviri navales*, commissioners for superintending ships, were for the first time appointed; in B.C. 311 an officer was appointed with the title of 'praefect of the sea coast'; and in B.C. 282, when help was sent to Thurii, it was conveyed or accompanied by ten war-vessels (*naves longae*) under the command of a duovir. Still there is no idea as yet of possessing a fleet which could fight at sea. We shall learn when we come to the Punic wars how Rome partially remedied this defect.

4. **The Roman Government.** Rome was a republic. There was no hereditary rank, no hereditary offices. To be born in one of the Patrician gentes gave no legal privilege of importance; and though to become a tribune a man must be a Plebeian, the tribuneship, like other offices, was elective, and no man had a claim to it. But Roman magistracies were 'honours' and carried no salary, and as most of them involved great expense, only men of wealth were as a rule candidates for them; and there was always also a presumption in favour of the members of the same families appearing again and again in the lists of consuls.

Therefore, though the Roman constitution was democratic in the fact that its magistrates were elected by the people, and the Senate to a great extent filled by ex-magistrates who had been so elected; yet, in practice, it approached nearer to what is called an oligarchy, or the rule of a few. This was a source of strength in dealing with foreign nations, so long as these men of the governing class were, on the whole, loyal to the constitution. But corruption gradually found its way in, and led to violent partisan contests, which eventually brought revolution and a return to the rule of one man, though he was never again called king.

5. **The Curule Magistrates.** At the head of the State were the two consuls, who originally had all the powers of the single king. They had authority over the citizens at home, commanded the armies, acted as judges, and had control of the treasury, and were preceded by twelve lictors carrying bundles of rods or fasces, with an axe, as symbols of supreme power (*imperium*). The checks upon their power were (1) that they were two and not one, and each acted as a restraint upon the other; (2) the Senate could control them in various ways, and even force them to name a Dictator to supersede them; (3) the tribunes of the people could veto their actions or judicial decisions; (4) persons sentenced by them as judges could appeal to the people. Gradually also some of their functions devolved on other magistrates. In B.C. 443 two new magistrates, called Censors, were appointed, who took over the duty of making up the list of the Senate and the other 'orders' in the State, performed the *lustrum* or official purification every fifth year, and had a general superintendence over public works, buildings, and roads. Again in B.C. 347, from which year consuls were again always elected, another curule magistrate was appointed, called *Praetor*, to preside in the law courts.

These five—consuls, censors, and praetor—now did what the two consuls used to do by themselves. They, with the curule aediles, formed something like what we call the 'government.' They became life members of the Senate, and were called *Curules*, from the *sellae curules*, ornamented chairs, set for them in the Senate house, as distinguished from the benches on which other senators sat.

CIPPUS FROM AVIGNON, SHOWING SELLA CURULIS AND FASCES.

6. **The other Magistrates.** Besides these there were the quaestors. Their duties were mainly financial. From B.C. 421 there were four (instead of two); of whom two remained in Rome in charge of the treasury, and one accompanied each of the consuls on military service, had charge of the military chest, and generally managed the money affairs of the legions; as new provinces were added to the Empire their numbers were increased.

When tribunes were first appointed (B.C. 494), two new officers were also annually elected from the Plebeians, called

Aediles, who acted as magistrates in petty causes, and superintended the police of the city, the corn market, and the games. However, when the praetorship was established (B.C. 367), two new aediles were also appointed from the Patricians, called *aediles Curules*. They did much the same duties, and before long the curule aedileship also was thrown open to Plebeians. But being curule magistrates they obtained a life membership of the Senate, and so their office was regarded as the first step in an official career.

The Dictatorship was an expedient in a time of difficulty, temporarily reviving the single kingship. A Dictator was supreme over all other magistrates, who continued performing their functions, but under his direction. If he was appointed for carrying on a war, he became at once commander-in-chief. Sometimes, however, he was appointed for some special purpose of a civil nature, such as holding an election. In that case he abdicated as soon as he had done what he was appointed to do. In any case he only held office for six months. He was named by one of the consuls, generally by order of the Senate, and himself nominated a second in command, called Master of the Horse.

7. **The Senate.** For a long time, however, the most powerful body in Rome was the Senate, the normal number of which was 300. Under the kings it seems to have been a mere council for advising the king, and he was not bound to take its advice. Under the consuls it was nominally the same, but it gradually acquired in practice a number of powers, which, though they rested on no law, and might be always overborne by a law, yet in reality were undisputed. It controlled the treasury; assigned to the magistrates their spheres of duty (though this was also done in ordinary cases by drawing lots); voted or withheld triumphs; issued commissions to try and determine cases of difficulty in subject towns, or (in later times) to arrange the constitution of new provinces; authorized or

forbade new laws; decided, in some cases, the validity of disputed elections; extended the command of generals in charge of armies, or superseded them by others; received and answered foreign ambassadors, and frequently settled questions of peace or war. No law gave the Senate these powers, but it absorbed them by a kind of general assent, and for a long time no one thought of disputing them. Still it was certain that a decision of the Senate could be overridden by a vote of the people, and every now and then some magistrate did override it by this means. So that the Senate was unable to push its authority too far.

8. **Carthage.** The rival with which Rome was now to try her strength was Carthage. The Phoenicians, who lived in Tyre and the country round, had from very early times been great navigators and merchants. In various places on the shores of the Mediterranean they had erected factories, which had grown into towns. The most important of these was Carthage (in Greek Καρχηδών, a corrupted form of Kart-hadasat, 'New Town'), on the coast of Africa where the shore first bends to the south opposite Sicily.[1] Tradition assigned its foundation to Dido, who fled from her native Tyre after the murder of her husband, with a band of followers who established themselves round the Byrsa, or fortress, which they purchased from the natives. As to the time at which this took place tradition varied between about the epoch of the foundation of Rome and two or three hundred years earlier. At any rate, about the time of the expulsion of the kings of Rome, we find Carthage a powerful commercial State, supreme over her neighbours, and in possession of settlements in Sicily and Spain, some of which had been founded by earlier Phoenician settlers; and before the period of the Punic wars the city was said to

[1] The Roman words Poeni and Punicus are corruptions of Phoenix (Φοίνιξ), 'Phoenician.'

contain 700,000 inhabitants. Its territory in Libya embraced 300 cities; it held two-thirds of Sicily, the Balearic Islands, Corsica and Sardinia, and many settlements in Spain south of a line joining the Tagus and Ebro.

9. **The Constitution of Carthage.** The constitution of Carthage was not unlike that of Rome in externals,—there were two Suffetes or kings (*Shofetim*, 'judges'), a Senate, and an Assembly. But in reality the chief power had long been exercised by a small body called the 'Hundred' (actually 104). This body, originally formed by popular election, had by some means got into the hands of a few rich families and formed an oligarchy like that of Venice. But there was a democratic party also, headed by the great family of Barca, and about the time of the Punic wars this party was in the ascendant; and so the historian Polybius looked upon Carthage as an instance of mob-rule, not as a well-ordered state like that of Rome, where each rank and order served as a check upon the rest, but subject to irregular and sudden bursts of popular excitement when things were going wrong.

10. **Rome and Carthage compared.** As compared with Rome, Carthage was much the stronger as a naval power. She had the best vessels, and the most experienced pilots and sailors of any people; and Rome (as we have seen) can scarcely be said to have had any navy at all as yet. Secondly, she was immensely wealthy, while Rome at this time was only beginning to use silver coins, and could have had but small store of money. But as a military power it turned out that she was inferior to Rome. To a great extent she depended on mercenary troops which her wealth enabled her to hire from different countries. These were often good troops in themselves, but they did not prove equal in the end to the citizen soldiers of Rome.

CHAPTER VII.

THE FIRST PUNIC WAR, B.C. 264-250.

1. *The Carthaginians in Sicily.* 2. *Causes of the First Punic War.* 3. *The First Punic War:* **1st period** (B.C. 264-262)—*Fall of* **Agrigentum**; *alliance with Hiero.* **2nd period** (B.C. 262-255)—*The Romans build a fleet; battles of* **Mylae** *and* **Ecnomus**; *defeat and capture of Regulus.* **3rd period** (B.C. 254-250)—*Capture of* **Panormus**; *fruitless proposals for peace; Carthaginians strengthen* **Lilybaeum.** **4th period** (B.C. 249-242)—*Blockade and siege of Lilybaeum; fighting at Eryx and Drepana; Hamilcar on Mt. Hercte; victory of Duilius at the* **Aegusae** *Islands.* 4. *Sicily the first Roman province.* 5. *The Mercenary War, and the reduction of Sardinia.*

1. **Carthage and Sicily.** The Carthaginians had long been the enemies of the Greek cities in Sicily. They had held without dispute the west of the island, as far east as the River Halycus; but they were always trying to extend their dominions, and for this purpose had engaged in several great wars, generally with Syracuse, which, being the most powerful of the Greek cities, offered the most strenuous resistance. Thus in 480 B.C. Gelo I., tyrant of Syracuse, defeated a great Carthaginian invasion. Dionysius (tyrant from B.C. 405-367) was constantly engaged in a similar struggle. Timoleon of Corinth (being invited to aid Syracuse) conquered the Carthaginians in a great battle on the Crimisus (B.C. 340). Agathocles (tyrant B.C. 317-278) not only drove them back to the west, but

even invaded their dominions in Africa. And Pyrrhus, when invited in B.C. 278-276, also forced them to keep to the west for a time, and took and besieged some of their chief possessions in Sicily. But after his retirement they had not only recovered their cities in western Sicily, but were again struggling to spread their power to the east. And now, as before, their chief opponent was Syracuse, at this time under the rule of an able sovereign, Hiero II. Some Sicilian states, however, were jealous of Syracuse, and were willing to welcome even Carthaginian aid against her, or to look elsewhere for support. There was always therefore an opportunity for a foreign power to interfere; for the Greek states were often at enmity with each other, and in the several cities there were opposing parties, each ready to appeal to an outside power to crush the other. Before long a circumstance happened which brought on such an interference.

2. **The Causes of the First Punic War.** The Campanian mercenaries, who called themselves Mamertines, have been already mentioned (p. 63). They were in Sicily at the time of the death of Agathocles, tyrant of Syracuse (B.C. 289). Left to themselves they seized on the town of Messana, expelled or killed the men, and took possession of the women, children, and property. They established themselves as a regular state, but as they were a terror to their neighbours by their constant freebooting expeditions, it became one of the chief objects of the Syracusan sovereigns to suppress them. When Hiero II. grew strong and defeated them severely at Mylae (B.C. 270), they were in great fear for their safety and looked out for help. Some of them appealed to the Carthaginians, whose chief towns in Sicily were Panormus (*Palermo*) and Agrigentum, and others sent to Rome. The Carthaginians, however, were nearest, and while it was still uncertain what the Romans would do, a Carthaginian general named Hanno arrived

and occupied the citadel with a garrison. The Romans had to consider what steps they should take. The cause of the Mamertines was a bad one; but the increase of Carthaginian influence in Sicily they looked upon as a danger to Italy, and as a perpetuation of their own exclusion from the trade of Africa and Sardinia, from which they had been barred by a treaty made about B.C. 306. They determined therefore that they would undertake the cause

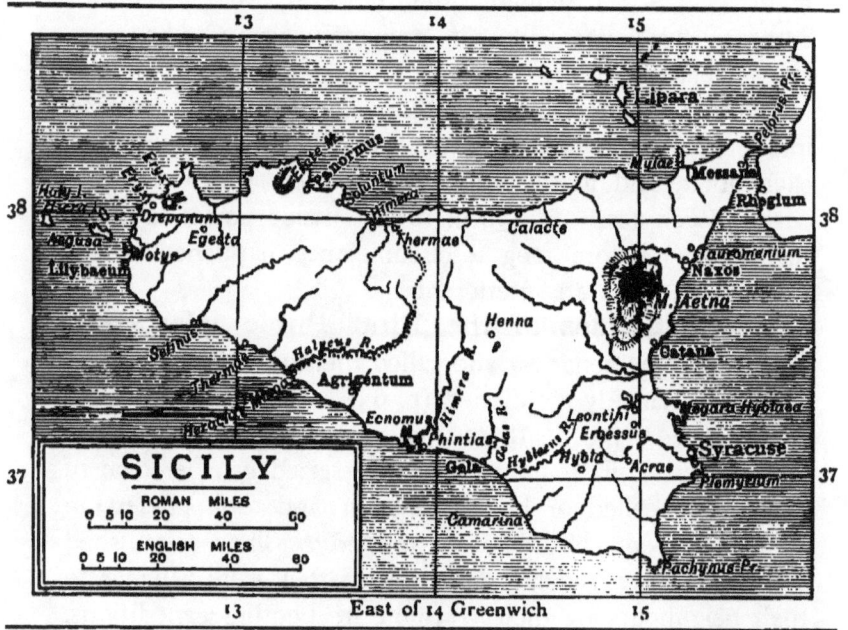

of the Mamertines, and refuse to let it be settled either by the Syracusans or Carthaginians. They hired or borrowed ships from the Greek maritime towns, Tarentum, Locri, Elea, and Naples, and sent an army by sea to Messana. Hanno by an act of imprudence allowed himself to be ousted from the citadel, and a Roman garrison was introduced instead. And when the town thus guarded was besieged by another Carthaginian army, and by Hiero of Syracuse, the Roman commander, Gaius Claudius, sallied out and defeated both. When the consul Appius Claudius arrived he even proceeded to besiege Syracuse; and though he did not succeed in taking it, Hiero was so much impressed by the superior strength of the Romans that he made a treaty with them, and remained a faithful ally to the end of his life. This was the beginning of a war which was to last nearly twenty-four years, and the object of which was to decide whether Rome or Carthage was to be paramount in Sicily.

3. **The First Punic War,** B.C. 264-242.

First Period, B.C. 264-262. The first two years of the war decided that Syracuse was to be the ally of Rome and not of Carthage; and, secondly, drove the Carthaginians back to the west of the Halycus by the fall of Agrigentum after a seven months' siege (B.C. 262), which was followed by the adherence of many other towns in Sicily; and this was done in spite of the fact that Carthage made great efforts to strengthen her hold, collecting mercenary troops from the Ligurians, Gauls, and Spain.

Second Period, B.C. 262-255. From this time the Romans began to aim at more than they had first intended, namely, to expel the Carthaginians from Sicily altogether. But to do this they now learnt that they must possess a fleet. They might conquer inland towns, but they could not win those on the western and northern coasts; for they were dominated by the Carthaginian fleets, which not only scoured the coasts of Sicily but made descents upon Italy, and held Sardinia in a firm grasp. The Romans therefore determined to build a fleet which should not merely be capable of conveying troops, but should fight the ships of Carthage at sea. It was a strangely daring thing to do, for the Carthaginians had long been masters of the sea, and their navy and crews were the best in the world; while the Romans had scarcely any ships of war, and were obliged to go to the allied cities in southern Italy for most of their crews.[1] The attempt was made however: ships were built on the model of a Punic quinquereme which had been stranded and captured, and rowers (it is said) were trained on wooden platforms. By the spring of B.C. 260 the fleet was ready and set sail for Sicily under the command of Cn. Cornelius Scipio, one of the consuls: the other consul, Gaius Duilius, going to Sicily in the ordinary way to command the army which was to relieve Segesta, then being besieged by the Carthaginians. Scipio, however, was captured while attempting to take the island Lipara. Duilius therefore took command of the fleet, and defeated the Carthaginians near **Mylae**. The victory was a triumph of force over skill. The Roman notion of fighting at sea was to run their ships alongside the enemy, hold them fast with a contrivance consisting of a swinging gangway and iron grapples (which they called *corvi*, or 'crows'), and fight it out as though on land. But the victory however obtained enabled Duilius to go to the relief of Segesta, and to make descents at various places on the coast. It naturally caused great exultation at Rome, where for the first time a naval triumph was celebrated and a column adorned with beaks of captive ships set up in the Forum (*Columna rostrata*). It encouraged the Romans also to take the offensive. Corsica and Sardinia were attacked in B.C. 259-8; and after an indecisive battle off Tyndaris in B.C. 257 they resolved to transfer the war to Africa, thus forcing Carthage to act almost wholly on the defensive. The two consuls of B.C. 256 therefore were despatched to Africa with a large fleet and army. They conquered a Carthaginian fleet which tried to intercept them off **Ecnomus** in southern Sicily, and

[1] Hence the name of *socii navales*, applied to sailors in the Roman fleets.

landed in Carthaginian territory. During the remainder of the season they harried the country and repulsed Carthaginian troops sent to withstand them. But in the winter one consul went home, and the other (M. Atilius Regulus) was next spring defeated and made prisoner, chiefly by the means of a certain Xanthippus of Sparta, who had taken service in the Carthaginian army (B.C. 255). The remains of the Roman army still held Clupea, a town on the coast, but were presently withdrawn and were being conveyed home by a fleet sent to fetch them, after winning another naval engagement off Hermaeum, when they were caught in a storm off the coast of Sicily, in which nearly all the ships were wrecked.

Third Period (B.C. 254-250). The Romans, undismayed by this double disaster, built and fitted out another fleet, and went on patiently sending armies year after year to Sicily. The fortunes of the war varied continually, and neither side gave in. At one time, by the capture of Panormus (B.C. 254), the Romans seemed to be getting the upper hand; for Panormus had the finest harbour in Sicily, and the Carthaginians had used it as a starting-point against Italy. They adopted Lilybaeum in its place as their chief port and harbour, and this they made so strong that it was practically impregnable. Still they failed to dislodge the Romans from Panormus; and, though in B.C. 253 the Roman fleet suffered again so disastrous a wreck that for a time Rome abandoned naval warfare, the Carthaginians got so discouraged by constant failure on shore that, in B.C. 251, they made a proposition for peace, sending the captive Regulus as envoy under oath to return if he failed to get it. Tradition said that he advised the Senate against granting peace, and returned to meet a cruel death at Carthage.

Fourth Period, B.C. 249-242. The interest of the last eight years of the war centres round Lilybaeum, Mount

Eryx, and Mount Hercte. During the whole time Lilybaeum held out in spite of every contrivance of blockade and siege which the Romans could bring to bear upon it. The summit of Mount Eryx and the town of Eryx, on its slope, were seized by the Romans in B.C. 249; but the latter was recovered the next year by the Carthaginians, who also held Drepana, on the coast immediately below. On Mount Hercte, overlooking Panormus, Hamilcar Barca (father of Hannibal) posted himself in B.C. 247, keeping up communication outside by sea from a bay and beach below, which could not be approached except over the mountain, while the Romans still held Panormus. At these three points the war went on for six weary years, which witnessed every kind of surprise, skirmish, and assault, but no decisive battle. A defeat and destruction of a Roman fleet at Drepana, under Publius Claudius, in B.C. 249, followed by the loss of a still larger fleet in a storm on the south of Sicily later in the year, had discouraged the Romans from continuing a naval war on which they had again ventured. Consequently they again found that their attacks on coast towns were futile, for they could be relieved and supplied by the Carthaginians at will. In the seventh year, therefore, after their last naval disaster, they again resolved to build a fleet. Early in B.C. 242 a fleet of 250 quinqueremes was ready, under the command of the consul, C. Lutatius Catulus. In March he fell in with the Carthaginian fleet, coming as usual with supplies and reinforcements for the year; and on the 10th of that month decisively defeated it, off the **Aegusae** islands, capturing seventy and sinking fifty ships. The effect of this was that the Carthaginian garrisons at Lilybaeum and Eryx would be left without supplies, and would be obliged to surrender. It was necessary to make terms, and Hamilcar Barca, with whom the government left the arrangement, agreed to evacuate Sicily, to pay a large war indemnity, and to promise not to attack the king of Syracuse or his allies, both sides undertaking not to molest each other or each other's allies; to which the Senate added the evacuation of the Liparae islands (Corsica having been already occupied), and an increased amount of war indemnity,—3000 talents (about £720,000) in ten years, instead of 2200 in twenty years.

4. **The First Roman Province.** The chief fruit of the war was that all Sicily, except the kingdom of Syracuse, became the property of the Romans. It was their first possession outside Italy, and there was no precedent to go upon as to the arrangement to be made. Ten commissioners were sent to decide what was to be done. They decided that it should be permanently a 'province' of a Roman magistrate. This word had been always employed for any sphere of duty of a Roman magistrate. It was henceforth used specially (though the old use also continued) for the governorship of a country outside Italy, which had to be administered according to principles and methods laid down by a decree of the Senate. This decree was usually drawn up in accordance with the arrangements made by the commissioners sent to the spot. In the case of Sicily the plan was to take it over as nearly as possible as it was before, substituting Roman for Carthaginian supremacy. The States in it were to retain their own laws and local institutions, but were to pay a tenth of their yearly produce, and five per cent. on exports and imports to Rome, as they had paid to Carthage, or in some cases to Syracuse. Each year a praetor would be sent out from Rome to whom there would be an appeal in all cases of dispute, and a quaestor to administer the finances. But certain towns which had been specially loyal to Rome were placed in a better position as *civitates foederatae*, being regarded as entirely independent

except for the one obligation of supplying sailors for the Roman navy.

Rome had thus begun the system of governing countries outside Italy, which before long was to extend to a large part of the known world.

5. Sardinia taken by Rome becomes a Roman Province, B.C. 238. The reduction of Sicily to the form of a Roman province was not the end of the changes brought by the Punic war. Immediately after the peace was effected, the Carthaginians withdrew their mercenary troops from Sicily to Africa, intending to pay them, and dismiss them to their several countries. But the treasury was low, and they were tardy in producing the money. The mercenaries mutinied, and were presently joined by Libyan cities subject to Carthage. A terrible war was the result, which taxed the resources of Carthage to the utmost, and endangered her very existence; and it was not till it had been going on for nearly two years that the ringleaders, Spendius and Mathos, were killed, and the country saved (B.C. 241-239). A similar disturbance broke out in Sardinia, and the Romans, being appealed to, undertook to restore order in the island. Now Sardinia was a most cherished possession of Carthage, for, though unhealthy, it was rich in corn. The Romans, by treaty, were precluded from even trading there, much more from interfering in its government. But they caught at this opportunity, which the weakness of Carthage, after the late long war and the mutiny of her mercenaries, gave them. When the Carthaginian government therefore (having got the better of their revolted mercenaries) made preparations for an expedition to Sardinia, the Romans treated it as an act of hostility to themselves, demanded the cession of the island, and an addition of 1200 talents to the war indemnity. The Carthaginians felt this bitterly as an ungenerous advantage taken of their weakness, but

VII. THE PROVINCE OF SARDINIA AND CORSICA.

were obliged to comply. The native Sardinians, however, were rebellious, and a Roman consul with an army was sent there every year, till about B.C. 225, when, like Sicily, it was with Corsica made a province, and thenceforth two extra praetors were elected each year, one for Sicily and one for Sardinia.

THE EARLIEST FORM OF THE TOGA. STATUE, DRESDEN.

CHAPTER VIII.

BETWEEN THE FIRST AND SECOND PUNIC WARS

B.C. 241-218.

1. *Roman power consolidated in North Italy.* 2. *War with Queen Teuta and the Illyrian Pirates.* 3. *Increase in the population of Rome; the new nobility; the* ager publicus; *increased number of slaves; the spread of Greek influence.* 4. *Political changes; decline of the influence of the Senate; the* Comitia Tributa; *change in the character of the Tribunate.*

1. **Struggles with the Gauls and Ligurians in North Italy,** B.C. 235-218. We have seen Rome become mistress of Italy south of the Rubicon, and of Sicily, Sardinia, Corsica, and other islands near the shores of Italy. For a time there was peace, and the temple of Ianus was closed for only the second time in Roman history (B.C. 235). But soon her great position involved her in other struggles. The Gauls in the north and the Ligurians in the north-west were both constant dangers to her quiet possession of Etruria, and sometimes even threatened the city itself. The most restless and dangerous tribe was now the Boii, and either with them or the Ligurians Roman armies were engaged nearly every year. The war with the Boii and their neighbours, the Insubres, was dictated by a desire to protect the northern frontier: and towards the end of the period (about B.C. 220) it was resolved to secure this by establishing colonies at Cremona and Placentia (on the Po), and to put garrisons

in Bononia, Parma, and Mutina; while one of the great routes to the north, from Rome to Ariminum, was made fit for the passage of armies by Gaius Flaminius about the same time and called the *Via Flaminia*. With the Ligurians the object of the wars was primarily, no doubt, to prevent their giving assistance to the Gauls; but soon the Romans had another object—the securing of a safe and quiet route to Spain by the coast road of the Riviera, between the maritime Alps and the sea. Neither of these objects had been fully obtained before the beginning of the Second Punic War, in spite of more than one hard-fought victory.

2. **The Illyrians.** At the same time the power of Rome began to be known and respected in the East. The Illyrians, living on the east coast of the Adriatic, were in a great degree a nation of pirates. They not only plundered the shores of Greece, but those of Italy too. Their long Liburnian galleys threaded the maze of islands along the Illyrian coast, and darted out to stop and plunder Italian merchants. Rome's naval superiority since her victories over the fleets of Carthage caused her to be appealed to for protection on many sides. Her ambassadors to the Illyrian Queen Teuta, who was engaged in blockading Issa, were answered contemptuously, and one of them even murdered on his way home by the order, it was believed, of the Queen herself. A Roman army was accordingly sent, which took possession of Corcyra (Corfu), admitted Epidamnus (Durazzo) as a 'friend and ally,' and forced Queen Teuta to submit (B.C. 229). She was allowed to retain a small part of her dominions: the rest was given to her young stepson, with a guardian named Demetrius of Pharos, who had joined the Romans against the Queen, but afterwards proved a traitor to the Romans also. The whole country, though left nominally free, had to pay a fixed tribute, and the Illyrians had to promise not to sail south of the promontory Lissus in a ship of war. An interesting fact in

regard to this war is that it first brought Rome into direct communication with Greece. At that time the two most powerful states in Greece were the Aetolian League in the north-west, and the Achaean League in Peloponnesus. Their territories had both suffered from Illyrian piracies; and now the Roman government sent ambassadors to inform them what terms they had imposed on the Illyrians, and these ambassadors were received with great honour and respect. At Corinth, for instance, they were admitted to take part in the Isthmian games, as though of Hellenic descent; and at Athens they were admitted to citizenship and to initiation in the Eleusinian mysteries. This is to be noted, because it meant that some Greeks were already prepared to look to Rome for protection; and all through Roman history that was only a preliminary to the Romans exchanging such protection for absolute dominion. Moreover, the Romans were beginning about this time, since their conquest of Magna Graecia, to know something more of Greek customs, thought, and literature; and when they became masters of the East, as of the West, they always treated the Greeks in a somewhat different spirit to that in which they treated the rest of the world.

3. **Some Changes in Rome between the two Punic Wars.** (1) The great success of the Roman arms and her increasing dominion was reflected in the city. Large numbers of people came to live there who were not citizens, but *peregrini*, 'foreign residents.' They came for trade or pleasure, and their transactions with the citizens became so numerous that a new Praetor, called *praetor peregrinus*, was appointed each year to judge cases between citizens and foreigners. (2) The old quarrel between Patricians and Plebeians had died out because the Plebeians had got virtually everything they wanted: but a new nobility was growing up, consisting of rich men who got nearly all the offices and places of authority; and a new

set of questions had arisen between them and the lower orders. The chief of these was the now often-recurring question as to what was to be done with lands taken from conquered peoples in Italy. The upper class wished them to remain *public land*, let out to capitalists, who made much by it and soon came to regard it as their own property on which there was an easy rent or tax payable to the State. The lower classes wished it to be allotted to themselves in full ownership and in fixed proportions. The settlement of citizens on lands at a distance from Rome had a tendency to weaken the notion of the supremacy of the city, and of the government as an urban State, and the conservatives objected to it. (3) A sign of growing wealth and success was the increased number of slaves. This was in many ways a bad thing, for it tempted people to leave the country, where farming could be carried on most cheaply by slaves who were not liable to be taken off to serve in the army, and to crowd into the city, where there was more amusement and greater chances of success in trade and commerce. It filled Rome with an idle and often turbulent populace, which afterwards caused much trouble. (4) Luxury and love of display were beginning to take the place of the old simplicity of life, and several sumptuary laws were passed to restrain it. (5) Greek influence was beginning to be felt in some of the habits of life, but, above all, in education and literature. Greek was the 'common dialect' of a great part of the world east of Italy, and boys now began to learn it as part of an elementary education, instead of, as before, the Etruscan language. Schoolmasters and doctors were mostly Greeks; and, as the Romans as yet had very little literature of their own, some men—especially Livius Andronicus (about B.C. 240) and Cn. Naevius (about B.C. 235)—began the fashion of translating Greek plays into Latin, to be acted in Rome. And when, at length, some Roman writers were found to compose regular histories, instead of mere dry annals, they wrote in Greek, as though that were the only language suited to such books. The earliest to write in Latin, either poetry or speeches, of whom we know anything was App. Claudius Caecus (about B.C. 312), but he does not seem to have had any imitators for sixty or seventy years.

4. **Senate, Comitia, and Tribunes.** There had been no great constitutional change at Rome since the series of laws which gave the Plebeians full rights and admission to all the magistracies. But some of the effects of that legislation were beginning to show themselves. The influence of the Senate was declining. The magistrates felt themselves strong enough, with the support of the people, to defy its orders if they seemed inconsistent with the powers which they had received from the people. They were no longer quite so much all members of a narrow clique of families, and felt less the traditional authority of the Senate; and the old device whereby the Senate could practically supersede the consul by forcing him to name a Dictator fell into almost complete disuse. The dangers so near home, which arose in the Second Punic War; the difficult questions, so often arising in its course, which the magistrates were glad to refer to the Senate; and, above all, the government of the rapidly-increasing foreign provinces, for which there were no constitutional provisions, afterwards combined for a time to increase the Senate's power and influence once more, but for the present they were declining. Another change of importance was in regard to the comitia. The will of the people was expressed in two ways—voting by centuries and voting by tribes. But the legislation which gave the votes of the tribes (*plebiscita*) the force of law had had this result, that, while in electing magistrates the people still voted by centuries, in making laws they generally voted by tribes, that is, in the

Comitia Tributa. There was no law making this distinction, but it was becoming the prevailing custom. Now the tribunes summoned and did business with the *Comitia Tributa*, and it was often the habit of the consuls, when proposing some law, to entrust it to a tribune to bring forward. The tribunes for this reason, and because the cases requiring their *auxilium* were rarer now that all citizens had equal rights, became much more engaged in politics than in their original business of protecting individuals from magisterial oppression. They had gradually got admission to the Senate, and the right of stopping business there as elsewhere, and could therefore influence acts of imperial policy. As trials ceased also to be held, except on special occasions, by the consuls, and were decided by the people themselves, they had few occasions for interference in the administration of the law. Still they were regarded as the proper persons to champion popular grievances, or to withstand the Senate, if necessary; and it was against the Senate, rather than against the consuls, that they now most often exercised their powers. They became, in fact, more and more political partisans.

ROMAN COUNTRY HOUSE.

CHAPTER IX.

THE SECOND PUNIC WAR, B.C. 218-204.

1. *The importance of the Second Punic War.* 2. *Events leading to the war; the Carthaginians in Spain; fall of Saguntum.* 3. **The First Period of the War in Italy** (B.C. 218-216); *Hannibal crosses the Alps; battles of the Ticinus and the Trebia, Lake Trasimene, Cannae.* 4. **The Second Period of the War in Italy** (B.C. 216-207); *siege and capture of Capua; loss and recovery of Tarentum; death of Marcellus; battle of the Metaurus.* 5. **The War in Sicily**; *siege and capture of Syracuse by Marcellus* (B.C. 214-212). 6. **The War in Spain**; *campaigns of Publius and Gnaeus Scipio; their death; arrival of P. Cornelius Scipio Africanus* (B.C. 210); *capture of New Carthage; battle of Ilipa; Spain cleared of Carthaginian armies.* 7. **The last period of the Punic War** (B.C. 207-202); *Scipio Africanus in Sicily and Africa; Hannibal recalled from Italy* (B.C. 203); *defeat of Hannibal at the battle of Zama* (B.C. 202). 8. *The first war with Philip V. of Macedonia* (B.C. 214-205).

1. **The object and importance of the Second Punic War.** The first Punic war had been fought for the possession of Sicily; the second was for that of Spain. It did indeed leave the Romans supreme in Spain, but its accidental results were still more important. It brought Rome into collision with Macedonia, with the result that she eventually became mistress not only of that country but of Greece also. Her presence in Greece brought her into conflict with the king of Syria, and into close relations with other Asiatic princes and peoples. Lastly, the

possession of Spain compelled her to secure the route thither by occupying Gallia Narbonensis. That within a century from the end of the second Punic war, therefore, she became ruler of all Europe south of the Rhine and Danube, of all islands in the Mediterranean, and of a large tract of country on the coast of Africa, as well as of Asia Minor and Syria, may be traced directly to this great struggle with Carthage. Hardly any of these countries to this day are without traces of the supremacy once exercised over them by Rome. Judging by results, therefore, this is one of the most important wars ever waged. The Romans of course had no prophetic feeling of the great things it was to do for them. To them it seemed a fearful struggle for bare existence. They had expected that it would be confined to Spain and Africa; but the most terrible and disastrous part of it was really fought in Italy. This was due to the genius of one great man, Hannibal, son of Hamilcar.

2. **Immediate causes of the Second Punic War.** By the loss of Sardinia and Sicily the commerce of the Carthaginians was much hampered, and their prestige lowered. They looked out, therefore, for other means of expansion. Spain was easily reached from Africa, and they already had settlements and factories there. From Spain too they were not debarred by any treaty with Rome, for the Romans as yet had nothing to do with Spain beyond having some trading connexions with Tarraco in the North East. In B.C. 238, therefore, Hamilcar Barca, who had made the great stand on Mt. Hercte in the last war, was sent with an army to secure the African coast as far as the Pillars of Hercules, and thence to cross into Spain, with general orders to promote the interests and extend the power of Carthage there. Taking his young son Hannibal with him he crossed to Spain, and there laboured patiently and successfully with this object

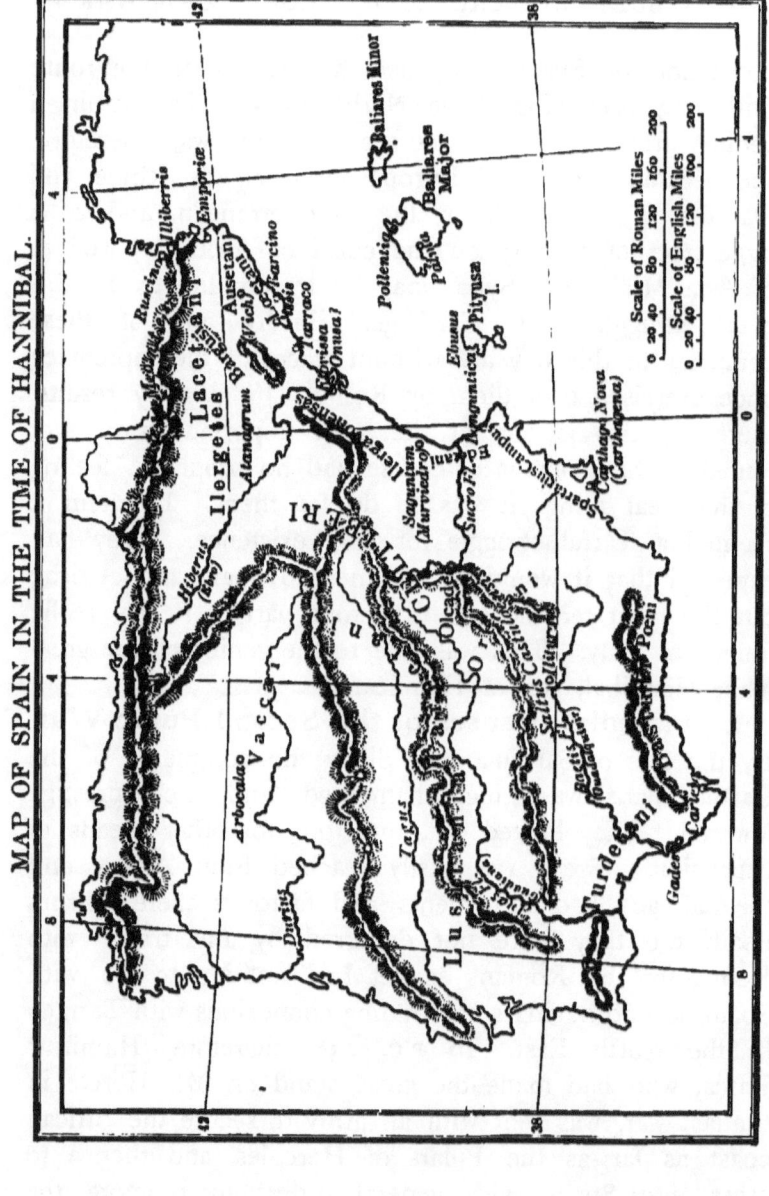

in view. At his death in B.C. 229, Southern Spain was mostly Carthaginian as far as the *Saltus Castulonensis* (Sierra Morena). He had administered the country well, had encouraged his men to settle and marry among the natives, and had done much to develop its wealth by working the mines on an improved system. His son-in-law Hasdrubal succeeded him (B.C. 229-221), and founded New Carthage to be the capital of Carthaginian Spain. At his death the army elected Hannibal (then about twenty-seven years old), who had served under his father and brother-in-law and become very popular among the soldiers, and the home government was forced to confirm the election.

But the progress of the Carthaginians had already roused the jealous suspicions of the Romans, who feared that their commercial relations in the North East at Emporiae and Tarraco might soon be endangered or eclipsed by their encroaching rivals. They were, however, at the time engaged in war with the Illyrian pirates and the Boian Gauls, and therefore were content to exact a treaty from Hasdrubal, or perhaps a mere verbal declaration on his part, that the Carthaginians would not go in arms north of the Ebro. But about the same time they made terms of 'friendship and alliance' with Saguntum, which was considerably south of the Ebro, and was therefore in the 'sphere of influence' of Carthage. Such an agreement was always held by the Romans to mean that they might proclaim war upon any people that attacked their ally.

Now Hannibal had inherited a passion for resisting, and if possible, taking vengeance on the Romans. His father had always cherished bitter resentment for the ungenerous use they had made of the weakness of Carthage to wrest Sardinia from her; and when starting for Spain had consented to take the young Hannibal (then nine years old) with him only after causing him to swear that he would never be friends with Rome. Hannibal now had an excellent army, devoted to him, and long trained in actual war; and the existence of a city in alliance with Rome in a country which his arms and diplomacy were winning more and more completely, seemed to him intolerable. Circumstances gave him an excuse for interfering. There had been violent party contests in Saguntum, and one of the parties had called in the help of Rome. The Roman commission sent in answer to this request had treated the other party with great severity. Hannibal therefore determined to take Saguntum, in spite of an embassy from Rome ordering him not to attack it (B.C. 220). The command, however, was not backed up by any military aid sent to Saguntum (for the Romans were engaged again in a war in Illyria) and by the late summer of B.C. 219 after a desperate resistance and a seven months' siege Hannibal took Saguntum. The Romans at once sent an embassy to Carthage demanding redress, and the surrender of Hannibal with his chief officers. The Carthaginians argued that no treaty barred them from attacking Saguntum, for though in B.C. 241 they had promised not to attack the allies of Rome, that applied only to allies existing at the time. But the Roman ambassadors would listen to no arguments. In a dramatic scene Q. Fabius Maximus (afterwards called Cunctator) is represented as standing up in the Carthaginian Senate with his toga folded across his breast, and saying, as he pointed to the folds, that 'he carried there peace and war, which would they have?' The Senators shouted in answer that he might produce whichever he chose. 'Then I give you war,' he said, shaking out the folds of his toga. 'The majority of the Carthaginian Senate cried out that they accepted it.

3. **First Period of the Second Punic War.—Ticinus and Trebia,** B.C. 218-216. War being now

determined on, the Romans proceeded to make preparations for waging it in Spain and Africa, using Sicily as a base of operations for the latter. But an unexpected movement of Hannibal quite disconcerted this scheme. He had during the winter of B.C. 219-218 laid his plans carefully for a march into Gaul and thence over the Alps into Italy. His object in following this route, rather than going by sea to the south, was to rally the Gauls of the Po valley to his side. He knew how hostile they were to Rome, and had interchanged messages with them and received promises of help. He felt that to attack Rome unaided was hopeless: and though he intended to work also on the hostility to Rome which he believed to exist among the Italians generally (in which he found himself to a great extent mistaken), he was not so sure of that as he was of the feelings of the Gauls. The passage of the Alps he knew to be difficult, but he knew also that many Gallic tribes had already accomplished it, and he probably underrated the real terrors of it. The Romans apparently knew of his march up to the north of Spain, but they did not fully grasp his plan and trusted to stop him on his way. Accordingly one of the consuls (P. Cornelius Scipio) was ordered to proceed to Spain, while the other went to Sicily. But a sudden movement of the Boii, who swooped down upon the new colonies of Placentia and Cremona, while it warned them that danger was to be looked for in the North, delayed the march of Scipio. To confront this immediate danger one of the praetors, Gaius Atilius, was sent with the legions enrolled by Scipio to the relief of the Roman colonists who had taken refuge at Tannetum, near Parma; and Scipio had to wait till two more legions were enrolled. Accordingly when he touched at the mouth of the Rhone on his way to Spain he was surprised to find that Hannibal had already passed the Pyrenees and

had reached the Rhone higher up. He sent out a body
of cavalry to reconnoitre, who fell in with some of
Hannibal's Numidian horse sent out by him on a similar
errand. After a brush with these troops the Roman
cavalry got near enough to see Hannibal's camp, and
hastened back with the news to Scipio. Marching hastily
up the left bank of the Rhone, Scipio hoped to force
Hannibal to fight him there. But when he arrived at the
point at which Hannibal had crossed, he found that he
was three days in advance. He hurried back to the coast;
sent his brother on to Spain with the greater part of the
fleet; and returned himself to Italy. There he took over
the legions commanded by the praetor, and crossing the
Po awaited Hannibal on the **Ticinus**. Meanwhile Hannibal
with terrible difficulties and losses had effected the
passage of the Alps. By which of the passes he came is
to this day uncertain: but whichever it was, soon after
reaching the plains he had to engage with the Taurini and
take their chief city (*Turin*). He then advanced down the
Po along its left bank; defeated the Roman cavalry on
the Ticinus, wounding Scipio himself; and followed the
retreating Roman army to the right bank of the Po till
he found them entrenched on the upper Trebia, one of
the southern tributaries of the Po flowing from the
Apennines. Here Scipio was joined by his colleague
Sempronius, who had been recalled from Sicily when
Hannibal's arrival in Italy was known. Scipio wished to
avoid a battle, but Sempronius was anxious to fight, and
allowed himself to be tempted out by Hannibal. He
crossed the **Trebia** on a cold rainy day and brought his
men wet and hungry into collision with an enemy well
fed and unwearied. He was badly beaten, but a large
part of the army was got off to Placentia, and there
remained safely entrenched. For the rest of the year
only skirmishing went on between the two armies: and

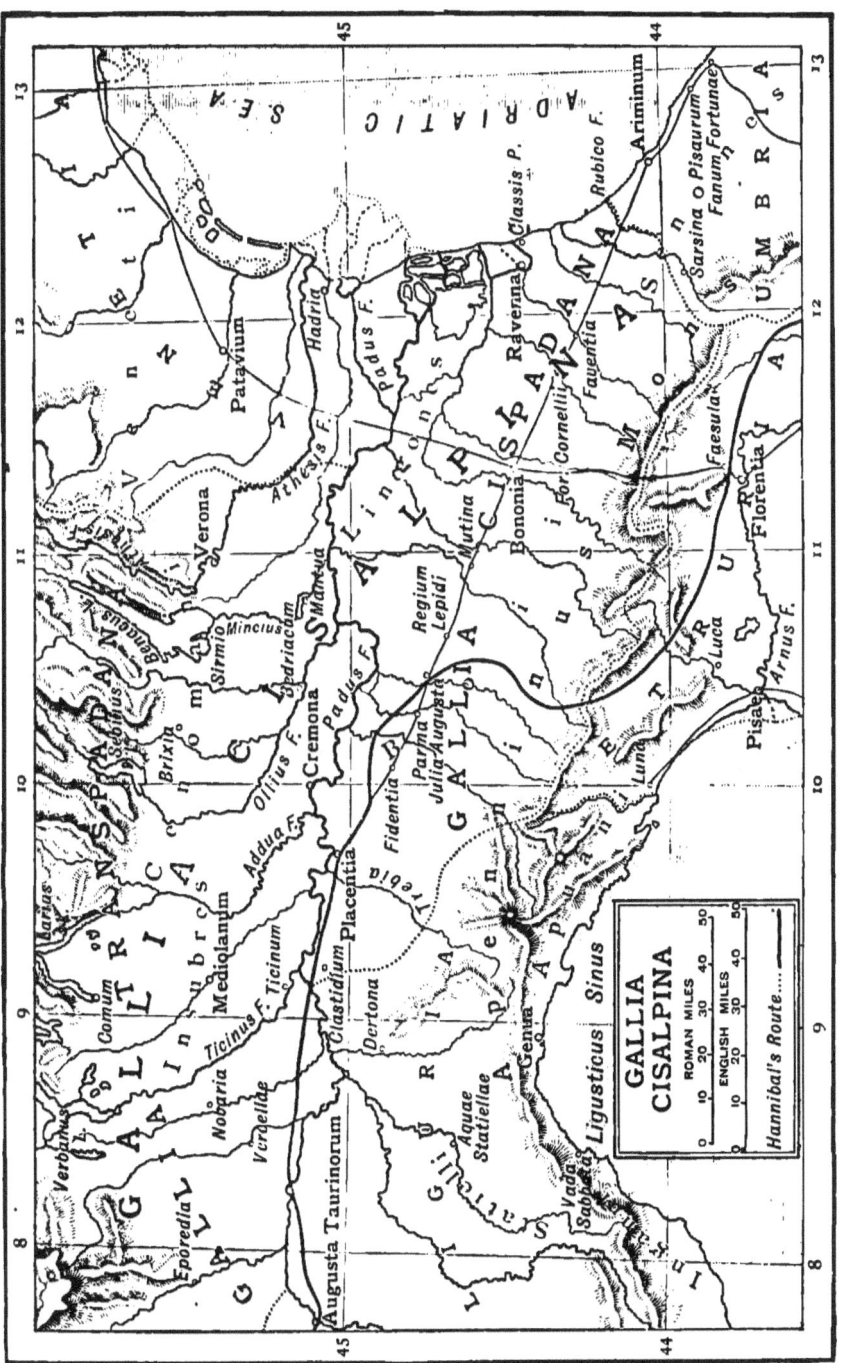

Hannibal had some difficulty in retaining the fidelity of the Gauls who had joined his standard.

Battle of the Trasimene Lake, B.C. 217. In the following Spring, as soon as the weather permitted, Hannibal, with a large contingent of auxiliary Gauls, started for the South, and marching past Faesulae (Florence) arrived in the neighbourhood of the **Trasimene Lake**. He had suffered greatly since he reached the Rhone in the previous year. Nearly half his men had been lost in the march into Italy, and now he lost a great number more in the marshes near Faesulae, which were specially dangerous from the unusually wet winter that had preceded. All but one of the elephants had perished; horses and men were in a sad state of disease and emaciation; and he himself lost the sight of one eye by ophthalmia. But the mismanagement or misfortune of the Consul opposed to him (Gaius Flaminius) gave him a victory which made up for these losses. He passed the camp of Flaminius, wasting the country far and wide as he marched. This Flaminius could not brook; he had been sent into Etruria to stop Hannibal's march upon Rome, and he felt that he would be wanting in his duty if he allowed him to push on while he hung idly on his rear. Without waiting for his colleague who had been posted at Ariminum to block the coast road, but who had started to join him on hearing that Hannibal was in Etruria, he broke up his camp and followed. Hannibal had turned to the left and was going along the north of the Trasimene Lake towards Perusia (*Perugia*), but finding the narrow road between the lake and the mountains well fitted for an ambuscade, he concealed his men at various points commanding the road. Flaminius arrived soon afterwards, and without making proper reconnaissances, started along the narrow road. Then from every point in the surrounding mountains the enemy rushed down, and the Romans found themselves attacked on three sides at once. They fought desperately, but were, for the most part, cut to pieces, or taken prisoners, though about 10,000 in all managed to escape in various ways, and straggling over the country found their way back to Rome. Flaminius was killed, his army annihilated, and the way to Rome lay open to Hannibal. There was no chance of the other consul, Servilius, from Ariminum catching him up; and, in fact, 4000 horsemen whom he sent in advance were intercepted by Hannibal's cavalry and killed or made prisoners.

Hannibal in South Italy, B.C. 217-216. But though the Romans expected now to see Hannibal under their walls, he turned from the road leading to the capital and marched through Umbria and Picenum to Arpi on the borders of Apulia. He did not feel fit as yet to attempt the capture of a large city. His plan was to raise the Italian states against Rome, and up to this time not one had joined him. At Arpi he found himself confronted with a new army under Q. Fabius Maximus, who had been named Dictator on the news of the battle of Trasimene. Fabius adopted, and persisted in tactics which got him the name of Cunctator, 'the Delayer.' The plan was to follow Hannibal at every movement, cutting off stragglers and marauders, but keeping himself on high and safe ground, and avoiding a pitched battle. Hannibal tried to irritate him by marching in every direction, plundering as he went: but nothing moved Fabius from his policy of caution. He followed Hannibal through Daunia, Samnium, and into Campania. There he thought he had trapped him by blocking up the narrow gorge between Mount Tifata and the river Volturnus. But Hannibal, who had been misled by his guide, and found himself in an unfavourable position, extricated himself by a ruse. Taking advantage of a dark night, he ordered cattle with burning torches attached to their horns to be driven up the mountain, followed by some light-armed troops, with instructions to make their way to the ridge with all the commotion possible. This drew away the 4000 who were guarding the gorge, through which Hannibal promptly led his main army. This was distinctly a failure on the part of Fabius, and it encouraged the feeling growing against him in the army and at home. His Master of the Horse, Minucius, presently obtained some minor advantages against Hannibal in Apulia, whither they had followed him; and this induced the people to name him also Dictator with powers equal to Fabius. His rashness, however, put him at a disadvantage when he ventured to offer Hannibal battle; and he was only saved by the timely interposition of Fabius, to whom he thereupon surrendered his powers.

The Battle of Cannae, B.C. 216. But in the following year it was determined that a great army should be collected and that battle should be given to Hannibal near his chosen quarters in Apulia. Naples and Paestum, and Hiero of Syracuse, had offered gold and other contributions; but if Hannibal were left undisturbed, the Romans must expect a combination of South Italian States against them, which would endanger not only their supremacy in Italy, but their very existence. They had failed to effect a diversion of Hannibal's Gallic auxiliaries by sending an army to the Po. The summer was wearing away: Hannibal had captured the Roman magazines at Cannae, and as harvest time had come he was securing the corn supply of the whole district. The consuls of the year B.C. 216, C. Terentius Varro and L. Aemilius Paulus, were ordered to go as soon as possible to the seat of war. But they differed as to the plan to be followed: Paulus wished first to draw Hannibal to ground less favourable to cavalry, in which he was the stronger; Varro wished to fight at once. The latter prevailed, and the disastrous battle of **Cannae** (2nd August) was the result. The Roman heavy armed troops charging the centre of the Carthaginian line broke triumphantly through it; but they pursued too far, and the two

CIPPUS OF PINTANIS, A STANDARD BEARER.

CIPPUS OF L. PATILIUS, A LEGIONARY SOLDIER.

wings of the enemy faced to left and right and charged their flanks. They fought desperately, but the arrival of the Numidian cavalry, which had been pursuing the Roman light-armed troops routed at the beginning of the day, decided the event of the battle. Of 70,000 infantry barely 10,000 escaped: about 3000 to some neighbouring towns, and the rest in scattered groups wandering through the country, till they were able to rejoin Varro who had made his way to Venusia with 70 horsemen. Aemilius himself had fallen; and though Varro was mainly responsible for the disaster, he did much to redeem his error by the vigour and spirit which he showed in collecting the scattered remains of his army: so that, when later on he returned to Rome he was met by a procession of senators and other citizens and thanked for 'not having despaired of the republic.'

4. **Second Period, from Cannae to Metaurus** (B.C. 216-207). **Capua and Tarentum.** Again the way to Rome seemed open to Hannibal, and again he declined to take it, in spite of the pressure of his officers, and especially of his Captain of the Horse, Maharbal, who promised that, if Hannibal would send him forward, he should 'on the fifth day feast as conqueror on the Capitol.' But Hannibal still waited for adhesions, and preferred to advance slowly into Campania, and secure possession of that district before venturing to undertake the siege of Rome. We cannot tell what would have been the result if he had taken Maharbal's advice: but we can see that he never had another real chance, although his victory at Cannae was followed, as he hoped it would be, by the adhesion of nearly all southern Italy. He entered Campania indeed, and received the submission of its chief city Capua, but he found himself in the presence of two Roman armies under M. Claudius Marcellus and Q. Fabius Maximus Cunctator. He did not succeed in taking either Nola or Naples (thus failing to get what he wanted—a sea-port), and such successes as he had in the capture of towns did not advance him on his way to Latium; while his winter quarters at Capua proved so pleasant and seductive that the state of his army was

seriously impaired and its discipline relaxed. In the years that followed Hannibal won many battles, and probably lost none, though his generals did; but he hardly made any progress in his chief purpose of attacking Rome or permanently alienating any great part of the country from her. His attention was distracted between the East and the West—now hovering round Tarentum, now promising relief to Capua, to the siege of which the Romans were directing all their energies. Tarentum fell into his hands in B.C. 212, but the Roman commander (M. Livius Macatus) maintained himself in the citadel, and thereby prevented Hannibal from using the harbour. The Roman siege of Capua went on during B.C. 212 and 211, and in the latter year Hannibal attempted a diversion by making a sudden and rapid march on Rome. He actually pitched a camp within three miles of the city, and rode round part of its walls. But he was closely followed or checked by two Roman armies, which he could not bring to a pitched battle; and, finding that the city walls were impregnable with such materials as he had been able to bring with him, he as suddenly resolved to retire, and effected his retreat to the south, inflicting a severe repulse on a pursuing army as he went. He did not, however, return to Capua, which, thus left to its fate, was forced to surrender to the Roman consuls (B.C. 211). A farther blow to his hopes was the recovery of Tarentum by Fabius in B.C. 209; and, though in the course of the years B.C. 210-208 he held his own in the field, and in three days' fighting near Canusium (B.C. 210) reduced Marcellus to remain inactive for the rest of the season at Venusia, and in B.C. 208 surprised and killed him near Bantia, yet he was steadily losing his hold on the country and becoming more and more confined to the Lacinian promontory, where he was to stand at bay for four or five years. He had failed, above all, to obtain a good port for troops arriving from

Africa to reinforce him: and now his one hope was that supplies of men and money should be brought him from Spain by his brother Hasdrubal, who in B.C. 209 had crossed the Pyrenees with large supplies of gold, and had spent B.C. 208 in Gaul collecting allies and hiring mercenaries.

The Battle of the Metaurus. Early in the summer of B.C. 207, Hasdrubal had crossed the Alps, and, having spent some time in an attack upon Placentia, arrived at Ariminum, intending to march down by the eastern coast road and effect a junction with Hannibal, who was near Venusia on the borders of Lucania and Apulia. Hannibal was being watched by a Roman army under one consul C. Claudius Nero, while the other, M. Livius, was encamped on the river Sena, to bar the march of Hasdrubal. But some horsemen sent by Hasdrubal to announce his arrival to Hannibal, and to request him to advance to meet him, fell into the hands of Nero, who resolved to go to the assistance of Livius without Hannibal's knowledge. Leaving enough men to defend his camp and keep up appearances, he marched away by night. On the day after his arrival the consuls determined to attack Hasdrubal, who was encamped between the rivers Metaurus and Sena. Now Hasdrubal had perceived that the one consul had been reinforced by the other; and thinking that this must mean that Hannibal had fallen, resolved to retreat. But he lost his way and could not hit the ford of the Metaurus, and was at last forced to fight on unfavourable ground. His army behaved with great gallantry, but was outnumbered and out-manœuvred; and seeing that all was lost, he charged a Roman cohort and died sword in hand. Nero carried his head back with him to Venusia, and caused it to be thrown in front of the Carthaginian lines, allowing two African prisoners at the same time to escape and carry the news to Hannibal. This really ended the

Hannibalian war in Italy. The news which those Gauls and Ligurians who escaped from the Metaurus carried back to their countrymen made it certain that no more help would come to Hannibal from the North: and Hannibal himself was obliged to retreat again to his headquarters on the Lacinian promontory, from which he no more made any effectual advance; and though he held his position there, and retained the loyalty of his army, he was isolated, and hopeless of support from home, or of any farther rising in his favour in Italy. It was natural, therefore, that the victory of the Metaurus should be hailed with transports of joy at Rome as the signal of relief from a long agony of danger and suffering.

5. **The War in Sicily.** One of the side issues raised by the Hannibalian invasion was fought out in Sicily, with the result of putting that island entirely in the hands of the Romans, and giving them a securer base of operations against Africa. Hiero of Syracuse died at the end of B.C. 216, and was succeeded by his grandson Hieronymus, a young man of feeble character and in the hands of advisers opposed to Rome. He was assassinated in B.C. 214, but had had time to break the Roman alliance, encouraged by the disasters sustained by the Romans in Italy. After his death two Carthaginian agents sent to Syracuse by Hannibal, Hippocrates and Epicydes, contrived to be elected generals, and to commit the republic of Syracuse to the same course of hostility to Rome. The consul Marcellus (B.C. 214), who was in Sicily, resolved to besiege that city. The siege lasted till B.C. 212, the city being defended with engines contrived by the famous mathematician Archimedes, and more than once relieved by reinforcements and supplies sent from Carthage. At length, however, it fell: the city was plundered of its wealth and works of art, and the old kingdom of Syracuse was added to the rest of the island as part of a Roman

province, though a few places, especially Agrigentum, held out for about two years longer.

6. **The War in Spain,** B.C. 218-206. While the Romans in Italy were struggling for life against Hannibal, they had been steadily keeping up another struggle in Spain, which was destined to have a still more decisive influence on the final result. The war with Hannibal is best known to us. It impressed the imaginations of the Roman writers most deeply, as no doubt it seemed to the men of the time the most pressing and important. But it was in Spain—where it had been originally expected that the war would be entirely waged—that the future conqueror of Hannibal gained his reputation and experience, as well as the material resources which enabled him to transfer the war to Africa. We saw that when Publius Scipio in B.C. 218 had to return from the mouth of the Rhone to Italy to meet Hannibal, he sent his brother Gnaeus on to Spain (p. 98). Gnaeus captured Hanno and much of Hannibal's heavy baggage which he had left behind in Spain; and though Hasdrubal had done some damage to his fleet, Scipio had firmly established himself in the district north of the Ebro. In B.C. 217 he was joined by his brother Publius with fresh ships and troops; and for four years the two brothers steadily pursued their object of pushing the Carthaginians farther and farther south. They were not invariably successful. If we divide Spain roughly into three districts, first, that part of it which is north of the Ebro; second, the country between the Ebro and the Saltus Castulonensis (*Sierra Morena*); and, thirdly, *Baetica*, the country between these mountains and the sea, and watered by the Baetis (*Guadalquiver*),—we may look upon the first as now almost entirely Roman, and the third as almost entirely Carthaginian; while the tribes of the central district sometimes joined one and sometimes the other according as they alternately prevailed, or in some cases were equally hostile to both. When the Romans are most

successful the fighting is on the Baetis, and the intervening tribes mostly favour the Roman cause; when the Romans are unsuccessful the Punic arms compel the adhesion of these central tribes and push the war up to the Ebro. Such was the general course of events: but towards the end of B.C. 213, though the Romans had a large auxiliary army of Celtiberians, and had prevented Hasdrubal from making his way to Italy, the Carthaginians seem to have been in unusual force. Three Punic armies were threatening the line of the Ebro; and when the Scipio brothers attempted to repel them, they perished separately within three weeks of each other. It was a great blow to the Roman cause in Spain, for the Scipios had been very influential there, and now even the position north of the Ebro was in danger. It was saved by the heroism of a young officer named L. Marcius, who secured the camp and headquarters at Tarraco until help could come from Rome. In B.C. 211 the praetor, C. Claudius Nero, arrived with an army, but did little. It was not found easy to get a successor to him, for the service was difficult and dangerous, and seemed to promise little credit. At last the son of the fallen Publius Scipio, who was to be famous as P. Cornelius Scipio Africanus, volunteered to take the command. He was only twenty-four, much below the age to which custom (though not as yet law) limited the enjoyment of consular work or command. But he had something about him which stirred enthusiasm and won confidence, and the people elected him without hesitation. He remained in Spain from B.C. 210 to B.C. 206, and in those four years quite changed the aspect of affairs. His first move was a sudden descent upon New Carthage, the chief seat of Carthaginian power in the south. Its capture gave him not only immense supplies of money and provisions, a considerable fleet of war and merchant vessels, with the use of many skilled artizans, but above all a base of operations in the very heart of the enemy's country, their best port and source of supplies. Its effects were immediately seen in the movement of the Spanish tribes to offer their submission to Rome. From this time forward the Roman cause in Spain seems to have advanced almost without interruption. But though Scipio, when he returned in B.C. 206, could declare that, after defeating the last great Punic army raised by Mago at the battle of Ilipa, he had left no Carthaginian soldier in Spain, yet he had allowed Hasdrubal to give him the slip in B.C. 209, and was only able to warn the home government of his intended march upon Italy. Still he had done more than merely win Spain: he had secured a valuable ally in Africa, whither it was now his object to transfer the war. Syphax, king of Western Numidia, long wavered between the Carthaginian and Roman alliance. To keep him quiet, the Carthaginians stirred up Gala and his son Masannasa. This last-named prince brought a body of Numidian horse over to Spain to support the Carthaginians. Scipio's success and diplomatic skill won both of them over. He even crossed to Africa to visit Syphax, and journeyed right across Spain to have an interview with Masannasa. The friendship with Syphax turned out to be useless; but Masannasa, his enemy and rival, remained devoted to the Roman side, and a few years later did valuable service. The last year of Scipio's command in Spain was marked by his own serious illness, and by a mutiny in the Roman army, leading to movements among the natives. Still when he handed over the province to his successor, the only chiefs who were formidable (Indibilis and Mandonius) had submitted, though they afterwards brought ruin upon themselves by renewing their rebellion.

7. **The War finished in Africa** (B.C. 207-202).—When Scipio returned to Rome in B.C. 206 he had resolved to transfer the war to Africa, where he had already secured allies. In spite of the opposition of the Senate, he was elected consul for B.C. 205, and had the 'province' of

Sicily assigned to him, with leave to extend his operations to Africa. After spending a year in Sicily collecting war material and strengthening and training his army, in B.C. 204 (with imperium extended as proconsul) he started

P. CORNELIUS SCIPIO AFRICANUS.

from Lilybaeum. He was at once joined by Masannasa; but Syphax had made terms with Carthage in the winter of B.C. 204-203, and was encamped with Hasdrubal near Utica, which Scipio now blockaded, after having plundered the country between it and Carthage. He deluded

Syphax by pretended negotiations, and then suddenly attacked and destroyed his camp and that of Hasdrubal. The Carthaginians in great alarm sent for Hannibal, who was thus reluctantly obliged to leave Italy. Before he arrived, Scipio had already defeated an army in the 'Great Plains'; Syphax had been captured by Laelius; and the last Carthaginian effort in North Italy had failed by the defeat of Mago in Gallia Cisalpina; and an embassy sent to Rome to propose peace on the basis of that made at the end of the first war had returned unsuccessful. There had been a short truce to enable this embassy to go to Rome and return; but the Carthaginians violated it by seizing some ships laden with provisions from Sardinia, which had been blown into the Bay of Carthage. The war therefore recommenced, and before long (18th October, B.C. 202) Scipio met Hannibal some days' march from Zama, and defeated him so decisively that the Carthaginians,—having no more troops, and not enough ships to keep their harbours open in face of the Roman fleets,—were obliged to submit to any terms Scipio chose to dictate. These terms were meant once for all to reduce Carthage to dependence on Rome, and to prevent her from rivalling the Romans in commerce or standing in the way of the extension of their foreign dominions. They were to retain their territories in Africa, but were to give up all their elephants, and all war vessels but twenty, with which they were, if required, to assist the Roman fleet. They were to wage no war outside Africa, and none within it without the permission of Rome; to pay 10,000 talents (about £2,400,000) in ten years, and meanwhile to give 100 hostages. Masannasa was to have all his dominions restored, with a great part of those of Syphax. This was really the hardest condition of all; for Masannasa would be on their very frontier, and there would be constant disputes as to the limits of the two dominions, in which

Masannasa would always be able to reckon on the support of Rome. The surrender of the ships also must ruin their commerce and destroy their wealth. Some of the more desperate spirits in Carthage wished still to resist, but were prevented by Hannibal. From this time Carthage ceased to be important, and the Romans were masters of the Mediterranean without a rival. In the period which followed Rome extended her empire eastward without any reason to fear opposition from Carthage. It was an unreasonable jealousy which, fifty years afterwards, made the Romans determine on her utter destruction. Scipio's triumph, on his return to Rome, was the most splendid that had ever been seen in the city; and the name of Africanus, which he adopted by general consent, was transmitted to his family. The exultation of the citizens was natural. The long agony of Hannibal's invasion was at an end. He had not only been driven to leave Italy, but had been beaten in his own country. Italy was free; Spain was open to Roman trade and Roman arms; the islands of the Western Mediterranean were occupied by Roman fleets and soldiers; and the question had been settled for ever as to whether Western Europe was to be Latin or Semitic.

8. **The War with Macedonia** (B.C. 214-205). It must be remembered that, while the Romans were engaged in their mortal struggle with Hannibal, and were maintaining a difficult and expensive war in Spain, and a shorter but still severe war in Sicily, they were also engaged in a quarrel with the king of Macedonia, destined to be even more important in its after results, though desultory and unimportant in the immediate incidents accompanying it. This king was Philip V., who was constantly seeking to make himself master of Greece, and had, in fact, garrisons in several of the strong places, such as Demetrias, Chalcis, Acrocorinthus—the three 'fetters of Greece.' The two

chief powers in Greece at this time were the Aetolian League, in the north-west, and the Achaean League in the south. In Peloponnesus, Sparta and Elis, and north of the Gulf of Corinth, Athens and Thebes maintained a nominal independence, but they had much declined from their ancient importance; and Thessaly was almost entirely in the hands of Macedonia. King Philip was usually inclined to be on good terms with the Achaean League, and to act as its protector against the Aetolians, whose desire of extending their power in Acarnania and Epirus brought them into collision with his interests. At the time of the Hannibalian invasion Philip was in fact engaged in war with the Aetolians; and his success was such as apparently to rouse his ambition, and make him look forward to the time when he might improve his kingdom by securing the coast line of Illyricum and the trade of the Adriatic, and even extend his dominion into Italy. When therefore he heard of the battle of Trasimene, he determined to negotiate a treaty with Hannibal, and take the first step by seizing the ports of Illyricum and building a large fleet. By his treaty with Hannibal, made after the battle of Cannae, he engaged to exclude the Romans from Corcyra and Illyricum. But the Romans got information about it by capturing Philip's envoys, and in spite of all which they had on their hands they proclaimed war against him also. It was not prosecuted with much vigour; but a fleet was kept permanently at Brundisium to prevent descents upon Italy, and some expeditions were made on the Illyrian coast and on the north shore of the Gulf of Corinth; and what proved a durable friendship was made with king Attalus of Pergamus, in Asia Minor, who had his own reasons for dreading the expansion of Philip's power. Philip was also hampered by new combinations against him in Greece, and when peace was made at Phoenice (B.C. 205) the chief result was that a considerable part of

Greece had come to look to Rome for protection,[1] and that she was therefore presently drawn into more decisive interference in Greece, and ultimately to supreme power there.

[1] Sparta, Athens, Elis, Messene in Greece,—Ilium and king Attalus of Pergamus in Asia, are in this treaty reckoned as on the Roman side. On the side of Macedonia are Achaia, Boeotia, Thessaly, Acarnania, Epirus.

PROW OF SHIP.

CHAPTER X.

SETTLEMENT OF ITALY AND CONQUEST OF MACEDONIA, GREECE, ASIA, AND CARTHAGE,

B.C. 202–146.

1. *The settlement of Italy after the Second Punic War.* 2. *Political changes in Rome.* 3. *The influence of Greece.* 4. *Depopulation of the country.* 5. *The Second Macedonian War and battle of Cynoscephalae* (B.C. 200-195). 6. *Greek towns declared independent.* 7. *War with Antiochus III. of Syria and with the Aetolians; battles of Thermopylae and Magnesia* (B.C. 193-188). 8. *Settlement of Asia after the war with Antiochus.* 9. *The destruction of Aetolia.* 10. *Contests with the Gauls and Ligurians* (B.C. 200-178). 11. *Organization of the Spanish provinces.* 12. *War with Perseus and subjection of Macedonia; battle of Pydna* (B.C. 175-168). 13. *Effects of her conquests on Rome.* 14. *Macedonia made a Roman province* (B.C. 147-146). 15. *Destruction of Corinth and subjection of Greece.* 16. *Destruction of Carthage* (B.C. 146). 17. *Viriathus and the Numantine war in Spain* (B.C. 153-133). 18. *The Roman Empire at the end of* B.C. 146.

1. **Settlement of Italy after Second Punic War,** B.C. 202-194. Rome was now again supreme in Italy, but her supremacy had to be secured and the traces of the struggle wiped out. The Italian towns generally returned to the same position which they occupied before. But to this rule there were some exceptions. The Brutii, who had set the example of revolt to Hannibal, were treated no longer as allies, but as subjects, at any rate for the present generation; they were not enrolled in the army,

and the whole country was regarded as a province ruled by one of the praetors. Campania suffered most; but the treatment of each town was carefully apportioned according to the loyalty or disloyalty it had shown during the invasion of Hannibal. Some were treated somewhat as Capua had been: that is to say, their inhabitants were either removed or sold into slavery, their territory was made 'public land,' in which Roman tenants, or *aratores*, were to be settled, paying a tithe to the Roman exchequer. They lost all independent or corporate existence, were to have no local magistrates or assembly, and were to depend for the administration of justice on a magistrate sent from Rome.

But besides these penal measures others were taken more calculated to fill Italy with communities loyal to Rome. The *civitates foederatae*, towns connected with Rome on fixed terms, generally preserved or resumed their former rights; and the Greek towns round the coast seem to have been treated with special indulgence. In the next place, the confiscated lands in Samnium and Apulia were divided among Roman citizens, who often settled on them and spread Roman customs and ideas. And, lastly, a considerable batch of colonies was sent out in B.C. 194, in Apulia, Campania, and Bruttium.[1] The two Latin colonies in the north, Placentia and Cremona, which had been founded just before the war, had suffered much from the Gauls while the Romans had been engaged in the south with Hannibal. Even after the end of the war Gauls and Ligurians ventured to attack them. But in B.C. 195 they were restored and protected by the consul at the head of an army, and after a time and some more fighting the Romans obtained a firm hold of the valley of the Po.

2. **Changes in Roman Politics.** Two or three

[1] See list of Colonies on pp. 55-57.

changes in the social and political state of Rome which were coming into prominence during this period may be noted here. In the first place the importance of the Senate revived. The foreign wars, and still more the foreign dominions secured by them, caused a great variety of new business: provinces had to be assigned to a larger number of magistrates; commissioners had to be named for settling their government, and constitutions to be drawn out founded on their reports; ambassadors had to be received and answered; trials to be held in regard to things happening in the Italian towns; disputes to be settled arising in the provinces. Now, though no law gave the Senate the power of managing all this business, and if a magistrate chose to appeal to the people he could always override the Senate's decree, yet by general consent it was usually left in the Senate's hands. Therefore the Senate became the most important authority in the Empire. It was generally filled by rich men who had been magistrates and whose interests began to clash with those of the poorer citizens, and therefore we shall soon see coming into existence a party of nobles, or *optimates*, and a party of the commons, or *populares*. The former were for supporting the authority of the Senate, and giving it the management of most business; the latter wished the magistrates to come to the people for directions, and take their orders as to what was to be done. The existing magistrates could do either, for from the aediles upward they were members of the Senate, where they spoke but did not vote; while the consuls could bring measures before the *Comitia Centuriata*, and the tribunes before the *Comitia Tributa*.

3. **Increase of Greek Influence.** In the next place, the war had filled Rome with works of Greek art, brought from Syracuse, Tarentum, and other places; and either because Greeks were forcibly brought to Rome as slaves,

or were attracted by the greatness and wealth of the city, Greek ideas, and Greek literature and philosophy, began to be better known there. Schoolmasters, as we said, were generally Greek, as well as doctors; and the work begun by Andronicus and Naevius (see p. 89) was farther continued by Q. Ennius (B.C. 239-169) and T. Maccius Plautus (B.C. 254-184), who not only translated more Greek plays, but wrote Latin poetry also on the model of Greek poems. All this, though it prevented originality, was an improvement to Roman literature, and in many ways to Roman life; but not in all ways, for Greek life was more luxurious than that of the old Romans, and many corruptions which had found their way among the Greeks now appeared in Rome also.

4. **Abandonment of Country Life.** Lastly, the old tendency to leave the country and crowd into the city was rising to a still more alarming pitch. Farming on a small scale did not pay, and the farmers were liable to be called from their work to serve in the army, or during the war often found their houses burnt and their cattle driven off. The only way it was thought that farming could answer was by having large estates (*latifundia*), and working them by slaves. The war made slaves cheap, because vast numbers of captives were sold, and they were not liable to be enrolled in the army, and so withdrawn from their work. Thus small properties were disappearing, and the city was crowded with people, some of whom indeed were successful in other ways, but many fell into great poverty, and clamoured for grants of land, though, when they got them, they often failed again to make them pay, and therefore sold them to the large proprietors.

5. **The Second Macedonian War**, B.C. 200-195. Scarcely had the Punic war closed when the Roman government determined that they must begin another with Philip, king of Macedonia. He had not observed the terms of the treaty of Phoenice. He had allowed one of his

nobles to take troops to Africa to help Hannibal at Zama; he was constantly making aggressions in Greece; and had made a bargain with Antiochus, king of Syria (B.C. 204), to divide between them the dominions of the king of Egypt, a boy named Ptolemy Epiphanes, who governed also at that time the Cyclades and many Greek towns in Asia. This led him into conflict with Attalus, king of Pergamus, and with the republic of Rhodes, which was a strong naval state. He won a battle over their combined fleets at Lade (B.C. 201), and in B.C. 200 was besieging Abydos when he was visited by legates from Rome demanding that he should abstain from attacking Greece or Greek towns, or any place under the authority of the king of Egypt. For the Romans had learnt the value of the Egyptian cornfields, and had made friends with the king of Egypt during the Punic wars, and regarded themselves as entitled to prevent all attacks upon him. Philip refused to listen to the Roman envoys, and proceeded to take Abydos. But this, added to his other aggressions in Greece, enabled the Romans to form a confederacy against him. The Rhodians, King Attalus of Pergamus, and the Athenians took the Roman side; and before the end of the year a Roman army was at Apollonia in Epirus ready in the following spring to invade Macedonia, and a detachment of it was sent forward to protect Athens. In the next year (B.C. 199), however, though the Roman fleet, joined with that of Attalus and Rhodes, took some islands in the Aegean and some towns in Euboea, the Roman army only approached the Macedonian frontier. It engaged in nothing more serious than some skirmishes, which, however, were sufficiently in their favour to induce the Aetolians to join the Roman alliance. But in B.C. 198 the command was taken over by T. Quintius Flamininus, the new consul, and before long the position occupied by Philip, at what was called the 'Gorge of the Aous' (*Stena Aöi*), was turned, and the king retreated through Thessaly, followed by Flamininus, and after some hesitation finally stationed his army near Tempe, to defend the entrance of Macedonia on the east. Flamininus did not attack him this year, which he spent in marching through Greece, and expelling Macedonian garrisons from the towns. He was then joined by the Achaean League, so that nearly all important States in Greece, except Corinth, Argos, and Sparta, were allied with Rome against Macedonia. The king thought it prudent to attempt negotiation, and three months' truce was arranged that Philip might send messengers to the Senate: but as they had no authority to promise that the king would give up the three 'fetters of Greece'—Demetrias, Chalcis, and Acrocorinthus—the Senate determined that the war should go on. In B.C. 197 the king entered Thessaly, where Flamininus met and utterly defeated him in the autumn at the battle of **Cynoscephalae** (Dog's Heads), so called from a low range of mountains south of Larissa. About the same time the Roman fleets, under the brother of Flamininus, subdued the Acarnanians; the Achaeans defeated the Macedonian general at Corinth; and the Rhodians were recovering territory which the Macedonian king had occupied. Philip's cause, therefore, was depressed on all sides, and he was obliged to submit to the Roman terms,—to evacuate all Greek towns, to give hostages, and pay a large war indemnity.

6. **Greek Towns declared Independent.** The only people in Greece dissatisfied were the Aetolians; for some of the Greek towns which Philip had occupied had once belonged to their League, and they expected to get them back again. But Flamininus meant that the word of Rome should now decide all such matters: and by and by at the Isthmian games (in July B.C. 196) he caused a herald to proclaim that all the parts of

Greece which had been held by the Macedonians were to be free and independent. This proclamation was received with great enthusiasm by the crowd attending the festival: and it was followed by a commission, sent by the Senate, which determined on local inquiries the several claims of the States as to territory and confederacies. In the next year Flamininus completed his work by forcing Nabis, tyrant of Sparta, to give up Argos, which had been assigned to him by Philip as a bribe to secure his adhesion; to surrender his fleet and all towns on the coast or outside Laconia; and to restore all whom he had exiled. Then he withdrew the Roman garrisons from Chalcis, Demetrias, and Acrocorinthus, and having received a large number of Roman prisoners, who had been ransomed as a compliment to him by the various States, he returned to Rome to celebrate his triumph. The general result of this war was to confine the king of Macedonia to his own frontiers (which underwent some rectification on the side of Illyria) and to leave Greece free indeed from Macedonian influence, but certain to look to Rome for the settlement of internal disputes, and practically debarred from seeking help elsewhere.

7. **The Wars with Antiochus, King of Syria, and the Aetolians,** B.C. 193-188. This peaceful state of things did not last long. There were elements of disorder working in Greece sure to provoke Roman interference. The Boeotians preferred Macedonian to Roman supremacy; the Aetolians were angry at losing some of the towns once joined to their League; Nabis of Sparta wanted to get back his harbours and his fleet. Accordingly the Aetolians, who were the first to stir, invited the help of Antiochus III., king of Syria, who had got the name of the Great from his victories in Asia, and who had already been in Europe to take possession of certain towns on the Thracian Chersonese, once dependent on the king of

Egypt. He also governed a number of Greek cities in Caria, in virtue of terms made with the king of Egypt. His legates had visited Rome in B.C. 194, and had been told that unless he abstained altogether from entering Europe, the Romans would free the Greek cities in Asia from his rule. Antiochus therefore was glad to show his anger against Rome, and his previous successes gave him an exaggerated notion of what that power was. While he was taking measures to answer the invitation of the Aetolians, he was joined by Hannibal, whom Roman jealousy had forced to fly from Carthage. On his again answering Roman envoys sent to him in B.C. 193-192, in an unsatisfactory manner, the Romans determined on war, and a fleet and army was ordered to be prepared. War, however, was not yet actually declared, and it was the Aetolians who finally brought it on by inviting Antiochus to Greece, and by occupying Demetrias and attempting to occupy Chalcis in Euboea. Thereupon Antiochus crossed to Demetrias with an army of 10,000, where he was received by the Aetolians as a liberator. But though when he met a congress of his Greek partisans at Lamia he received all kinds of promises, and was declared 'general' of the Aetolian League, practical support was slow in coming in. The Boeotians hesitated, the Achaeans declared for Rome, Philip of Macedonia was prepared to stand by the Roman alliance: and although the troops of Antiochus defeated a small detachment of Romans near Delium, and Chalcis fell into his hands, he spent the winter there in idleness, and in the spring of B.C. 191 found on going to Western Greece that, either from fidelity to Rome or fear of her, he could get no hearty support from any State. On the arrival of M'. Acilius Glabrio with an army of 22,000 men in Thessaly, even the places that had declared for Antiochus were quickly subdued or gave in their submission. He then endeavoured to block the famous pass of Thermopylae and prevent the Roman army coming south; but he was beaten, as Leonidas had been in the Persian war, by a portion of the Roman army making its way over the mountain and taking him in the rear. He fled to Chalcis and thence to Asia, and never returned to Greece. The Aetolians were still in arms, but the Romans felt strong enough to neglect them for a time, while they wreaked their vengeance on Antiochus. In B.C. 190 another large army under L. Scipio (accompanied by his brother Africanus) arrived in Greece, marched to the Hellespont, and, having crossed to Asia, utterly defeated Antiochus late in the year at **Magnesia ad Sipylum**. During the previous year the fleet of Antiochus, as well as another which Hannibal had been sent to fetch from Tyre, had been more than once defeated by the Roman ships. The king therefore was obliged to submit to the Roman terms. He was to abandon all territory west of Mount Taurus, that is, all Asia Minor, and the Greek cities in it, all his elephants, and as many ships of war as the Senate should demand, give up all deserters, and above all Hannibal, and pay a huge indemnity.

8. **Settlement of Asia after the War with Antiochus**, B.C. 189. The result therefore of the war was that the Romans destroyed a great protecting power in Asia Minor, and were compelled to provide in some way for a substitute. They did not, however, wish to undertake this themselves. Their plan was to put most of it in the hands of king Eumenes of Pergamus, who was a firm friend and ally, except certain parts which were assigned to Rhodes, and some Greek cities which were to remain independent. It was not a fair proceeding, because (whatever his faults) Antiochus had protected this country from surrounding barbarians and robber tribes. If the Romans destroyed his power

they were bound to take his place. But they did not understand that as yet, and did not desire greater responsibilities. They sent the usual ten commissioners to carry out in detail the scheme which the Senate had determined upon, and they expected that the country would maintain itself. The consul Cn. Manlius Vulso (B.C. 189) did indeed carry out the duty of a protector of Asia by subduing the Pisidians, who were a nation of robbers and pirates, and the Gauls of Galatia, who were a constant source of danger to their neighbours; but his conduct was not approved of at Rome, and he was even impeached after his consulship for quitting his province. Yet it was certain that in Asia, as in Greece, every difficulty would in future be referred to Rome; and, whatever the ostensible arrangement as to government or nominal freedom might be, a new province had practically been added to the Roman Empire (though the Romans at present refused to administer it), and the confidence felt in that being the case, was shown by the country being rapidly filled with Roman merchants and bankers, who found a new and safe field for their enterprise.

9. **The Aetolian War Concluded**, B.C. 190-189. While Asia was thus being settled, the truce accorded to the Aetolians expired and the war was recommenced. It was brought to an end by M. Fulvius Nobilior who captured Ambracia, the old capital of Pyrrhus, now garrisoned by Aetolians. The Aetolians were obliged to submit, to surrender all towns they had taken since B.C. 192, and to bind themselves to follow Rome in war and peace, and not to add any city to their League henceforth: that is, they lost the right of making external alliances, and were obliged to become members of the Roman military and foreign system. The country seems after this to have rapidly lost all traces of unity or prosperity. Its inhabitants declined in number, and it became

a haunt of lawlessness and piracy. Ambracia, which was robbed of many of its works of art, was left free on the condition that Roman ships should be exempt from tolls or dues.

10. **Wars in North Italy**, B.C. 200-178. While Rome was thus becoming more and more supreme in the East, she was also consolidating her power in the West. In the first place, from B.C. 200 to B.C. 181, she was constantly engaged in contests with the Gauls living in the basin of the Po, especially the Boii and Insubres; and side by side with this was an ever recurring struggle with the Ligurians, who inhabited the country between the Maritime Alps and the sea, and thus barred the way along the Riviera, which the Romans wished to be open that they might reach Spain. The consuls and their armies year after year were sent to North Italy, and either attacked these two enemies separately, or, if one of them was quiescent, combined in attacking the other. At last in B.C. 191 P. Cornelius Scipio Nasica finally subdued the Boii. The whole tribe were forced to become Roman subjects, and to see half their territory become domain land open to Roman colonists. Thus within the next three years we find colonies sent to various places of importance. Potentia and Pisaurum secured the road along the north-east coast; Parma, Mutina, Bononia guarded the via Aemilia across the North of Italy through the heart of the country of the Boii; and Aquileia, in the territory of the Veneti, proclaimed the intention of holding that district against invading Gauls; Luna, Pisae, and Luca were advanced posts against the Ligurians. All were intended to thoroughly secure North Italy and Gallia Cisalpina, which in fact became so far Romanized that it was popularly called 'toga'd Gaul' (*Gallia Togata*). Still it was not yet treated as a part of Italy; it was a 'province' to which for some years one of the consuls went with an army, until in B.C.

181 the practice of sending a *praetor* there, on the analogy of Sicily and Sardinia, was begun, who sometimes stayed on as *propraetor*: and a few years later (B.C. 177) it was found necessary to send two praetors, who divided the province between them. The Roman colonies in it had the same rights as colonies elsewhere in Italy as to self-government, and the same duties as to military service.

The Ligurian wars followed much the same course as that with the Gauls. Sometimes there were expeditions every year against them, sometimes there was a year or two of quiet. Sometimes they threatened Pisae, which the Romans used as a port, or even the colony Bononia; sometimes they were driven back; but it was not till B.C. 181, that L. Aemilius Paulus finally crushed the Ingauni (on the Riviera near Albenga) in a bloody battle, which was followed by the submission of most of the Ligurian tribes. They surrendered their piratical vessels, and in many cases were obliged to demolish the walls of their towns; while one tribe (the Apuani) were in B.C. 188 transferred bodily to a vacant district in Samnium, where they settled peaceably. It was to maintain the hold thus gained over the Ligurians that Pisae and Luca were occupied. Yet even after this some tribes held out, and wars are often recorded up to B.C. 117. Liguria cannot in fact be considered to have been thoroughly pacified till the time of Augustus. Yet the Romans did secure their passage through the district, and in B.C. 109 M. Aemilius Scaurus made a military road (*via Aemilia Scauri*) from Pisae to Vada Sabbata (*Vado*), afterwards extended along the coast into Gallia Transalpina, being united to the *via Aemilia Lepidi* by way of Aquae Statiellae and Dertona; and some of the chief Ligurian towns were gradually admitted to the position of municipia.

11. **Organization of Spain**, B.C. 205-177. Contemporaneous with this settlement of North Italy was the

gradual organization of Spain. From B.C. 205 (after Scipio's departure) there was comparative quiet there. Some rebellious chiefs had to be suppressed; but on the whole it was peaceful. Two Roman armies were in occupation north and south of the Ebro, and the men when they had served their time often settled in the country and married native wives, thus gradually Romanizing parts of Spain. But the central tribes, the Celtiberians, were not subdued, and from time to time made raids on districts under the care of Rome. From B.C. 197 a regular provision began to be made for these two 'provinces' of Spain, which came to be called *Hispania citerior* and *ulterior*, one of the six praetors (or ex-praetors) being sent to each. When the outbreaks of the natives were more serious than usual, a consul with a consular army was sent, as M. Porcius Cato in B.C. 195, who compelled many of the restless tribes to demolish the walls of their towns, which were little better than nests of robbers. After Cato's departure, however, outbreaks were again of frequent occurrence, and it was not until B.C. 179-8, when Tib. Sempronius Gracchus was praetor, that much impression on the rebellious tribes was made. He won many victories, destroyed many robber castles, and dismantled many towns, as Cato had done. But he did something more. He inquired into the grievances of the people, endeavoured to relieve their poverty by a better division of the lands, and made with the several communities a treaty, similar to that enjoyed by Italian towns, whereby they enjoyed a local independence on certain fixed terms as to tribute and military service. This 'Gracchan settlement' was so just, that during troubles in after times it was often appealed to as the best charter of their liberties.

12. **Macedonia becomes Subject to Rome,** 195-166. Thus Rome was becoming undisputed mistress in the West. She was soon to extend her rule in the East as

well. There were many disputes between the States in Greece after the settlement of Flamininus, and in Asia after the settlement effected at the end of the war with Antiochus. These were usually referred to Rome; but Philip of Macedonia was always on the look-out to assert his own authority, and secretly plotted to recover his old influence in Greece. At the time of his death therefore, in B.C. 181, he was on the brink of a rupture with Rome. His son and successor, Perseus (B.C. 179-168), pursued or was believed to pursue the same policy. The king of Pergamus (Eumenes) was his enemy, and denounced his designs to the Roman Senate; and commission after commission was sent to Macedonia to find out what was going on. This irritated Perseus; and when he had, as he thought, secured a sufficient army, he resolved to risk a breach with Rome (B.C. 171). The Romans, who had secured the adherence of most of the States surrounding Macedonia, were ready; and, though the war which followed was protracted by the incompetence of the generals sent out, which enabled Perseus to baffle and even defeat the Roman arms for a time; yet in B.C. 168 an able man was consul, C. Aemilius Paulus, and on his arrival at the seat of war in South-eastern Macedonia, he restored discipline, and, having turned the position of Perseus on the River Enipeus, between the range of Mount Olympus and the sea, followed him to **Pydna**, and there decisively defeated him. Perseus fled to Samothrace, but was there made prisoner, and brought to Rome. No new province, in the technical sense, was made in consequence of this victory. But the whole of Macedonia, Greece, Epirus, and Illyria were treated as conquered, and reduced to a state of complete weakness and dependence on Rome, though their internal freedom was nominally respected. They all paid tribute in return for military protection, and were not allowed to keep soldiers or make any leagues with each other or with other nations; and though Roman magistrates were not yet sent, as in provinces, to administer justice, they were, in fact, subject countries and liable to be occupied by Roman troops at any time. Macedonia was still more effectually weakened. The dynasty of its kings was ended. The country was divided into four regions, each with a capital. These four regions were to have a separate administration. The people living in one district were not to own property or money in any of the others. They were not to have soldiers except in a few places on the border of barbarous tribes; they were prohibited from cutting timber for shipbuilding or working mines, except copper, which paid the Roman treasury a royalty; and a fixed tribute (half the amount formerly paid to the king) was to be paid to Rome.

The first step therefore towards turning these countries into Roman provinces was taken; they were subjected to tribute, and in return were under the protection of the Roman army, which therefore of course could be sent to them at any time.

Greece and Egypt. Greece was in a way better treated. The various States and Leagues were left as they were; but as in each of them there had been parties friendly or opposed to Rome, the members of the latter were treated as guilty of treason, and were ordered (to the number of over 1000) to come to Italy to stand a trial. There they were detained in various towns, without the trial being ever held, for sixteen years, when the 300 who survived were contemptuously allowed to return. Egypt was treated as a friendly State, and protected. When Antiochus Epiphanes (son of Antiochus the Great) ventured to invade it, he was met by a Roman legate, C. Popilius Laenas, who commanded him to withdraw; and when the king hesitated, Popilius drew a circle in the dust round him with his vine staff, and bade him

give his answer before he stepped out of it. Even the
Jews, when attacked by this same Antiochus, looked to
Rome for help. Thus free states and sovereigns, as well as
conquered countries, became the clients of Rome.

13. **Effects of these Conquests on Rome.** One
effect of these conquests was so greatly to enrich the
Roman treasury with tribute, spoil, and rents of State
domains, that Roman citizens were no longer required to
pay the property tax or *tributum*, which was not again
collected for several centuries, except once in the year
of Caesar's murder. This made the possession of the
citizenship valuable, and led afterwards to a determined
attempt of all Italians to obtain it. Another was that
a great many men became rich, and sought all kinds
of luxuries and works of art to adorn their houses; and
as these were mostly got from the conquered countries
which became Roman provinces, a great deal of oppression and robbery of the provincials took place. Again,
as holding office at Rome led to the governorship
of provinces, men became very anxious to get office, for
the sake of the wealth they might get from the provinces.
Consequently bribery at elections began to be common,
and many laws were passed between B.C. 182 and B.C. 137
to punish bribery and to establish secret voting by ballot.
Cases of oppression and extortion in the provinces became
so common that a separate court was established to try
such cases (*de repetundis*) in B.C. 149 by a *lex Calpurnia*,
in which the praetor presided and the jury was to consist
of senators. It was hoped that they would be impartial
and above bribery or intimidation; but that was not long
found to be the case. This was the first court established
permanently to try one particular kind of offence, and
was called a *quaestio perpetua*, as opposed to the *quaestiones*
('commissions of inquiry') which had been generally
appointed to try each crime committed against the laws

as it occurred. Another way of trying to stop the luxury which led to these crimes, was by passing what were called 'sumptuary laws,' which limited the amount which it was lawful to spend on dress, ornaments, banquets, and funerals. But such laws are always evaded, and do little good.

ROUND DINING-COUCH (SIGMA OR STIBADIUM). POMPEIAN WALL-PAINTING.

14. **Macedonia made a Roman Province,** B.C. 147-6. The arrangement made as to Macedonia in B.C. 168 did not prove successful. Several pretenders to the old crown of the whole country appeared: first Andriscus pretending to be a son of Perseus (B.C. 152), and then Alexander (B.C. 147) making the same pretence. Naturally the Macedonians, who found that the fourfold division weakened them very much, and was a very expensive way of being governed, felt sympathy with any one who offered to unite them and make them again a great nation. The Romans, therefore, determined to abolish the division, and make the whole country a province, adding to it parts of Epirus and Thessaly, to be governed by a propraetor sent annually from Rome. A great road suitable for the passage of an army was made from one shore to the other beginning at Dyrrhachium and ending at Thessalonica.

This was called the *via Egnatia*, and helped greatly the commerce and prosperity of the country. At any rate, protected by Roman troops from surrounding barbarians, Macedonia recovered much of its former wealth, though it never became again an independent country.

15. Destruction of Corinth, and further Reduction of Greece, B.C. 146. The formation of the province of Macedonia was followed by a great change in Greece. There had been constant disturbances in the Achaean League, because Sparta had against its will been forced to become a member of it. These quarrels led to frequent appeals to Rome, and the Roman Senate came to the conclusion that it would be best to weaken if not dissolve the Achaean League, and in B.C. 147 ordered that Sparta, Argos, Corinth, and Orchomenus in Arcadia should be separated from it. Irritated by this the partisans of the League were guilty of riots at Corinth and elsewhere, and the 'General' of the League for B.C. 147-6, named Critolaus, even ventured to raise a combined army to resist the authority of Rome. The Roman consul who was in Macedonia, Q. Caecilius Metellus, therefore marched into Greece, defeated Critolaus on the way near Thermopylae, and shut up his successor, Diaeus,[1] in Corinth. The consul for B.C. 146, L. Mummius, now arrived to take over the command; defeated Diaeus in a battle under the walls of Corinth, and then completely sacked and destroyed the town. It was full of famous statues and pictures, and such of them as were not destroyed were transported to Rome, adding greatly to the art treasures there already. It was said that the smelting of gold, silver, and copper caused by the fire produced a peculiar bronze known afterwards as *aes Corinthiacum*, which was much prized by

[1] Critolaus perished after the battle near Themopylae, it was never known how. Diaeus, the general of the previous year, according to the Achaean constitution, became thereby *ipso facto* general.

Roman collectors. Corinth sank to the level of a village and did not recover any importance till a hundred years afterwards, when it was colonized by Iulius Caesar. But this was also the occasion of a great change affecting all Greece. It was not made one province as Macedonia had been; but the Achaean League, and all lesser combinations, were dissolved. Each State with a small territory was treated separately; some, like Athens, Sparta, and Sicyon, were left with a certain semblance of independence, and Roman magistrates entering them did so without their lictors. They were *liberae civitates*, and paid no tribute. But they, no less than others, were really subject; and all others were so in form as well as in reality. They had their own institutions indeed and magistrates, such as the ten commissioners sent as usual, laid down for them; but they paid tribute, were forced to serve, if called upon, in the army, and were, in the last resort, under the authority of the Roman governor of Macedonia. The lands of Corinth, Euboea, and Boeotia became public land, the property of the Roman people (as well as the lands of some other cities which had resisted and had been taken by force), and those who worked it paid a rent or *vectigal* to the Roman treasury. Greece was not yet made formally a province, but it was completely subject to Rome from this time forth.

16. **Destruction of Carthage**, B.C. 146. In the same year as the burning of Corinth the Romans confirmed their hold on Africa by the cruel destruction of Carthage. Since the end of the Second Punic War, Carthage, though obliged by its treaty with Rome to remain practically unarmed by land and sea, had recovered a great deal of her wealth and commercial activity. The Romans had established Masannasa in an extended Numidian kingdom for the express purpose of keeping her in check, and being a continual menace on her borders. In the

quarrels that rose between them, appeals were constantly made to Rome, and always decided in favour of the king. There was therefore naturally a patriotic party in Carthage who looked on this as intolerable: and at length after one of these decisions rather more iniquitous than the rest, the Carthaginian Government refused to recognize a Roman Commission, and resolutely continued to fight Masannasa. The Romans therefore (most unjustly) resolved to make war on Carthage; and the famous Cato, now at a great age, continually urged the Senate to do so, ending (it is said) every speech he made in the Senate house with the exclamation, "Carthage must be destroyed." It was a purely selfish measure, instigated by downright greed and the desire to monopolize the trade of Africa, and nothing that Carthage had done justified it in the least. It was carried out also with cold-blooded and deliberate cruelty. First (B.C. 149), in view of the threatened invasion they surrendered their city to the discretion of the Roman people, *per deditionem* as it was called, trusting that the Romans would not exercise the full rights which this gave. Then they were ordered to give 300 boys as hostages, the Roman army being at Lilybaeum in Sicily ready to cross. After some hesitation they consented to do this. Yet the army crossed all the same to Utica, and there the legates of Carthage were told that they must give up all their arms of every description. This was done. And then at last they were told the full extent of their misery. They were to abandon the city altogether, and settle somewhere else ten miles from the sea. Driven into passionate despair by this cruel decree they resolved at last to resist. The whole city was turned into a workshop of arms, in which men and women in relays laboured night and day; and a vast number of shields, swords, catapults, and missiles were turned out each day, the women even cutting off their hair to be twisted into cords for the engines. But all was

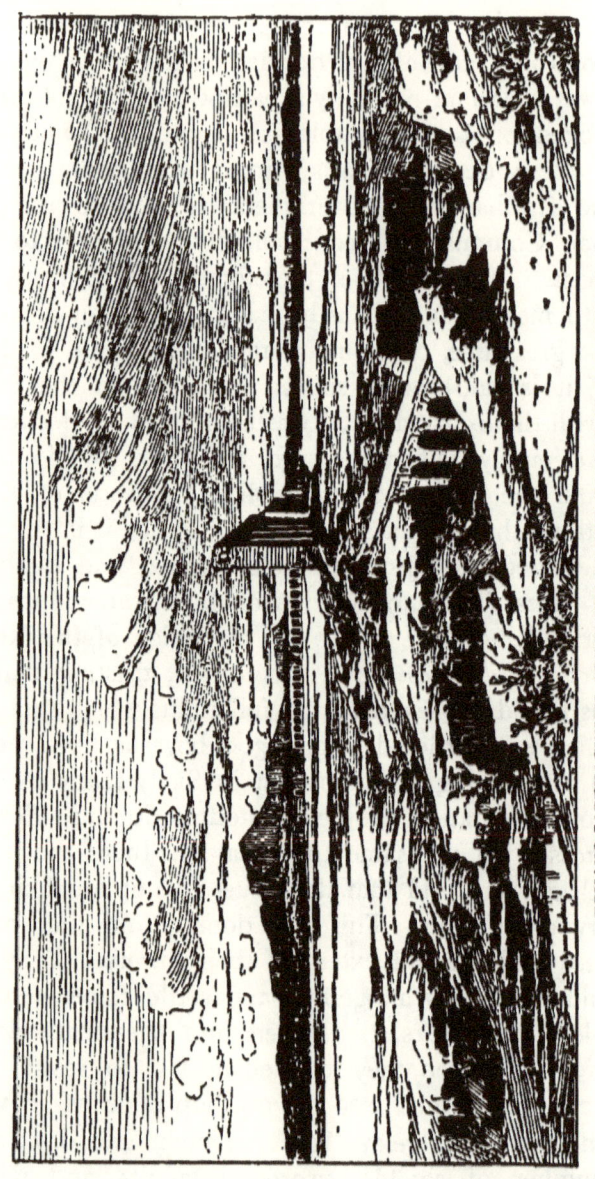

ROMANO-CARTHAGINIAN AQUEDUCT IN THE VALLEY OF UAD-MELIAN.

in vain; after an heroic resistance lasting nearly three years, protracted no doubt by the incompetence of some of the Roman commanders, the city fell. Publius Scipio Africanus, nephew and adoptive grandson of Africanus, the hero of Zama, who took command as consul in B.C. 147, succeeded in blocking up the mouth of the harbour, and thus cutting the Carthaginians off from getting supplies by sea, and in the spring of B.C. 146 delivered his final assault. Only about 50,000 people remained to surrender out of probably more than half a million. The city was ordered to be burnt and dismantled, and remained a scene of desolation and ruin (in spite of an attempt about twenty-five years afterwards to restore it) for a century. Having thus deliberately destroyed her ancient rival, the Romans made its territory a province, to be called Africa, of which the capital and seat of government was to be Utica.

17. **Wars in Spain,** B.C. 155-137. Though the Roman Empire was by B.C. 146 thus extended and organized, there were parts of it in which much fighting had still to be done. For some twenty years there was almost continuous war in Spain, where the **Lusitani,** who inhabited part of what is now Portugal, continually harassed the southern part of the Roman province, and were at length (B.C. 150) treacherously cut to pieces by the praetor, Sulpicius Galba. But from this massacre a certain shepherd, named **Viriathus,** escaped, who three years afterwards became a great leader among the dispersed survivors of the tribe. He collected them again from their mountain retreats, gained allies from Spanish tribes in the centre of the country, and for seven years, till his treacherous murder at the instigation of the consul Q. Servilius Caepio (B.C. 179), defied the Roman arms. Another enemy with whom the Romans had to struggle in Spain were the **Celtiberians** in the centre. The war was so fiercely contested that it was called the 'fiery war.' It arose from the Roman government

insisting that (in accordance with the arrangement of Gracchus) they should not build walls round their towns, which were the places of refuge for robbers and bandits. So dangerous was the war that the consuls often found it difficult to get officers or soldiers to enrol themselves in the legions for it. It went on with varied results for six years, from B.C. 153 to 148. Then it was renewed by the Arevaci, and centred round the siege of **Numantia**, their chief city. This siege lasted nearly ten years, and witnessed the defeat of more than one Roman commander. At length Africanus, the conqueror of Carthage, was elected consul for the second time in B.C. 134 and sent to Spain. He found the Roman army demoralized by this long and unsuccessful siege; discipline relaxed; and the camp filled with all kinds of loose characters, as well as traders making a profit of the war. He first restored discipline; expelled non-combatants from the camp; and accustomed the soldiers to labour and military activity. Numantia was then closely beleaguered, and, after horrible sufferings on the part of the inhabitants, finally surrendered in the autumn of B.C. 133. The survivors were sold as slaves, and the town entirely demolished. After this there was a long period of comparative peace in Spain, though several tribes still remained hostile and caused trouble afterwards. Three men were engaged in the Numantine war at different times who afterwards became notable in Roman history—Tib. Gracchus was there as quaestor in B.C. 137-136; and in B.C. 134 C. Marius was in the army of Scipio, where he may have met Iugurtha, grandson of Masannasa, whom, as king of Numidia, he was afterwards to conquer.

18. **The Roman Empire in** B.C. 146. We have now traced the rise of Rome from a small city with a narrow territory in Latium till she has become supreme first in Latium then in all Italy south of the Alps. Next we have seen how she acquired one foreign possession after another—

Sicily, Sardinia, Spain, Macedonia and Greece, Africa—and organized them as provinces. She has also exercised a kind of protectorate in Asia and Egypt, which we shall see was capable at the first provocation of being turned into a similar dominion. It has taken many centuries to do all this; yet there has been on the whole steady progress all the time. One thing led on to another, and it seemed almost impossible for her when she had taken one step not to take the next. Her career has been marked by much bloodshed, and what we may often call crime. But her people have shown great qualities,—not only dogged persistence and invincible perseverance in the face of disaster and defeat, but, what better accounts for her success, a real faculty of government and, on the whole, an enlightened view as to the management and improvement of her acquired dominions. Local customs and local self-government have been generally respected and fostered; but as yet little has been done to weld even Italy into one State. It is still in theory and largely in practice the people of one city governing others, that is, between three and four hundred thousand controlling about five millions.[1] But settlements of citizens forming part of this governing body have been planted in various parts of Italy, and this is to lead soon to larger ideas of nationality.

Internally we have seen an amalgamation of the inhabitants of the city in regard to their civil rights. At first there were two classes of such inhabitants: the original *gentes* and the Plebeians, the former alone being full citizens. The distinction has not been forgotten, but the inequality of rights has disappeared. All have a share now in the election of their magistrates, and theoretically in the magistracies themselves. But prosperity has emphasized the eternal distinction between riches and poverty. A new

[1] The census from B.C. 142 to B.C. 115 varies between 328,342 and 394,336 citizens.

nobility has grown up, founded not on birth but on wealth. High descent has still its reputation and influence, but wealth has still greater power; and though in theory the Roman government is democratic, in practice, office and power, and the influence which they bring, are getting more and more confined to a small section of the people. The period to which we have now come sees the beginning of the troubles caused by this difference between theory and practice, leading up to the next great change whereby both political parties, after fierce contests, fall under the rule of one man as the only means of ending the strife.

"TRICLINIUM" CIPPUS AT ESTE.

CHAPTER XI.

THE BEGINNING OF DISRUPTION, B.C. 150-120.

1. *The position and hardships of slaves.* 2. *Slave rising in Sicily.* 3. *The miserable state of Italy* (B.C. 140). 4. *Reform proposed by* **Tib. Sempronius Gracchus.** 5. *Tib. Gracchus wishes to be re-elected tribune; his death in a riot.* 6. *Results of the fall of Tib. Gracchus.* 7. *The new province of Asia.* 8. *The tribunate of* **Gaius Sempronius Gracchus**; *his laws as to the law courts; the province of Asia; the distribution of corn and the soldiers; his public works and colonies.* 9. *The* **ordo equester.** 10. *Other measures of Gaius Gracchus.* 11. *The proposal to enfranchise the Italians, and the murder of Gaius Gracchus.* 12. *General results of the movements and fall of the Gracchi.*

1. **Position of Slaves.** It has been already noticed that one of the effects of the numerous wars and conquests on the part of the Romans had been the increase of slaves, their consequent cheapness, and the extensive use of them in cultivating the land. This was an evil in itself, since it tended to withdraw free men from the country and to increase the pauper population of the towns, but it also involved more direct and immediate dangers. The position of a town slave, often in personal attendance upon his master, enjoying his confidence, and frequently possessed of useful accomplishments, was not intolerable, though it put him at the mercy of caprice, anger, and cruelty. But considerable comfort and profit might be, and often were, enjoyed by him, and he had before him the hope of

emancipation by favour or purchase as by no means an unlikely reward for skill and fidelity. But the position of the country slaves in many parts of Italy and Sicily was much harder. The worst and most unruly slaves were generally reserved for this service. They worked in gangs, often in chains, and at night were shut up in slave-barracks or *ergastula*,[1] which were practically prisons, and in which the overseer could exercise any tyranny he chose unchecked. There were no doubt masters who lived on their estates and treated their slaves with humanity, and in some parts of Italy the practice of working slaves in fetters never obtained; but in others, especially the south, *ergastula* were so common as to become a danger, not only by the congregating of so many men rendered desperate by crime or suffering, but as affording unscrupulous masters the power of entrapping and withdrawing from freedom men over whom they had no legal right.

2. **Rising of Slaves in Sicily**, B.C. 139 and B.C. 109. The result was a number of outbreaks of slaves in various parts of Italy and Greece about this time. But the most serious of all was the rising in Sicily, where not only had a large number of natives been reduced to slavery, but owing to the profitable nature of the corn lands, often owned by absentee Roman landlords, large importations of slaves from the east had taken place. The conduct of their owners, Roman and Sicilian, seemed to court danger. For the slaves were left without proper supplies of food and clothing, and encouraged to supply their necessities by open brigandage. They were therefore prepared for violence, and ready to exact vengeance for their sufferings. It began in B.C. 139, under the leadership of a Syrian slave named Eunus, who had gained influence among his fellows by professing to have magic powers. Finding himself soon

---

[1] Connected with ἐργάζομαι, 'to work on a farm,' whence Mommsen deduces that the use of the ergastulum came from the Greek Sicilians.

at the head of a large force he seized Henna, and was proclaimed king. Runaway slaves joined him from all parts, and they scoured the country, plundering and slaying. One praetor after another sustained defeat at their hands, and even a consul with a regular consular army fared no better. Finally they seized Tauromenium and fortified themselves there (B.C. 132), but were eventually starved out by P. Rupilius. A new constitution was provided for Sicily under a *lex Rupilia*, and some of those who had been illegally enslaved were released. But the condition of the slaves was not much improved, and thirty years later there were outbreaks again in Campania and Sicily. In the latter once more a slave, Tryphon, was proclaimed king, and gathered a large army not only of other slaves, but of poor men and fliers from justice, and doing great damage on the Leontine plains, held out for three years. They were at length subdued by M'. Aquillius in B.C. 101-100: and were so strictly forbidden the use of arms that L. Domitius Ahenobarbus, praetor in B.C. 96, crucified a slave for killing a wild boar with a hunting spear.

3. **Miserable State of Italy.** The decrease of the rural free population and the increase of poverty in Italy by the side of great wealth and luxury had, as we have seen, been for some time becoming serious. It is said to have attracted the observation of Tiberius Sempronius Gracchus as he was journeying through the country on his way to Spain, where he served as quaestor in B.C. 137. The country was cultivated by gangs of slaves, and seemed bare of free inhabitants, while the towns, and especially Rome itself, were crowded with citizens struggling with poverty. As he afterwards expressed it, 'The wild beasts of Italy had lairs and sleeping places, but those who fought and died for her had no share of anything but air and light.' The problem is one which has often recurred: how to get the people back to the

land? Great estates had spread out in every direction, but the small farmer or peasant proprietor had disappeared or was rapidly disappearing.

4. **Legislation of Tiberius Gracchus.** Gracchus was a young man of high family and his sympathies might be expected to be with the rich. He was son of the Sempronius Gracchus who had done so much to pacify Spain in B.C. 179, and of Cornelia, daughter of the elder Africanus, who was famous for her dignity of character and literary accomplishments, and who had devoted herself to the education of her sons. Tiberius and Gaius were the only survivors of a large family, and had already shown that they possessed powers of eloquence and energy of character worthy of their high descent. As Tiberius reflected on the distress in Italy, and its causes, it occurred to him that it might partly be remedied by means of the public land (*ager publicus*)—the land which in various parts of conquered Italy had remained nominally in the ownership of the State. According to the law the amount of this land that any one man might hold was strictly limited, as well as the number of cattle and sheep which he might feed on the pastures. But such regulations had been allowed to fall into abeyance. Sometimes the land had been granted to the holders (*possessores*) on such easy terms, that the idea of undisputed ownership naturally grew up, and the small payment to the State came to be regarded rather as a tax than a rent. It had often changed hands by sale, had mortgages upon it, or was the subject of marriage settlements. To disturb the holders would raise deep resentment, and more than one attempt to do so had failed. Yet this is what Gracchus determined to do. He was elected tribune for B.C. 133, after his return from Spain, where he had distinguished himself in the Numantine war, and immediately brought forward his scheme of legislation. He first proposed that holders

of more than the legal amount of the public land (500 jugera, with 250 for each son) should surrender the surplus and receive a fair compensation: a commission was to be appointed to distribute the land, and the people who received the allotments (for which they would pay a small rent) were to be forbidden to sell them, lest they should again be bought up by the rich. But the landholders were not conciliated by the offer of compensation, and they persuaded one of his colleagues in the tribuneship, M. Octavius, to veto the proposal being brought before the people. Then Gracchus brought in another law without the compensating clauses, and when Octavius again vetoed it, Gracchus first retaliated by stopping all public business by his veto, and finally caused Octavius to be deposed by a vote of the people. This last measure was quite unconstitutional; for a tribune's authority could not lawfully be resisted during his year of office, though he might be impeached afterwards. However it was done. Gracchus brought in his law and got it passed, and a commission of three was named to decide what land was 'public land' and to divide it out. This was a novelty, which secured the execution of the law, whereas other laws of the same sort had not been really carried out. The men who got the allotments were to have grants of money from the treasures of king Attalus of Pergamus, who had died the year before, leaving all his wealth to the Romans.

5. **Fall of Tiberius Gracchus, B.C. 133.** Gracchus attempted to get people on his side by other proposals, such as limiting the length of military service, and allowing the equites, or rich middle class, to sit on juries that tried governors of provinces accused of extortion. But in order to carry these laws, and to see to the proper execution of his agrarian laws, he wished to be re-elected tribune for the next year. It was doubtful whether this was lawful, and the Senate determined to resist. Two of the tribes

had already voted, when the presiding tribune postponed the election because of the Senate's protest. The next day there was great excitement and uproar, and the Senate passed a vote authorizing the consuls to suppress the riot.[1] While this was passing in the Senate, a report was brought that the followers of Gracchus, armed with clubs and broken benches, were congregated on the Capitol, and that Gracchus, addressing them, had been seen to raise his hand to his head. He had really meant by this, as he could not make himself heard, to indicate that his life was in danger. But his enemies explained it to mean that he was asking for a crown. Thereupon one of the extreme party, Scipio Nasica, called on the consul to put 'the tyrant' to death. The consul refused to execute a citizen uncondemned. 'Then,' shouted Scipio, 'since the consul deserts the State, let the friends of the constitution follow me!' Many senators, rolling their togas round their arms by way of shields, rushed out to the area in front of the temple of Jupiter, and in the general mêlée Gracchus was struck down and killed. Popular feeling was so greatly in favour of Gracchus, and Scipio Nasica was so hated for his share in this riot, that, though he was Pontifex Maximus, he was obliged to leave Rome. It was an evil example set by the nobles, and recoiled on themselves afterwards; but for the moment the senatorial party triumphed.

6. **Results of the Fall of Tiberius Gracchus.**—The body of Gracchus was thrown into the Tiber, and many of his followers were brought to trial by the consuls of B.C. 132 and condemned. The land commission also,

---

[1] This was called *senatus consultum ultimum*, 'final decree of the Senate.' It was in the form *videant consules etc. ne quid detrimenti respublica capiat*, 'let the consuls [and other magistrates] see that the Republic take no harm.' It was held to give the consuls absolute power of life and death, like that of the Dictators in the old times, though there was really no legal ground for this.

which was still at work—and on which a partisan of Gracchus, M. Fulvius Flaccus, took his place, while that of his father-in-law, Appius Claudius, who died in B.C. 132, was filled by C. Papirius Carbo—before long was brought to a standstill. At first it had dealt only with public land held by full citizens; but a good deal was also held by Italians from various causes, and when the commissioners began to touch this, the Italians objected on the ground that, not having the privileges of citizens, they should not be involved in their disadvantages. Their cause was supported by the younger Scipio Africanus, who carried an order in the Senate transferring the decision in cases of dispute from the commissioners to the consuls; and this seems to have practically put an end to their proceedings. Shortly after this, Scipio Africanus, who had been on the day before addressing the people, and had been enthusiastically received, was found dead in his bed, not without grave suspicion of an assassination to which Carbo was privy. Nothing, however, was ever proved. His death (B.C. 129) removed a moderating influence. The party which had supported Tiberius Gracchus now formed a regular opposition to the nobles or Optimates, who kept power and office to themselves as much as they could; and the younger Gracchus was soon to come forward as the leader of this opposition.

7. **Asia a Province**, B.C. 129. Meanwhile a new province was added to the Roman empire, the management of which gave a great field to the greed both of the senators and equites, and caused much dissension between them afterwards. The will of king Attalus of Pergamus (which has been partly preserved) left the Romans his personal wealth and estates, and also, it seems, the right to the tax paid to him from his various dominions, most of which had originally been given to the ruler of Pergamus by the Romans after the defeat of Antiochus. The internal

government of Pergamus was to be free. At first the Romans were content with this, and even lowered the tax. But a pretender appeared—Aristonicus, a natural son of king Eumenes, the predecessor of Attalus, who claimed the sovereignty and all its rights. The Romans took three years to conquer him, and one at least of their generals showed himself corrupt, and was beaten in a disgraceful manner. At length he was defeated and brought to Rome, and the Senate determined to form the dominions of Attalus into a province to be called Asia. M'. Aquillius was sent out to settle it, but behaved with such dishonesty that he was impeached on his return, and only got off by bribery. These acts of misconduct by nobles sent out to fight or govern made the opposition more determined than ever to bring about some change. Gaius Gracchus therefore had both an opportunity and a party ready to support his reforms.

8. **Gaius Sempronius Gracchus**, B.C. 123-121. The measures of Tiberius Gracchus had been chiefly directed to the relief of poverty by means of the public land. Though his deposition of his colleague and his attempt to be re-elected tribune (which cost him his life) had been somewhat revolutionary, he had no deliberate scheme for changing the constitution or lowering the position of the Senate. But Gaius Gracchus (tribune from December B.C. 123 to December B.C. 122) introduced measures which, though not properly speaking revolutionary either, were of much more far-reaching effect, and were intended to shift power from the Senate, and the families who were getting exclusive possession of office, to the middle class,—the equestrian order, as it now came to be called.

9. **The Ordo Equester and the Judicia.** The 'equites,' originally serving as cavalry in the Roman army, and divided for voting purposes into eighteen centuries, had always been the wealthiest men in the country. As the

number of wealthy men increased there were many possessed of the equestrian census (400,000 sesterces) who could not get admission to the eighteen centuries, and who, while cavalry service was still required of them, served on their own horse (*equo privato*) instead of the 'public horse' supplied to those in the privileged centuries. When they ceased to really form the cavalry, the custom of having the *equus publicus* was still maintained; and also those rich men who wished to serve their ten campaigns in order to qualify for office, but were not in the centuries, still did so on their own horse. Thus in time all men who had the required census, and were thus capable of doing their military service either on a public or private horse, were spoken of generally as the *ordo equester*. As the senators and their sons were excluded from commercial enterprises, the members of this order had generally undertaken public contracts, collection of payments from mines, public land, and the like. Only those however who had the *equus publicus*, or had served on their own horse (*privatus*), were legally recognized. Those who had not had the horse or had not so served were not legally *equites* at all. Yet all who had the equestrian census (equal to that of the first 'class') were conventionally included under the general title of the *ordo equester*. But the law of Gracchus gave them legal recognition: for up to this time *quaestiones* ordered by the people were formed by the Senate, and senators alone sat on them as jurors or *iudices*. There was only one permanent *quaestio* as yet, the *quaestio de repetundis*, or court for trying cases of malversation in the provinces. This only applied to senators, because the governors, being all ex-praetors or ex-consuls, were, with their *legati*, members of the Senate. Gracchus and his party thought it unfair that accused persons who were always senators should be tried only by senators, most of whom hoped some day to have similar chances of enriching themselves. His *lex iudiciaria* therefore ordered that in making up the list of *iudices* (*album iudicum*) for these trials the praetor should only enter names of those of the first class who were not senators. This included what was now reckoned as the *ordo equester*, and so the only title to be reckoned in that order henceforth was the census of the first class, or equestrian census. When other *quaestiones* were established afterwards, up to the time of Sulla, a similar clause was inserted in the laws, so that the equites got entire control of the courts. It did not turn out to be a good regulation, for many of the equites held public contracts in the provinces, and if the governor of the province tried to control their extortions, their fellow equites at Rome were apt to join them in their revenge by condemning the governor when impeached at home.

10. **Other Measures of Gaius Gracchus.** Gracchus also at once promoted the interests of this order by throwing open the new province of Asia to their enterprise. At first the taxes in Asia (at a reduced rate) were collected locally: but he now made the reduction of the country after the war with Aristonicus an excuse for selling the taxes, like other contracts, to the highest bidders at Rome. That is to say, certain companies of *publicani* paid the treasury a fixed sum, trusting to make a great profit by collecting the tenths of the produce, the rents of the public pastures, and the customs. Farther, he carried a law which deprived the Senate of another hold possessed by them over the government of the provinces. The consuls and praetors drew lots for the provinces which they were to hold during or after their year of office; but the Senate had been used to settle which were to be drawn for by the consuls, and which by the praetors. Thus if a consul were in office whom the senators disliked, only the less important pro-

vinces might by a vote of the Senate be assigned to the consuls of that year. The law of Gracchus ordered that this arrangement as to the provinces should be made before and not after the consular elections,—thus preventing the Senate from so manipulating the governorships. Again his law *de provocatione* prevented the Senate from doing again what they had done in the time of his brother, *i.e.* arming the consuls with the power of life and death, by passing the *senatus consultum ultimum* (p. 146, *note*); the law gave every one the right of appeal to the people (*provocatio*), even after this decree had been passed.

This curtailment of the Senate's powers of course roused its indignation and opposition. But Gracchus was able to defy it by purchasing the support of the Equites and the Plebs. He secured the favour of the latter (1) by his corn law, which provided for the distribution of corn somewhat below the market price to all residents in Rome; (2) by a law relieving the common soldiers from the expense of purchasing their arms and clothing, and it seems also, by allowing an appeal from sentence of death in the army; (3) by providing work for many in building roads and bridges, which also made easier the transport of farming produce; and (4) by proposing a number of new colonies where landless men could get allotments of land,—such as Fregellae (under the name of *Fabrateria*), which had been ruined in a recent rebellion; at Tarentum under the name of Neptunia; at Capua; and at Carthage to be called Iunonia.

11. **Death of Gaius Gracchus**, B.C. 121. Up to this time Gracchus had carried all before him; he had won to his side the equites, and the common people, and was influential even in the Senate. But of course the majority of the Senate disliked his laws and himself; and were only waiting to strike a blow at both. The opportunity came when he made his next great proposal, to admit

the Italians to citizenship. This was now desired by the Italians, because it gave them protection against the sentences of magistrates both at home and in the army; the right of claiming a share in allotments of land, and (if at Rome) in distributions of corn; and the right to be candidates for Roman magistracies. But the proposal was likely to arouse jealousy among the very classes of citizens whom his other measures had won over. The Senate therefore seized the opportunity. They set up one of his fellow tribunes, M. Livius Drusus, to outbid him for popular favour. Drusus proposed twelve colonies, the remission of the rent on lands allotted in the *ager publicus*, with a revocation of the regulation against their sale; and, lastly, as a concession to Italians, the protection of socii in the army from flogging on the order of Roman officers. This was a compromise by which the Senate hoped to avoid some of the worst evils that they foresaw from the laws of Gracchus. The colonies would be slow in forming, and, as a matter of fact, hardly any of them were actually made. The permission to alienate land would result in it again getting into few hands, and the concession to the Italians would perhaps prevent the question of their enfranchisement being brought forward for some time. The manœuvre was successful; the bill was passed, and that of Gracchus for giving citizenship to the Italians rejected. Gracchus ceased to be tribune on the 10th Dec., B.C. 122, and early in the next year (B.C. 121), a tribune named Municius proposed that the foundation of the new colony Iunonia, on the site of Carthage, the law for which had been carried by Gracchus, and which he had personally superintended, should be stopped, on the ground of the curse pronounced upon the rebuilding of Carthage by Scipio, at the time of its destruction. The project was offensive to many of those who otherwise supported Gracchus, because Italians were invited to take part in the colony: still the extreme partisans of Gracchus, led by M. Fulvius Flaccus, determined to resist the passing of this law. On the first day the *Comitia* were put off on pretext of rain, after the two opposite mobs had come to blows and one man had been killed. On the next day the Senate declared that there was a riot, and passed the usual decree (*videant consules*, etc.[1]), and when the followers of Gracchus, or rather of Fulvius Flaccus, occupied the Aventine, the Senate declared both Gracchus and Fulvius Flaccus public enemies (*hostes*), and offered a reward for their heads; and the consul with a company of soldiers and some Cretan archers went to attack them on the Aventine. Gracchus tried to escape, but was overtaken and killed in the Grove of the Furies on Ianiculum. Fulvius took refuge in a bath, but was also dragged out and killed. Many fell in the encounter, and 3000 were afterwards condemned by a commission presided over by the consul, L. Opimius.

12. **Results of the Movement, and of the Murder of the Gracchi.** The aristocrats had triumphed for the present, and used their triumph unmercifully. But the death of Gracchus caused a revulsion in popular feeling, and his opponents did not venture to repeal his laws. The colonial schemes however came to almost nothing. Carthage was not now made a colony, though citizens already there retained their lands. None of Livius's proposed colonies were made. Neptunia alone of those proposed by Gracchus flourished on the site of Tarentum. Livius's law allowing the sale of allotments was passed, and before long these lands became free of rent, and in all respects freehold property, though a large tract of country in Campania still remained *ager publicus*, and was let to tenants. The defeat of the policy of Gaius Gracchus as to the admission of Italians to the *civitas* led to the Social

[1] See p. 146.

154   DEFECTS IN THE POLICY OF G. GRACCHUS. CH. XI.

War of B.C. 90. The plan of extra-Italian colonies was carried out many years afterwards with good results; but it cannot be said that his legislation on the whole was favourable to internal peace or good government. The Equites proved more venal as jurymen than the Senators; the distribution of cheap corn exhausted the treasury without adequately relieving the poor, and was extremely mischievous in its effects; the arrangement as to the collecting the taxes in Asia made the Romans hated there, and did much to bring on the war with Mithridates; and a permanent quarrel or opposition was started between the Senate and the Equites, which helped on the civil war, ending in the rule of a single master. On the other hand, the murder of the two brothers and many of their followers in riots provoked by the nobles, and the judicial murder of many more in the trials which took place afterwards, set an example of violence and bloody party contests which rebounded upon these nobles themselves with disastrous results. Many therefore, with some reason, regard the agitation of the Gracchi as the beginning of the fall of the Republic.

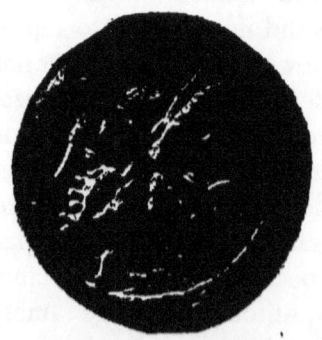

HEAD OF JANUS.

CHAPTER XII.

THE RISE OF MARIUS.

1. *Formation of the Province in Gallia Transalpina.* 2. *The* **Cimbri** *and* **Teutones** *appear on the northern frontier of Italy.* 3. *The war with* **Jugurtha.** 4. *Effect of the Jugurthine war on Roman politics.* 5. *Destruction of the Teutones and Cimbri.* 6. *Great position of* **Marius.**

1. **Gallia Transalpina,** B.C. 118. The struggles which the Romans had maintained year after year with the Ligurians in order to command North-west Italy and secure a safe road to Spain, now brought them beyond the Alps, and led to the formation of a province in Transalpine Gaul. This embraced the greater part of south-eastern France, from the Lake of Geneva on the north, to the Gulf of Lyons and the Pyrenees on the south, and was bounded on the east by the Alps, and on the west by the Cevennes and the Upper Garonne. As opposed to the rest of Gaul it was spoken of as 'the Province,'—a name which has survived in the modern Provence. Its acquisition was brought about by help given to Massilia (long in alliance with Rome) against the neighbouring barbarians, and it began as usual with military occupation, and the founding of towns to form military headquarters,—such as Aquae Sextiae (Aix) in B.C. 122-1 by C. Sextius Calvinus. When the province was formed in B.C. 118, Narbo Martius

(*Narbonne*) was made a Roman colony to be its capital, Massilia remaining a 'free state' in alliance with Rome.

2. **The Cimbri**, B.C. 113. But, while the Romans were thus securing the north-west frontier of Italy and farther extending their Empire and securing the sea from piracy, by annexing the Balearic Islands (*Majorca* and *Minorca*), and putting down risings in Dalmatia and among the barbarous tribes round Macedonia, a new and terrible danger threatened the Province of Gaul and the northern frontier of Italy both on the west and east. This was the appearance of the Cimbri, coming from the neighbourhood of Jutland, and joined by a German tribe called the Teutones. For years they hung like a cloud on the northern frontiers of Italy. They defeated one Roman army under Cn. Papirius Carbo near Noreia (*Neumarkt* in Styria) in B.C. 113, and another under M. Junius Silanus, in B.C. 109, and still another under Q. Servilius Caepio near Tolosa (*Toulouse*) in B.C. 106, their allies the Tigurini having defeated and slain L. Cassius Longinus in the previous year. They then separated into two great invading hosts,—the Teutones were to invade Italy by way of the province of Gaul, the Cimbri were to go east into the Tyrol, and enter Italy by the Brenner Pass along the Athesis (*Adige*),—and the two hosts were to unite again in the valley of the Po. For a time the threatened invasion was postponed by the Teutones making a fruitless expedition into Spain, but for nearly ten years it was a danger ever present to the minds of the Romans.

3. **The Jugurthine War**, B.C. 112-106. Contemporaneous with the threatened invasion of the Cimbri and Teutones was a long and difficult struggle in Africa. Masannasa died in B.C. 149, leaving his kingdom of Numidia between three sons—Micipsa, Gulussa, and Mastanabal. The two latter died, and Micipsa reigned alone till B.C. 118. On his death he left his dominions between

two sons—Adherbal and Hiempsal—and Jugurtha, a natural son of his brother Mastanabal. Jugurtha was accomplished in all manly exercises, and had served with credit with the Romans at Numantia, and made many friends among the Roman nobles. He had the qualities to win favour, and the cunning to conceal his unscrupulous ambition till the time came for gratifying it. He had learnt, it is said, from intercourse with Roman nobles that anything could be got at Rome for money; and, trusting to be able by this means to do anything he chose without interference from the Senate, he resolved to destroy his cousins and rule alone. He first got rid of Hiempsal by assassination, and bribed the commissioners sent from Rome to divide the kingdom between himself and his other cousin, Adherbal; and finally picked a quarrel with him also, besieged him in Cirta, and, having forced him to surrender, caused him to be murdered. All this was done in spite of several commissions sent from Rome with orders to force Jugurtha to submit to their arbitration; and such great indignation was caused at Rome by the idea that these commissioners had been bribed, that the Senate was forced for shame to order one of the consuls to enrol an army and proceed to Numidia (B.C. 111). But for the first two years little was done, and the consuls and their *legati* so notoriously took Jugurtha's gold, that a public investigation was demanded, and Jugurtha brought to Rome with a safe conduct to give evidence. There he pursued his course of bribery; but was eventually obliged to fly secretly from the city when it became known that he had secured the assassination of his cousin, Massiva, whom it was proposed to set up in his stead. In B.C. 109-108 the war was prosecuted by Q. Caecilius Metellus with more success, and, at any rate, without suspicion of corruption. But the chief credit of this success fell to his legatus, C. Marius, a man of obscure birth, but who had already distinguished himself at

Numantia, and had been tribune, praetor, and propraetor in Spain. He was married to Iulia, aunt of Caesar, the future Dictator, and was looked upon as a leader of the popular party. Encouraged by the favour of the soldiers and by predictions of fortune-tellers, whom he was fond of consulting, he demanded leave to go to Rome and stand for the consulship. Having taken care that it should be known in Rome that he thought Metellus might have been more energetic in the war, he was elected, and returned in B.C. 107 to take command, with L. Sulla as his quaestor to follow with the cavalry, who was afterwards destined to be his great opponent and the leader in a political reaction which was to undo much of the work of Gaius Gracchus. Marius acted with great energy and success; but, after all, Jugurtha was not conquered, but was delivered into the hands of Sulla by the treachery of his friend and ally, Bocchus, king of Mauretania (B.C. 106). He was taken to Rome to adorn the triumph of Marius, and afterwards, with his two sons, thrust into the vault of the Mamertine prison, and there left to starve. Numidia was handed over to his cousin, Hiempsal II.

4. **Effects of the Jugurthine War on Roman Politics.** Two results of this war it is necessary to note. First, the corruption and mismanagement of several of the consuls and their legati did a great deal to ruin the credit of the aristocratic faction, and to bring into prominence a popular party of opposition, which aimed at lowering the prestige of the Senate and getting a fuller share of office and the wealth that office now brought. Secondly, in regard to the army. Though, since the introduction of pay, men serving in the army had come more and more to regard it as a profession instead of a duty to the State, after performing which they had returned to their usual way of life, yet military service was still in a sense a privilege not open to every one. All whose property was below the

census of the fifth class were still excluded. But in forming his army for the Jugurthine war, Marius neglected this custom, and enrolled all freemen without distinction; and thus made a military career more the profession of a man's whole life, from which he looked to get support and maintenance after he had served his time.

5. **Destruction of the Teutones and Cimbri**, B.C. 104-101. By the time that Jugurtha had been taken, the danger from the Cimbri and Teutones was becoming imminent; the defeat and destruction of Q. Servilius Caepio in the Province took place in the next year (B.C. 105), during which Marius was still in Africa as proconsul. In great alarm the people resolved to elect Marius again consul for B.C. 104, and send him against the Teutones in the Province, whilst Q. Lutatius Catulus was sent to resist the Cimbri in the east, who were about to enter Italy by the Brenner Pass. During this year and the next nothing was done, for the Teutones and Ambrones were engaged in a fruitless expedition into Spain, and were not ready for a forward movement. At length, late in B.C. 102, Marius found them encamped near Aquae Sextiae (*Aix*) and determined to give them battle. There were two days' fighting; the first with the Ambrones was brought on by a struggle for the possession of a stream, and ended in the capture of their laager of wagons, which the women defended as desperately as the men; and a second with the Teutones. Both were defeated with immense slaughter. More than 100,000 are said to have fallen, the plains on which they lay produced extraordinary harvests for some seasons afterwards, and the people of Massilia are said to have used the bleeding bones to fence their vineyards. Even now remnants of the battle are found, and the village of Les Pourrières (*campi putridi*) recalls the memory of the slaughter.

Meanwhile the Cimbri had descended the Adige into

Italy, and forced Catulus to retreat south of the Po. In B.C. 101 Marius, now consul for the fifth time, hastened to meet Catulus as he marched up the right bank of the Po, while the Cimbri were marching up the left bank to meet as they thought their allies the Teutones, of whose destruction at Aquae Sextiae they were not fully informed. The Romans, crossing the upper Po, met them in the Raudian Plains near Vercellae, and again won a great victory. The whole horde seems to have been destroyed, and the women killed themselves with their children.

6. **Great Position of Marius.** Thus the danger that had been overshadowing Italy for twelve years was dispelled. Marius was the hero of the hour, and his success as a soldier gave him for the moment immense political power. For already scenes of violence at elections and legislative assemblies were becoming common, and the popular party were beginning to look to the army as ultimately the means of enforcing their aims and of securing the reforms which they desired.

CHAPTER XIII.

CIVIL WARS (FIRST PERIOD, B.C. 100–83).

1. *Political parties at Rome; the Optimates and Populares.* 2. *Policy and death of Saturninus.* 3. *The origin of the* **Marsic** *or* **Social War.** 4. *The course and result of the Social War.* 5. *The Sulpician laws; rivalry of* **Marius** *and* **Sulla.** 6. *The flight of Marius.* 7. *Return of Marius to Rome; the massacre of the Optimates.* 8. *Death of Marius and policy of Cinna.* 9. *The Optimates take refuge in Sulla's camp.*

1. **Political Parties at Rome.** We come now to a period of Roman history in which the division of parties became so bitter as to lead to civil war, and even, when there was not actually civil war, to scenes of violence and bloodshed. We may call the two parties the aristocratic and the popular, or, as they presently began to be called, the Optimates ('partisans of the best'), and the Populares. The former wished to keep up the practical monopoly of office enjoyed by certain families and to strengthen the authority of the Senate. The Populares wished to break down this monopoly and to bring all sorts of details of government at home and in the provinces before the popular assembly rather than leave them to the management of the Senate. But the chief question which was now in the front—the admission of the Italians to citizenship—introduced a somewhat different division. The Optimates were against it, as they were against any measure that

tended to multiply voters at a distance from Rome; but the Populares were generally not in favour of it either, for many of them were jealous of having their privileges shared by others. So that the statesmen who usually led the Populares sometimes found that they were deserted by their own followers on this point; and the Optimates used this jealously to keep things as they were, and even to ruin those who wanted to introduce changes too quickly. Thus the Equites, who were constantly estranged from the Senate on the question of the juries in trials for malversation, sometimes acted with it in attacking a leader who desired this measure. Marius was strongly in favour of the admission of the Italians, and in fact his reforms in the army had made it almost inevitable. Not only had he, as we have seen, admitted the lowest class of citizens (*capite censi*), and arranged them in the legions irrespective of their property qualifications, but he had also done away with the distinction of citizens and socii—that is, he had allowed the Italians to serve in the legions instead of under their own officers, making the number in the legions 6000 instead of 3000 (plus an equal number of socii) as before. When these men served side by side with citizens in the legions it must have seemed intolerable to them that they should not have the same rights. As a matter of fact service in the army became one of the ways of obtaining citizenship, which Marius, for instance, on one occasion bestowed as a reward on 1000 men of Camerinum, excusing himself by saying that in the midst of arms he could not hear the laws. But though Marius possessed the confidence of the army and therefore was looked up to as necessary for the popular cause, he was in many ways unsuited to be a political leader, and presently lost credit with both sides.

2. **Policy and Death of Saturninus**, B.C. 101-100. The first important outbreak was connected with L.

Appuleius Saturninus. He had once been of the party of the Optimates, but had been, as he considered, injured by them and had joined the Populares. He tried to make a coalition of three to consist of himself, Marius, and C. Servilius Glaucia, to get hold of the chief offices, and thereby the control of legislation. After the murder of his successful competitor for the tribuneship he was elected tribune for B.C. 100, and immediately proposed laws for the division of lands in Gallia Transalpina among citizens, with a special clause forcing every senator to take an oath of obedience to it. It was in regard to this that Marius first lost men's confidence. As consul he told the Senate that nothing would induce him to take such an oath, but when the law was passed he immediately took it; while Metellus Numidicus, the most respected of the Optimates, refused and went into exile. Saturninus proceeded to carry laws for colonies in Sicily, Achaia, and Macedonia, in which Italians were to share; and, in order to reconcile the Populares to this, he passed another law fixing the price of distributed corn at one *as* for a modius, instead of allowing it to vary with the market value. All these measures were odious to the Senate, and were passed in spite of hostile decrees in it. It was necessary to strain every nerve to keep the coalition together if he was to push his legislation farther. But Marius had incurred general contempt by his vacillating conduct, and had no chance of being elected a seventh time consul. Therefore Saturninus was all the more anxious that the other member of the trio, Glaucia, should obtain the consulship of B.C. 99. Accordingly his most formidable rival, C. Memmius, was killed, and most people believed that this was done at the instigation of Saturninus. He and Glaucia and their followers found themselves in danger and took refuge on the Capitol. The Senate voted them public enemies, and authorized Marius as consul to arrest and punish them. Marius was thus in a difficulty; he did not wish to appear as a patron of murder and disorder, and at the same time these men were his friends and partisans. He tried to play a double game, admitting emissaries of the Senate by one door and members of the popular party by the other. But finally he had to arrest them: and when he put them in the Curia for safety a mob of Equites broke in and killed them—a murder expressly approved by the Senate. The whole policy of Saturninus was disliked by the Senate; but it was his proposal to give the Italians a share in the Gallic lands on an equality with the citizens that armed the middle class against him.

3. **The Origin of the Marsic or Social War.** But though the policy of granting justice to the Italians was thus checked, and though Marius had lost the credit necessary for a party leader, the question was not dead. It was brought into prominence again by the mistaken zeal of the consuls for B.C. 95, L. Licinius Crassus and Q. Mucius Scaevola, who, finding that many Italians had obtained citizenship by doubtful means, or were exercising its rights without legal authority, passed a law appointing a commission of inquiry into such cases. This measure showed the Italians that they were as far as ever from getting the citizenship. Though no outbreak took place immediately, secret communications were passing from city to city, and preparations were being made for a combined movement. In B.C. 91 one of the tribunes, M. Livius Drusus, determined to bring about the enfranchisement of the Italians. In order to get the necessary influence he attempted to secure the favour of all parties,—that of the Senate and Equites, by proposing a compromise as to the *iudicia*, and that of the lower orders by proposing new colonies in Italy and Sicily and new distributions of corn. But he failed to please any of the orders, or to induce them to stand by him. Jealousy of the Italians was too

strong in all alike: and his sudden death (whether from natural causes or assassination) left the question still unsettled, and the city full of rumours of a secret conspiracy organized in the Italian towns, in which certain Romans of position were believed to be involved. Many were in fact tried and condemned for treason (*maiestas*) under a law proposed (B.C. 90) by the tribune, Q. Varius, but with such violence and contempt of legal forms that a recall of the 'Varian exiles' remained for some time a point in the policy of the popular party. The actual war—called sometimes the Social War, *i.e.* the war of the Italian socii, and sometimes the Marsic War, because the Marsi took a leading part in it—was begun by an outbreak at Asculum in Picenum. A Roman proconsul and his legate were there murdered by the populace when he harangued them in threatening terms as to their supposed complicity in a secret conspiracy. This was followed by a massacre of Roman citizens in the town; and before long the old nationalities which Rome had done its best to break up, divide, and reduce to uniform subjection, showed that they still existed and possessed a power of combination:—the Vestini, Marsi, Peligni, Marrucini, Samnites, and Lucani, all joined in the movement, which spread like a conflagration from one end of Italy to the other.

4. **The Course and Result of the Social War**, B.C. 90-88. The war itself was a scattered one. But it may be roughly divided into two departments—of North-Central Italy from Umbria to Picenum, and South Italy from Picenum to Apulia. An attempt was made to form an entirely new republic, with a new capital city at Corfinium, which was to be called Italica. A forum and Senate house were planned, a Senate of 500 named, and two consuls, with six legates apiece to conduct the war. They were to attack Roman colonies wherever they were, and such *municipia* as contained Roman garrisons or a large

proportion of Roman citizens. The war is said to have cost the lives of 300,000 men of military age in Italy. One of the Roman consuls, L. Iulius Caesar, was frequently beaten in the south; the other, P. Rutilius Lupus, lost his life in battle in the country of the Marsi; and, though Marius, who was serving as Rutilius' legate, partially retrieved the disaster, the first year's fighting was generally in favour of the rebels, so much so that the Umbrians and Etruscans, who had hitherto held aloof, declared on their side. But the Umbrians were defeated, and the timely concession of the *lex Iulia* (carried by the consul L. Iulius Caesar in B.C. 90) pacified the Etruscans; for it gave the franchise to all Italian communities who had not been in arms, and who would accept it.[1]

The tide was turned in the next year (B.C. 89), mainly by the victories of Sulla in the south, and of Gaius Pompeius Strabo (father of Pompey the Great) in Central Italy. Corfinium (Italica) was taken, and the seat of the Italian government transferred to Bovianum, which Sulla also took. The one town of importance that held out into the year B.C. 88 was Asculum, the place where the war originated; and when it fell to Pompeius Strabo, little further resistance was offered except by the Samnite forces at Nola, in Campania. But the Romans were now wise enough to remove completely the cause of the war. A vote of the people, proposed by two tribunes—C. Papirius Carbo and Marcus Plautius Silvanus—gave the full citizenship to every member of a municipium or civitas foederata as far north as the Po who, within two months, declared before a praetor his desire to receive it; and another law, proposed by Pompeius Strabo, gave the imperfect citizenship (*Latinitas*) to all cities between the Po and the Alps. From this time, though the government of the Empire was still in theory that of a single city, where alone

[1] These communities which accepted it were called *Populi Fundi*.

imperial magistrates could be elected, laws made, and treaties confirmed, yet Rome and Italy are now one, or rather Italy, as compared to the rest of the world, is an extended Rome.

5. **Rivalry of Sulla and Marius. The Sulpician Laws**, B.C. 88. The Social war had settled one difficulty, and had united the whole of Italy in a common citizenship; but so far from lessening the differences between the Optimates and the Populares, it had made them more pronounced. For the Italian question had divided the popular party, which could now once more unite and strive for the objects at which it had always been aiming—the lowering the prestige of the Senate, and depriving the noble families of the monopoly of office. In the very year in which the war was ended (B.C. 88) one of the tribunes, P. Sulpicius, brought in a series of measures, which the Optimates regarded as revolutionary. The enfranchised Italians were to be spread through all the thirty-five tribes, and would thus influence an election much more than if, as was at first proposed, they were confined to eight tribes; the exiles condemned under the law of Varius (p. 165) were to be recalled; freedmen were also to be enrolled in any tribe, and not, as before, in only the four urban tribes,—thus spreading their influence, and not concentrating it in the city where the nobles had most power; bankruptcy was to exclude a senator (thus weakening the influence of rich senators, who controlled the poorer); and, lastly, Marius instead of Sulla was to have command in the war with Mithridates, king of Pontus, which was already begun. This last order was a reversal of a decree of the Senate, which had assigned the command to Sulla. To make such appointments was a function usually left to the Senate, but it could always be resumed by the people, and the popular party aimed at doing so on every possible occasion. The origin and course of this war must be left to

another chapter. At present we must see how the quarrel as to the chief command in it affected Roman politics. The Senate resolved to resist the laws of Sulpicius; but his followers appeared in arms, killed the son of one of the consuls (Pompeius Rufus), and forced Sulla, the other consul, to take refuge in the house of Marius, and thence retire to the camp at Nola, where his army had been stationed to complete the reduction of the Samnites, and thence to go to Asia. The laws of Sulpicius were then passed, but they were passed by violence, and Sulla was determined that he would not submit to being superseded by Marius in his command by such means. His army was devoted to him, and ready to support his claim. The tribunes sent by Marius to take over the command in his name were murdered, and Sulla advanced on Rome, joined by the other consul Pompeius Rufus. Sulpicius fled to a villa outside the city, but was betrayed and put to death by a slave, who was rewarded by emancipation, and then hurled from the Tarpeian rock by Sulla's order.

6. **Flight of Marius**, B.C. 88-7. Marius escaped to Ostia, where he found a ship and set sail. He was, however, forced by a storm to land near Circeii, where he wandered helplessly, until, being warned by a peasant that horsemen were scouring the country in search of him, he concealed himself in the woods. Forced by hunger to descend to the beach, he was again taken on board a vessel. The master of the ship did not deliver him to the horsemen on the shore, but, alarmed at the risk of what he was doing, insisted on landing him near Minturnae. Making his way with difficulty over the bogs and ditches of that marshy district, he at last reached the hut of an old labourer, who concealed him under a heap of reeds and wood. When the pursuers arrived and threatened the old man, Marius in terror tried to hide himself more completely in a pool of water, but was dragged out covered with mud, and taken to Minturnae

There the magistrates, after long deliberation, decided to put him to death, and ordered a Gallic slave to do it. But the slave remembered him in his glory during the Cimbric War; and when he entered the room, the well-remembered form rose, the fierce eyes glared in the dim light, and the stern voice of the old hero dismayed him. He threw down the sword, and rushed from the room, exclaiming, "I cannot kill Gaius Marius." The citizens of Minturnae repented of their resolve, and decided to put him again on board ship, and thus free themselves of the difficulty. This time the wind was favourable, and he touched at Aenaria (*Ischia*), where he found friends, and thence crossed to Africa, whither his son had already made his way in safety. He remained in the neighbourhood of Carthage, and sent his son to ask the protection of Hiempsal, king of Numidia, who owed his sovereignty to Marius's victory over Iugurtha. But that king, though professing friendship, was secretly intending to gratify the Sullan party by delivering up his suppliants; while the propraetor of the province of Africa insisted that they should leave his province. They accordingly again took ship and landed on the island Cercina, where they were joined by other exiles of their party, and collected some Mauritanian soldiers by promises of pay and future rewards.

7. **Marius returns to Rome**, B.C. 87. Meanwhile at Rome the course of affairs had made it possible for them to think of returning and taking vengeance on their enemies. Sulla and his colleagues on entering Rome from Nola at the head of their troops, had at once proceeded to revoke the laws of Sulpicius, to fill up and strengthen the Senate, and to rearrange the centuries voting in the *Comitia* so as to give those of the first class a preponderating influence; and to curb the power of the tribunes by renewing a condition which had once been established by custom,

though not by law, that they should not propose bills in the *Comitia Tributa* without previous sanction of the Senate. This done, and the consuls elect for B.C. 87 being compelled to take an oath not to propose a reversal of these regulations, he put the command of the troops still employed near Nola in the hands of his two legati. The army still on foot in Picenum remained under the command of Pompeius Strabo: for Pompeius Rufus, who had been sent to supersede him, had been murdered by the troops. Early in B.C. 87, therefore, Sulla left Italy for Greece to carry on the war with Mithridates. No sooner was he gone than the consul, L. Cornelius Cinna, proposed to recall Marius and his friends, and at the same time to complete the enfranchisement of the Italians by enrolling them in the thirty-five tribes, as the law of Sulpicius had done. His colleague, Gn. Octavius, resolved to resist. Hearing that a crowd of armed Italians were in the Forum to overawe the citizens into voting for Cinna's bill, and were driving opposing tribunes from the rostra, he led an armed force into the Forum, killed many of the rioters, and drove the rest through the gates. Cinna fled, was declared by the Senate a public enemy, and no longer consul. But he found support in many Italian towns, and was joined by a great part of the army at Nola, and at Capua found himself at the head of considerable forces. The news of these events determined Marius to return to Italy; and as soon as he landed in Etruria, Cinna, as consul, nominated him as his legate with proconsular power. Two other of Cinna's legates, Q. Sertorius and Cn. Papirius Carbo, were also at the head of troops from Campania. There were, therefore, four armies advancing on Rome. The consul Octavius and the Senate in alarm sent to Sulla's legates Metellus and Appius Claudius from Nola, and Pompeius Strabo from Picenum, to come to their defence. They came, but a great part of their forces joined Cinna; Metellus, refusing to take command at Rome, retired from Italy; while Appius Claudius submitted to the invaders. The walls were in a dilapidated state, unfit to stand a siege. Pompeius Strabo fought an indecisive battle near the Colline gate with Sertorius, but was soon afterwards killed by lightning; and when Marius advancing along the Appian road (for he had come to Ostia, thence to Antium, and then up the Appian road to Arsia) joined Cinna on the Ianiculum, the Senate humbled itself to invite Cinna and Marius into the city, only begging that they would spare the lives of the citizens. Cinna made fair professions, but Marius, who stood by the consul's chair, said nothing, and his grim look gave no promise of mercy. The first demand of Cinna on entering the city was that Marius and other exiles who had joined him should be formally recalled. But Marius without waiting for this formality entered the Forum surrounded by a band of ruffians, and the work of blood began. The consul Octavius had already been killed on his curule chair, and his head brought to Cinna; and now every one whom Marius pointed out, or as some said, every one whose salutation he did not return, was cut down by his attendants. Catulus, his former rival and colleague in the Cimbrian war, in vain asked for mercy; and the famous orator, M. Antonius, grandfather of the Triumvir, who took refuge in the house of a humble client, was betrayed and put to death. Everywhere the trackers of blood were sent out in search of refugees, and no man's life who had opposed Marius was safe. Cinna soon got disgusted with these cruelties, and, with the help of Sertorius, put to death some of Marius's ruffians who were revelling in murder and robbery and every kind of excess.

8. **Death of Marius.** The election of consuls for B.C. 86 was then held, and Cinna and Marius were of course

returned. But the old man did not survive many days the realization of his cherished hope of a seventh consulship. The conqueror of Iugurtha and the saviour of Italy had lived too long for his fame, and the great services he had done his country were forgotten in the horror of the last weeks of his life. Worn out by fever and excitement he died on the 13th of January (B.C. 86). His successor, L. Valerius Flaccus, was sent out to supersede Sulla in the command against Mithridates; and Cinna meanwhile was all-powerful at Rome, and getting himself and Carbo named consuls for B.C. 85 and 84, proceeded to carry out a kind of revolutionary programme,—enrolment of Italians in the thirty-five tribes, free distributions of corn, assignments of land near Capua, abolition of three-quarters of private debts, appointment of his partisans to the government of provinces. Finally, he caused Sulla to be declared a *hostis* and his town house to be pulled down.

9. **The Optimates retire to Sulla's Camp.** The result of this was that many of the noble families retired from Rome, and took refuge with Sulla in Macedonia and Greece. He had with him so many senators that he could almost consider himself as acting in the name of the Senate. He let it be known that, when the war was over, he should come back to Rome with his army to protect him, and would ignore all Cinna's legislation except as to the Italian voters. The consuls, Cinna and Carbo, therefore enrolled troops and prepared to resist him. The rump of the Senate still left at Rome tried to compromise by proposing that Sulla should come to Rome under a safe-conduct. But when he made it a first condition that noble exiles should be recalled and authors of illegal massacres punished, the consuls decided to go on with warlike preparations. Cn. Papirius Carbo crossed to Epirus at the head of several legions: but late in B.C. 84, as Cinna was preparing to do the same, he was murdered in a mutiny of his soldiers,

who refused to cross to attack fellow citizens, and Carbo thereupon returned and wintered at Ariminum. In the spring of the next year Sulla returned to Italy, arriving at Brundisium (*Brindisi*) with 40,000 men and 1200 ships. To understand fully his position we must know something of the war in which he had meanwhile been engaged.

REMAINS OF PLATFORM OF CAPITOLIUM IN THE GARDEN OF THE CAFFARELLI PALACE.

CHAPTER XIV.

THE MITHRIDATIC WAR AND THE DICTATORSHIP AND LEGISLATION OF SULLA

1. *Origin of the Mithridatic war.* 2. *The history of Mithridates and his kingdom.* 3. *After long neglect the Romans became alarmed at the proceedings of Mithridates.* 4. *Rising in Asia Minor, and* **massacre** *of Romans.* 5. *Mithridates in European Greece.* 6. *Sulla's campaigns and siege of Athens* (B.C. 87-5). 7. *Battles of* **Chaeronea** *and* **Orchomenus.** 8. *Fimbria murders Valerius, sent to supersede Sulla, and is not recalled by the Senate.* 9. *Terms made with Mithridates, death of Fimbria, and settlement of Asia.* 10. *Sulla's advance on Rome* (B.C. 83-2). 11. *The proscriptions.* 12. *The* **Dictatorship of Sulla,** *his legislation and reforms.* 13. *Sulla's Criminal Code.* 14. *Sulla's retirement and death.* 15. *The Roman empire at the death of Sulla.* 16. *Foreign dominions.* 17. *The number and names of the* **provinces.**

1. **Origin of the Mithridatic War** (B.C. 88-84). After the war with Antiochus (B.C. 189) the Romans had established a kind of informal protectorate in Asia. No province was made, and no tribute levied except for the payment of the war indemnities. But they had rearranged the territories in it. They had declared the Greek cities free, and leaving the kingdoms of Cappadocia and Bithynia as they were, had put the rest under the king of Pergamus. In B.C. 133 the royal rights in this enlarged kingdom of Pergamus had been left to the Roman people by the will of Attalus III., and after a struggle with a pretender

Aristonicus (131-129), it had been organized as a province, officially styled Asia. Later still Cilicia on the south-east, where the people were dangerous to the commerce and peace of the Aegean from their piracies, had been conquered and also made a Roman province (B.C. 102). Rome had therefore a preponderating influence and interest in Asia Minor, and would be sure to interfere decisively in any changes there which would affect her provinces or give dangerous power to surrounding kings. Now the province of Asia had a special grievance. Originally it was proposed that it should be free from the tribute paid to the king of Pergamus, the Roman government contenting itself with the profits of the Royal Domains and the contributions invariably made even by 'free' States towards the expenses of the governors. But after the war with Aristonicus this promise was evaded. Henceforth farmers paid a tenth of their produce (*decumae*), a rent was levied on feeding cattle on public pastures (*scriptura*), and an ad valorem duty of 2½ per cent. was paid on imports (*portoria*). These duties proved a heavy burden to the people, which was made worse by the method of their exaction. We have seen that by a law of Gaius Gracchus in B.C. 123, instead of native taxgatherers, the collection of the various duties was sold every fifth year by the censors to companies of publicani. These men, having calculated the amount which the taxes and duties would produce, paid a fixed sum to the treasury and trusted for the margin over that sum for their profit. This must always have been somewhat speculative, for as the *decumae* were paid in kind a bad harvest might bring down the total amount to a ruinous figure; and in the same way the amount of the *portoria* would vary with the seasons and other circumstances affecting commerce. Therefore these publicani employed every device to increase the amount payable to them, exercised the most offensive kind of espionage, and set to work every engine of legal chicanery or personal violence. If the provincials appealed to the proconsul, they generally found that his interests or his fears were on the side of the publicani,—his interests because he might receive a percentage on the profits, and had besides exactions of his own to be tolerated; his fears, because, if accused of extortion (*de repetundis*) on his return, he would have to stand a trial before a jury of equites who had enjoyed or hoped to enjoy the chance of similar profits (p. 150). A scandalous instance of such a case had happened in B.C. 92, and had prompted the proposal of Livius to deprive the equites of their exclusive hold on the *iudicia*. P. Rutilius Rufus had in B.C. 95 distinguished himself (as legatus of Q. Mucius Scaevola) by repressing the extortions of the publicani, and had, in spite of his entire innocence, been prosecuted at Rome and condemned by an intrigue of the equites. It was natural that such men should be detested in the province; that the Roman government should be unpopular; and that the Roman residents generally, merchants, bankers, and money-lenders, should be the objects of dislike in towns and harbours. For thirty-five years, however (B.C. 123-88), all seemed going smoothly. The natives groaned and scowled, but the publican and money-lender returned gorged with wealth to plunge into the luxuries or vices of Rome. The opportunity for revenge came when the king of Pontus entered Roman Asia with an army, which had just defeated a combined force of Italians and Bithynians, bringing with him a Roman governor of Cilicia a prisoner, and a Roman legatus of consular rank in chains and treated with every kind of ignominy. This king was Mithridates, who succeeded to the kingdom of Pontus in B.C. 120 when twelve years old.

2. **Mithridates and his Kingdom.** Cappadocia Pontica was a district on the south shore of the Black Sea, which had been extended by the predecessors of Mithridates,

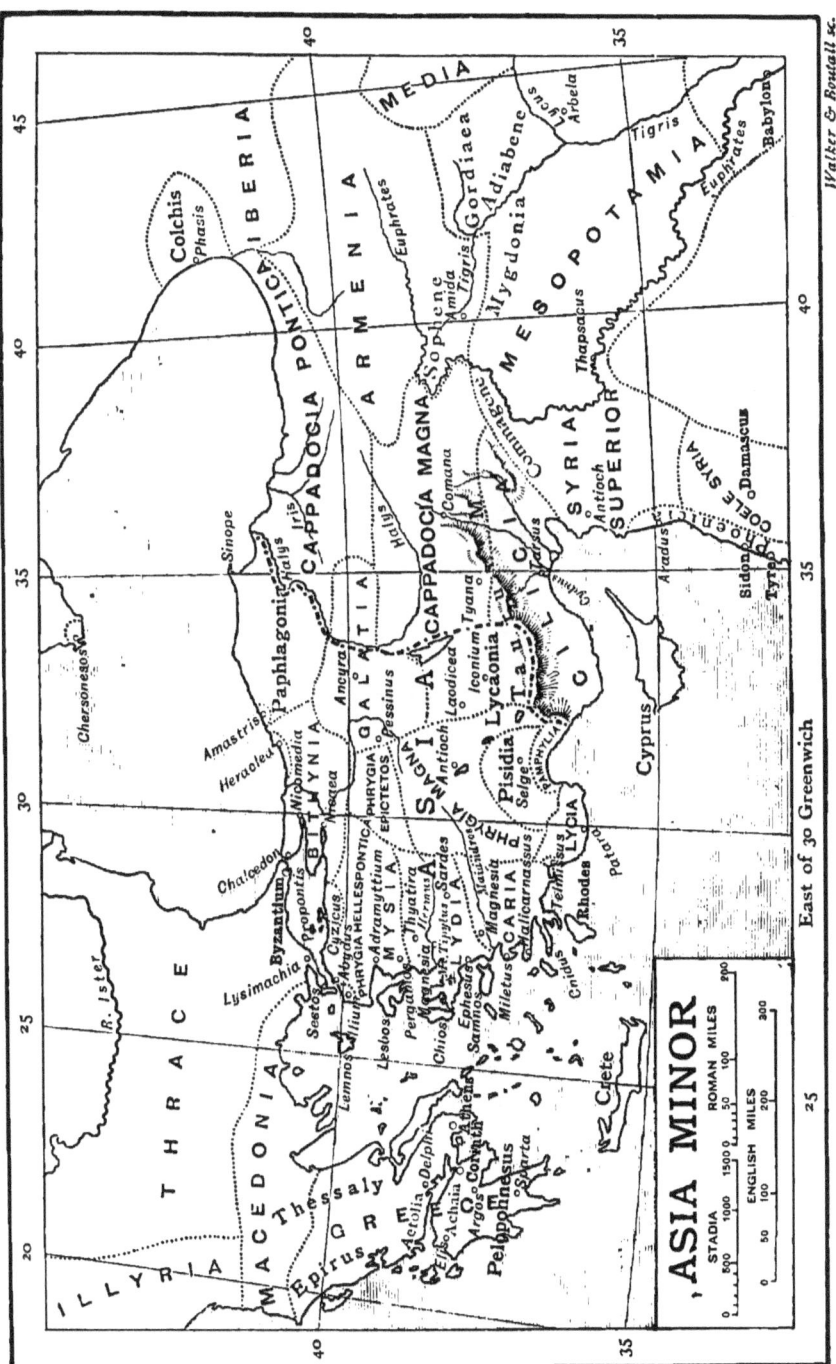

from the river Phasis in the east to the river Halys in the west, separating it from Paphlagonia. Attempts had been made to take in Paphlagonia also and the greater Phrygia, which had been defeated by Roman interference; and when Mithridates took over the government, in B.C. 111, he had reason to feel that the Roman power in Asia was the most formidable obstacle to the further extension of his kingdom. He had spent a youth of hardship and danger during his minority owing to the jealousy of his

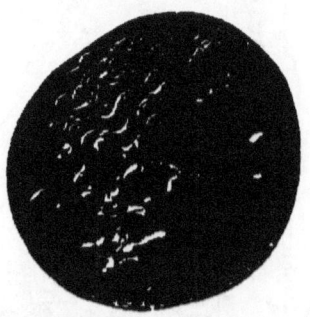

KING MITHRIDATES EUPATOR.

mother, who was acting as regent, and he was now a man of remarkable accomplishments and activity. He had some tincture of Greek learning and tastes, having a famous collection of engraved gems and other works of art, and was gifted with such powers of acquisition and memory that he was said to be able to converse in twenty-five languages. As soon as he took over the government he surrounded himself with Greek officers, paid great attention to the organization of his army, and in B.C. 110-107, had on the invitation of the Greek cities in the Tauric Chersonese (Crimea), established a protectorate there, while in the east he had reached the Euphrates by annexing the lesser Armenia. He was now the most powerful king in Asia, and desired to annex other parts of Asia Minor, and especially the Greek cities throughout,

3. **The Romans begin to be alarmed at Mithridates.** In B.C. 104, in conjunction with the king of Bithynia, he began by attacking Paphlagonia, Galatia, and Cappadocia. The Romans had been engaged meanwhile in the Cimbric war, and the political troubles that followed it. The Senate as a rule cared little for what was done in the East so long as the Roman province was untouched and the revenues from it secure. The nobles had no desire for a great war which might mean additional power and influence for some leader hostile to themselves (probably Marius). But at length the proceedings of Mithridates alarmed them for the safety of the province, and he was ordered to evacuate the parts of Cappadocia and Paphlagonia which he had occupied (B.C. 94). He obeyed for the time, as he did soon afterwards in the case of the Greater Armenia, in which he had set up a tool of his own as king. Sulla, propraetor of Cilicia in B.C. 92, was specially commissioned to restore the king of Cappadocia whom Mithridates had expelled. At the same time he received an ambassador from the Parthians, who desired the friendship and alliance of Rome. The Romans were now the most influential power in Asia, and when in B.C. 89, trusting to the difficulties brought upon Rome by the Social war, Mithridates again tried to interfere in the succession to the thrones of Cappadocia and Bithynia, he was forced to submit to the dictates of a Roman commission headed by Manius Aquillius. But Aquillius seems to have determined on forcing Mithridates to fight; and he instigated the restored kings of Bithynia and Cappadocia to attack him. The result was a war begun in B.C. 88, in which Mithridates not only defeated the Bithynians but also the Roman forces under Aquillius, as well as those under Q. Oppius, propraetor of Cilicia, and took both prisoners.

4. **Rising in Asia Minor against the Romans**, B.C. 88. This was followed by a general movement on the part of the Greek towns in Asia Minor to quit the Roman friendship and to attach themselves to the Pontic king. At his command a general massacre of Italian residents in these towns took place, and their confiscated property enabled him to relieve the cities from tribute for five years, thus making it their interest to stand by him. The cities indeed, especially those in the province of Asia, were glad to get rid of the Roman tax-gatherers, and were quite ready to join Mithridates, who now, having secured Asia, proceeded to extend his dominion over the islands and European Greece itself. The one great island that withstood him was Rhodes, which he therefore besieged in person, sending an army under Archelaus, one of his lieutenants, into Greece.

5. **Revolt joined by European Greece.** Athens was persuaded or forced to join him, and was followed by almost all the other States in Greece and the Aegean islands, except Delos; while an invasion of Thracians, instigated by Mithridates, kept the governor of Macedonia too much employed to interfere. Thus the whole Roman work of the last century in the East seemed to be undone. The Greek States indeed were nominally 'free,' but this freedom was such that they were precluded from foreign alliances; and the presence of a foreign army with their connivance or assent would seem to the Romans a just cause of war. It was a revolt in Greece, in which presently nearly the whole country joined, that Sulla with five legions was sent to quell in the spring of B.C. 87.

6. **Sulla's Campaigns**, B.C. 87-85. Sulla landed in Greece in the spring of B.C. 87, and found many of the Greek cities already prepared to revoke their submission to Mithridates, because his army had received a check at Demetrias at the hands of the proquaestor of Macedonia.

But Athens and the Peiraeus were strongly fortified and were in the hands of Archelaus, the general of Mithridates, and upon these places Sulla directed his full force. He had no doubt of being able to subdue Greece; but in order to carry the war into Asia and attack Mithridates himself, a fleet would be required capable of overpowering the formidable fleets of the king. The Romans were as usual ill supplied with ships, and the quaestor L. Lucullus was sent to collect them in Egypt, Cyprus, Rhodes, and other naval States. Meanwhile it was not till March, B.C. 86, that Athens yielded to Sulla's siege, and it was some weeks later still before the Peiraeus was forced to do the same. The former, though the inhabitants suffered greatly at the hands of the Roman soldiers, was not seriously injured; but the Peiraeus was dismantled and burnt and never recovered from the effects.

7. **Battles of Chaeronea and Orchomenus**, B.C. 86. Whilst the siege of Athens had been going on, another Pontic army had been engaged in subduing Macedonia, where there were very few Roman troops, and had in the spring of B.C. 86 come south to the pass of Thermopylae, secured it, and proceeded to besiege Elateia in Phocis. One of Sulla's legates, Hortensius, was in the district with 8000 troops, but was unable to move. Sulla had every motive for seeking a battle with this army. Attica could not supply him with sufficient support for his troops, and if Boeotia and Phocis remained in the enemy's hands he would be in great peril. Moreover Cinna had become all powerful at Rome; Sulla's party was being persecuted and driven into exile. It was necessary therefore for him to strike a blow which would secure his position. He effected a junction with Hortensius in Phocis, and, advancing towards **Chaeronea**, met the Pontic army commanded by Taxilus and Archelaus, who had come by sea from Peiraeus, in the plain of the river Cephisus and

utterly defeated it, in the summer of B.C. 86. This was followed by the submission of the greater part of Greece, and it encouraged the Greek cities in Asia Minor to throw off the rule of Mithridates, of which they had soon wearied. For a time the king checked this movement by severities or indulgences; but when another of his armies had been again defeated by Sulla at Orchomenus in Boeotia, the defection both in Greece and Asia became irresistible.

8. **Flaccus and Fimbria sent to supersede Sulla.** But Sulla was still in a difficult position in regard to the Roman Government. His enemy Cinna in B.C. 86 had secured that the consul L. Valerius Flaccus should be sent to Greece with an army and authority to exercise a command superior to that of Sulla. Flaccus had indeed withdrawn his first plan of proceeding to Southern Greece and there superseding Sulla, and had instead gone northward to the Bosporus, and there had been assassinated by his second in command, Fimbria, in the course of a mutiny stirred up by him (B.C. 85). But Fimbria, in spite of this crime, had not been recalled by the rump Senate unfavourable to Sulla, and had in fact crossed to Bithynia and won several successes against the officers of Mithridates. It was as important to Sulla that Fimbria should be suppressed as that Mithridates should be conquered; and Mithridates had to decide which of these two officers of the Republic he had most to fear. Sulla had been by this time declared a public enemy by the Senate, his town house had been pulled down, his wife and children forced to fly to his camp in Thessaly. But with them had come a large number of senators opposed to Cinna; and Lucullus had also arrived on the coast with a powerful fleet, which he had been collecting for a year and a half. Sulla was now in a position to cross to Asia, and the king concluded that he was the more formidable enemy of the two.

9. **Sulla makes terms with Mithridates. Death**

of **Fimbria, and Settlement of Asia** (B.C. 84). He therefore opened negotiations with Sulla, and eventually at a meeting at Philippi agreed to restore the deposed kings of Bithynia and Cappadocia, and to re-establish places that had been depopulated or destroyed by him in Greece and the islands. Mithridates was in fact to be reduced to his own kingdom, and as a 'friend' of Rome was to furnish ships and men for her fleet. This done, Sulla crossed to Asia to attack Fimbria in Lydia. But Fimbria's soldiers deserted him, and he fled to Pergamus and put an end to his own life. The rest of the year and the following spring Sulla spent in regulating the affairs of Asia Minor, capturing towns that still held out, and assessing the punishment to be imposed on those who had been guilty of acknowledging the supremacy of Mithridates and throwing off allegiance to Rome. The whole country was so heavily burdened by fines, and by the exaction of arrears of tribute, that the various communities had to mortgage their public buildings, and borrow on such usurious terms that Asia was reduced to a state of financial ruin, from which it was long in recovering. Nor for some time did the restored Roman government secure the country from the depredations of the pirate fleets which had grown to dangerous dimensions during the late troubles, and had seized islands and coast towns unchecked. Sulla now went to Greece, and in the spring of the next year (B.C. 83) returned to Italy with his army and a large fleet.

10. **Sulla's Advance on Rome**, B.C. 83-2. Sulla had a veteran army of 40,000 men, but the forces opposed to him were far superior; and though he met and defeated the consul C. Junius Norbanus, near Capua, he did not venture to continue his march upon Rome. Cn. Papirius Carbo, a third time consul in B.C. 82, was the chief leader of his enemies, and had at his command vast forces in several parts of Italy under his

legati. What favoured Sulla was, first, that these forces were somewhat widely separated; secondly, that the young Cn. Pompeius (afterwards called Magnus) had enrolled three legions, and, having declared for Sulla, was keeping a considerable part of Carbo's forces in play in Picenum; and, thirdly, that as the cause of his enemies was supported by the only half-obedient Italians, and especially by the Samnites, who had never laid down their arms since the Social war, Sulla was able to put himself forward as the champion of Roman authority. Nevertheless, it was not till after some very severe fighting, especially at the bloody battles of **Clusium** and at the **Colline gate**, in both of which Sulla was all but defeated, that he entered Rome. Carbo fled to Africa, where one of his partisans was governor, but was shortly afterwards caught on his way back to Sicily and put to death by Pompey; and the other consul, the younger Marius, killed himself at Praeneste, where he was besieged. Sulla entered Rome in November (he had been there for a short time earlier in the year), and immediately announced his intention of putting to death all whom he considered guilty of treason in opposing him since he entered Italy. The pretence was that they had broken a compact which he had made with the consul Scipio Asiaticus in the previous year (B.C. 83), but it soon became evident that he intended to get rid of practically the whole party of his opponents.

11. **The Proscriptions**, B.C. 82.—The names of forty Senators and about sixteen hundred Equites were at once announced as condemned, but he added that there were others whom he could not remember. The uncertainty thus left heightened the horror of the time. And when he adopted the suggestion of putting up a list in the Forum the uncertainty still remained; for the first list was followed by at least two others, and they were so carelessly supervised that his followers and partisans were able to insert the names of

their private enemies and of those whose possessions they coveted. For proscription involved confiscation of property, and when the dead men's goods were sold, Sulla's partisans were allowed to purchase for small sums estates which they afterwards sold at great profit. Sometimes the murder was first committed and the name afterwards put in the list, as the notorious Catiline was said to have done in the case of his own brother-in-law. These 'proscription' lists avenged, but went infinitely beyond, the similar executions ordered by Marius, and were imitated forty years later by the Triumvirs, Antony, Lepidus, and Octavian. They have blackened Sulla's reputation for ever, but they effected their object. He was now all-powerful, and at his own suggestion the obsequious Senate appointed an interrex to hold an election of him as Dictator.

12. **The Dictatorship of Sulla**, B.C. 82-79. The title was adopted as one known to the constitution, although the habit of naming a Dictator had long been in abeyance, for none had been appointed since B.C. 202. Moreover, the Dictator had in old times been nominated by a consul on the order of the Senate, not elected. His term of office had been limited to six months, and in practice had nearly always terminated in a much shorter time—as soon, that is, as the purpose for which he was appointed had been accomplished, whether it was the holding of an election, the suppressing of a sedition, or the command in a campaign. The office to which Sulla was now elected was unlimited in time, and its purpose was 'to settle the constitution' (*reipublicae constituendae causa*). In virtue of this he could make any laws he chose, and though in order to be binding after his dictatorship they had to be passed by the *Comitia*, his coercive powers were so great that this was merely a form. He was in fact a complete autocrat, and his measures were so important in their effect that they must be carefully noticed.

(1) First, he put an end to the remains of resistance still existing in Italy. Certain towns which had been in arms ever since the Social war were reduced by force and punished by disfranchisement and confiscation of land. Samnium, where rebellion was most obstinate, was almost depopulated, and its towns quickly sank to mere villages. In place of the old inhabitants Sulla established settlements of his veteran soldiers with large grants of lands, and thus Southern Italy became permanently Romanized, and no resistance was ever afterwards experienced there. In the north, as at Faesulae and its neighbourhood, the Sullan settlers do not seem to have been so successful. The country was not so stripped of its old inhabitants as Samnium, and we shall hear hereafter of troubles caused by the contests of the settlers with the dispossessed owners.

(2) Secondly, Sulla's object was to reinstate the Senate in its old position of power and influence. He filled up the vacancies caused by the civil war by admitting 300 Equites selected by himself and elected by the *Comitia*, and provided for future vacancies by giving a seat for life in it to every one who was elected among the twenty quaestors. In principle this was not a novelty, for the higher magistrates had for a long time, if not always, become life members. But this privilege was dropped one stage lower, that is, to the quaestorship instead of the curule aedileship; and it worked automatically instead of waiting for the next roll made up for the censors. The object was to keep up the numbers of the Senate and to fill it with men of position. So long as Sulla was supreme, the greater number of those who obtained office, and so an *entrée* to the Senate, would be in favour of his policy; and, even if they were not so, they would almost certainly be men of rank, members of the governing class, and it was with such men that he desired to fill the chamber.

(3) The power of the Senate was increased also by the

regulation (which was generally, though not always, observed henceforth), whereby the consuls and praetors stayed in Rome during their year of office, and only went to provinces with *imperium* in the next year; while the Senate decided which should be consular and which should be praetorian provinces, and could prolong a proconsul's or propraetor's stay in a province by withdrawing it from allotment. The governor was also forbidden to pass the boundary of his province in arms without leave of the Senate, and was to quit it within thirty days of the arrival of his successor.

(4) The continuance of power, such as Marius had obtained, was to be prevented by recurring to the old rule of an interval of ten years between two consulships. And though the ten years' service in the army before holding office was to be no longer compulsory, yet the rules as to age were to be enforced, and no one was to be consul until he had been praetor, or praetor until he had been quaestor.

The result of these regulations was on the whole to enhance the executive powers of the Senate and depress those of the magistrates. The censorship, for instance, was rendered almost objectless, as the list of the Senate was now made up automatically, and the affixing a *nota* to a man's name was no longer easy. It was one thing to omit a name from a list which the censor had to make up, especially as no one was technically a senator till the censors had so entered his name: it was another thing to strike out a name or affix a *nota* to one in a list for which the censor was no longer responsible.

(5) Another popular institution which Sulla depressed was the *Comitia Tributa*. We must understand that in the *Comitia Centuriata* and the *Comitia Tributa* the same persons voted or had the right to vote. It was only a different arrangement of the voters. In the *Tributa* the citizens were divided by tribes in such a way that the

wealthy had no preponderance; in the *Comitia Centuriata* the voting was by centuries, and the centuries were so distributed that the few wealthy could outvote the many poor. Gradually legislation had fallen chiefly to the *Tributa*, though both were competent by law; but by Sulla's arrangement nothing was left to the *Tributa* but the election of tribunes and the lower magistrates. Laws were to be brought before the *Centuriata*, while most prosecutions which used to come before the *Comitia* were arranged for in another way.

(6) The Tribunate was weakened in two ways. The tribunes were forbidden to summon and address the people, or to propose legislation without previous sanction of the Senate; and the office was rendered unattractive to men of ability by a rule which made tribunes ineligible to other offices; while their right of veto was restricted, though we do not know exactly how.

(7) Lastly, the sacred Colleges recovered the right of *cooptatio*; that is, vacancies were filled up by the existing members electing, not by the *Comitia*. These measures were meant to be permanent modifications of practice, mostly in the direction of a return to old customs, and all with a view to prevent excessive power of the democracy or abnormal influence of individuals. For the present the assent of the people was attempted to be secured by wide alterations among the voters themselves. The Italian towns were in many cases almost repeopled by large drafts of veterans; and the urban electorate (practically much the most important) was leavened by the addition of some 10,000 freedmen, whose masters had fallen in the civil war. They were enrolled in the urban tribes under the general name of Cornelii, following the usual practice of slaves taking the gentile name of their emancipator.

13. **Sulla's Criminal Code.** Sulla's constitutional arrangements, though they deeply affected subsequent

history, were not long fully maintained. But what he did as to criminal trials proved more lasting. Up to this time, if a crime had been committed, the *Comitia* either tried the case itself, or ordered a committee (*quaestio*) to try it, generally leaving the Senate to arrange the list of the jurors and other conditions of the trial. In one case, that of an accusation against a provincial governor for extortion or improperly retaining money (*res repetundae*), a permanent *quaestio* had been established by the *lex Calpurnia* (B.C. 149); that is to say, when such an accusation was brought the praetor had standing directions how to select the jury, how to conduct the case, and what sentence the court could inflict. Sulla extended this system by establishing similar standing committees to try a number of crimes of common occurrence, such as treason (*maiestas*), assassination, poisoning, murder, peculation, bribery, coining, forgery, riot. One common feature in all these *quaestiones* was that the jurors were not to be Equites, but Senators. He no doubt held that Senators were likely to be more impartial, and this regulation, of course, was meant to enhance their importance, and to depress that of the Equites. It was therefore the subject of constant struggles after his time between the two orders, which resulted in various compromises.

14. **Sulla's Retirement and Death,** B.C. 79-78. Sulla held his extraordinary office as Dictator only between two and three years (81-79), long enough to see that his new regulations were at any rate tried. Towards the end of B.C. 79 he abdicated, and retired to a villa near Cumae, where he spent the last year of his life in great luxury, in the company of men of letters, artists, musicians, and actors. He died calmly in B.C. 78, busying himself to the last with the composition of his memoirs. He is a rare instance of a man who, having obtained supreme power with great cruelty, and exercised it with severity, though also with wisdom and high policy, was able to

lay down his authority with safety. Perhaps if he had lived longer he would not have died so peacefully. It is interesting to notice that the two men destined in the next generation to be leaders in the civil war which brought the Republic to an end were both brought into contact with him and both defied him. Pompey had joined him on his landing in Italy, and had been employed after his success to secure the obedience of Africa and Sicily, and had, in spite of his opposition, celebrated a triumph for his African victories. Iulius Caesar, six years Pompey's junior, had been connected with the opposite party, was a nephew of the wife of Marius, and had himself married a daughter of Cinna, whom he refused to divorce at the Dictator's order. One of the earliest speeches of Cicero also was delivered in defence of a client accused of murder, in the course of which he ventured to speak plainly on the Sullan despotism.[1]

15. **The Roman Empire at the Death of Sulla,** B.C. 78. We shall now have to trace the course by which the constitution thus settled by Sulla broke down, and in between forty and fifty years gave place to a more complete and more lasting despotism. Before doing so it will be well to take stock of the progress made in the extension and organization of the Empire. And first let us notice that the whole of Italy from the Rubicon to the extreme south has now become an extended Rome. The various communities had long been joined to Rome in terms differing according to their origin or their separate agreement or *foedus*, and were called either municipia, coloniae (Roman or Latin), praefecturae, civitates foederatae, or mere fora and conciliabula (market towns). Some (as Roman colonies, and certain towns in Latium) had had the full franchise and a local government founded on the model of Rome; others had had governments of their own con-

---
[1] *Pro Sexto Roscio Amerino*, B.C. 80.

trivance, and were only bound to Rome so far as related to military service; some had had an imperfect citizenship called Latinitas; others had a constitution of their own but no jurisdiction, that is, the administration of justice was in the hands of an officer appointed by the Roman praetor. But as far as the full citizenship was concerned all these differences were done away with at the end of the Social war. All citizens in the various communities in Italy became alike citizens of Rome, though the variation in local and internal government remained as before.[1] It was now Italy (not Rome only) that was the governing body; but it was Italy as an extended Rome, not Italy with a capital city Rome. Therefore the name and official designation remained the same; it was still *Senatus Populusque Romanus* that governed; only the Populus Romanus now included many who did not live in or near Rome. It is necessary to keep this in mind, to understand why it was in Rome alone that magistrates could be elected, the Senate sit, and orders to the provinces go forth. Rome was still mistress though she admitted Italians among her citizens. One substantial advantage of the citizenship was the freedom from the land tax or *tributum* to which all provincials were liable; and another was the protection which it gave against arbitrary sentences of the magistrates.

16. **Foreign Dominions.** We have seen from time to time what countries external to Italy had been brought under the rule of Rome, and were now being governed by this enlarged city-state. They were called 'provinces,' that is, spheres of authority for certain magistrates. When Rome first began to have provinces (Sicily and Sardinia) additional praetors were elected to go to them, and, if they were in a disturbed state, one of the consuls often

[1] Sulla disfranchised whole districts, but this disability was only temporary.

went with an army also. But as their number increased, there were not enough praetors to govern them, and besides the increasing law-business at Rome required the presence of the praetors. Therefore it became the custom often to keep a man a second year in his province as *pro praetore* or *pro consule*, or to send him only when he had served his year of office at Rome. Sulla made this latter plan imperative, and after his time each consul and praetor drew lots during his year of office for the province which he was to govern in the next year. The Senate decided which province should have a propraetor and which a proconsul, but this was generally done according to a regular precedent; the easier provinces being praetorian, the more difficult consular. All alike were sometimes loosely spoken of as proconsuls. In their provinces these governors were in command of the troops stationed there, or of those they brought with them; had power of life and death over the provincials (who were not citizens); controlled the collection of tribute, and administered justice. The provinces consisted of certain defined territory containing a number of civitates or city-states, and the terms on which they were held, taxed, and governed, differed in each according to the original *formula* or charta drawn up when they became provinces by commissioners sent to settle their constitution (*redigere in provinciam*). The Romans usually respected local customs and laws, though in certain important points the principles of Roman law were applied to all alike. Above all they lost the power of making foreign alliances or wars, and were compelled to keep peace among themselves. They all paid tribute in one form or another, and in 'return were protected from foreign invasion or damage to their commerce.

17. **The Number of the Provinces.** There were now ten such provinces: I. Gallia Cisalpina, *i.e.* North Italy from the Rubicon to the Alps, which contained

several colonies enjoying full *civitas*. As far as the Po, indeed, the whole country had the *civitas* and north of it an inferior citizenship, which was yet on a higher level than that of other provinces. II. Gallia Transalpina, sometimes called Narbonensis, from the colony Narbo which was its capital, a district on the south-east of Gaul answering roughly to the modern Provence. III. Sicily. IV. Sardinia and Corsica. V. Hispania Citerior. VI. Hispania Ulterior. VII. Macedonia, to which was joined Thessaly, parts of Epirus, and, for certain purposes, the rest of Greece. VIII. Africa, that is, the territories of Carthage in Africa. IX. Asia, the old dominions of the kings of Pergamus,—Phrygia, Mysia, Caria, and Lydia. X. Cilicia.

Other places were so much under the influence of Rome that they were certain to become provinces in time. Thus Illyricum or Dalmatia, the district on the east of the Adriatic, paid tribute although it was not yet thoroughly organized as a separate province, being sometimes put under the governor of Cisalpine Gaul, sometimes under the governor of Macedonia. Greece, though many States in it were nominally free, was for practical purposes under the governor of Macedonia. In Egypt the kings depended on Roman support; and the next district in Africa to the west of Egypt called Cyrene, with Crete, had been bequeathed to Rome, though the Romans had at present refused to take it over formally. Thus the Roman Empire or protectorate already extended right across Europe and Asia Minor, and both the north and the south coasts of the Mediterranean were in her hands.

CHAPTER XV.

THE RISE OF POMPEY THE GREAT, B.C. 78–62.

1. *Signs of dissolution after the strong government of Sulla.* 2. *The two parties at Rome.* 3. *The revolt of Lepidus* (B.C. 78-7). 4. *Sertorius in Spain* (B.C. 83-72). 5. *Spartacus and the gladiators* (B.C. 73-71). 6. *Affairs in the East.* 7. *The second Mithridatic war.* 8. *The third Mithridatic war under Lucullus.* 9. *Pompey in the Mediterranean and the East.* 10. *War with the Cilician pirates.* 11. *Pompey sent against Mithridates* (B.C. 66). 12. *Death of Mithridates and settlement of Asia.* 13. *Pompey's return to Rome.*

1. **Signs of Dissolution.** The settlement of Sulla had been brought about with so much violence that a reaction was certain to follow; and the fierce passions roused by these scenes of blood were sure to produce others like them. We have now come therefore to a period of civil wars which, with little intermission, continued till the permanent peace secured by Augustus after the battle of Actium in B.C. 31. These wars and disturbances arose from different causes and in different places, but were all of them the result of political discontent or social grievances; of overgrown wealth contrasted with ruin and poverty; of disloyal ambition or extravagant partisanship. The legions serving at a distance from Rome began to regard allegiance to a successful commander as more binding than that to the State. The oppressions in the provinces inflicted by some of the

governors and by the *publicani*, or farmers of revenues, not only caused restlessness in the provinces themselves, but proved also the fruitful source of violent contests in Rome when the question of punishing powerful and guilty statesmen was mooted. The most notorious of these was Gaius Verres, who plundered Cilicia as pro-quaestor in B.C. 80-79, and was prosecuted by Cicero for extortions in Sicily, where he was pro-praetor in B.C. 73-71. Though obliged to go into exile to avoid condemnation, he was able to take most of his ill-gotten wealth with him, and lived in luxury till B.C. 43. Other causes nearer home were of dangerous omen, such as the shock to family life caused by the growing facility of divorce, the multiplicity of slaves, the large establishments of gladiators, the increased tendency to leave the cultivation of land to slaves, and to crowd into Rome, swelling the ranks of the needy citizens who were ready to take part with ambitious or unscrupulous nobles

2. **The Two Parties at Rome**. But even putting aside the distinctly disloyal or ambitious, the Romans were now sharply divided into two parties, the Optimates and Populares. The Optimates, as we have already seen, wished the republican forms maintained, but the offices to be chiefly in the hands of the nobles and men of high birth, and the magistrates to be thoroughly subordinate to the Senate, which was to direct Rome's foreign policy and the government of the provinces. The Populares wanted the offices to be easily attainable by all, as by law they were open to all; and though they did not aim at destroying the Senate, they wished to restrict its functions and bring as many details of government as possible directly before *Comitia*. In particular they wished the juries, who tried offending governors, to be composed of Equites instead of Senators, or at least of a mixture of the two. Both had some reason on their side. But the weak

point in the policy of the Optimates was that, though the Senate was a better body than a popular assembly for governing a foreign empire, yet experience had shown that it was not able to control members of its own order who were determined on enriching themselves at all risks; and that the family compacts which were made as to official promotion had often resulted in putting inefficient and corrupt men in positions of importance, and even in the command of armies. The weak point in the policy of the Populares was that not only were the *Comitia* unfit, as popular assemblies always are, to decide details of administration, but that the Roman *Comitia* were not even what they professed to be—assemblies of all citizens. A large number of citizens lived at a distance from Rome, and seldom came there. The voters were mostly the city populace, among whom the 'men of the pavement,' or what may be called the city rabble, formed a powerful element. For voting at elections indeed, distant voters sometimes were induced by leading men to come to Rome, but seldom for legislation. Office was now become so valuable from the provincial governorships to which it led, that it was fiercely contended for; and leading men on either side did not hesitate to incite their followers to riot and outrage in order to carry their election or their laws, or to interrupt assemblies at which measures they disliked were to be proposed or their political opponents to be elected. Of the two parties Pompey and Caesar came eventually to be heads respectively. Caesar had always been connected with the Populares; but it was only in later life, and owing to a long chain of events, that Pompey came to be regarded as chief of the Optimates. We must see now how the next thirty years brought on these changes, and, with them, the practical end of the Republic.

3. **The Revolt of Lepidus**, B.C. 78-77. Sulla's death

was followed immediately by an attempt to upset most of his legislation. This attempt was made by one of the consuls for B.C. 78, M. Aemilius Lepidus. He passed laws for cheap distribution of corn, and for recalling those exiled by Sulla, and proposed others to undo much of his legislation; finally, in the year after his consulship, when he was in command of troops in Etruria as proconsul (B.C. 77), he actually marched at the head of these troops to take Rome and enforce his views. He was, however, defeated by his former colleague, Catulus, at the Milvian Bridge, just outside the city, and retreated to Sardinia, where he died; whilst one of his chief legates, M. Brutus (father of the assassin of Caesar), was captured and put to death by Pompey at Mutina. This movement was nôt of great or permanent importance, but it showed to what lengths a party leader was prepared to go.

4. **Sertorius in Spain**, B.C. 83-72. Another movement which proved more troublesome and protracted was that of Sertorius in Spain. Q. Sertorius had been in the party of Cinna, and had shared in the defeat inflicted on the consul by Sulla near Capua in B.C. 83. He had not remained in Rome to witness the triumph of Sulla. He had been already named pro-praetor of Hispania Ulterior, and went there towards the end of B.C. 83. He was much above the average of his class in energy and uprightness, but he too was prepared to resist in arms the dominant party in the government at home. Knowing that Sulla would recall him, he made arrangements to hold the passes of the Pyrenees against his legates. When they were forced, he retired gradually to Africa; joined a fleet of Cilician pirates; landed in Spain at Gades (*Cadiz*); crossed again to Africa; and, finally, accepted an invitation of the Lusitani (Portugal) to lead them against the Roman army. His character won him great influence both in Lusitania and other parts of Spain. He was joined by

other malcontents from Rome in such numbers that he pretended to have the Senate with him; and from B.C. 79 to 72 maintained his ground against many Roman commanders and propraetors. He even negotiated with Mithridates as though head of the State, and sent a partisan to act as proconsul of Asia and assist the king. Finally his power in Spain became so formidable that, after he had defeated three Roman propraetors, Pompey was sent with a large army and the rank of proconsul to reinforce the Spanish governors (B.C. 76). But it was not for nearly four years that Pompey succeeded in putting down the insurrection, having in the course of them been driven back beyond the Ebro and suffered more than one defeat. The war dragged on, as wars in Spain always seem to have done, and became a series of assaults on isolated fortresses; but, on the whole, in this species of warfare Pompey and Metellus made steady progress. Even in B.C. 72 however, though deserted by many of his adherents, and losing popularity as he became embittered by the wearisome struggle, Sertorius was not defeated in battle, but was murdered by the treacherous Perpenna, a legate of Lepidus, who had joined Sertorius after the death of Lepidus, but was jealous of him, and hoped to secure his own pardon by thus destroying his leader. His treason was rewarded as it deserved: for Pompey refused to see him, ordered him to be executed, and some letters involving certain men of position in Rome in the crime of treasonable correspondence with Sertorius to be burnt unread. Few leaders of rebellion have had a purer and nobler record than Sertorius, or have made themselves more respected and beloved by those whom they ruled. There is a certain charm in the story of his intercourse with the simple Lusitani and the manner in which he impressed them with confidence. He was everywhere accompanied, it is said, by a favourite fawn presented to him by some hunters, but which he allowed them to believe came from Diana herself, and was a pledge of her favour. In some ways the history of Sertorius's rebellion foreshadowed the civil war of Pompey and Caesar. He had so many senators with him that he could pretend to have a Senate; he was still technically endowed with Imperium and the command of a province (for he had not laid down either); he professed to be acting for the Republic against a faction; and had the secret sympathy of many leading men at Rome. It showed the weak point in the senatorial government, and how it was possible for a provincial magistrate to defy it without being constitutionally quite in the wrong.

GLADIATORS FIGHTING.

5. **Spartacus and the Gladiators**, B.C. 73-71. If the movement of Sertorius betrayed the weakness of the constitution, that of Spartacus pointed to a danger nearer home, and springing from the social habits of the age.

Gladiatorial shows are first heard of in B.C. 264. Since then they had become the most popular of amusements. Wealthy men, wishing to secure public favour, vied with each other in keeping gangs or 'schools' (*ludi*) of them in training. They were selected from the most powerful barbarians, and their number was now so great that they might easily become dangerous, like a caged lion, if ever the bars were broken. A large school of this kind at Capua was owned by one Lentulus, in which a number of Gauls and Thracians were being trained. Two hundred of them broke loose, obtained arms, and under the leadership of a Thracian named Spartacus established themselves on a spur of Mount Vesuvius (B.C. 73). They were soon joined by other escaped gladiators and slaves, and during the next three years defeated more than one consular army, and traversed Italy at their will, plundering in every direction. Spartacus does not appear to have conducted his war with special cruelty or needless outrage; the one act of severity recorded is in B.C. 72, when, having defeated two consuls in Picenum, he forced three hundred Roman prisoners to fight as gladiators. But there was necessarily nothing stable in such a raid, however long continued. Spartacus himself wished to cross the Alps and make his way to his native country; but his followers were divided, and most preferred the life of plunder and adventure in Italy; and in the winter of B.C. 72-71 they were concentrated for the most part round Thurii, in the south. There he was at length overcome by L. Licinius Crassus, who had volunteered to take the command, when every one else tried to avoid it. Spartacus was driven to the extreme south at Rhegium, from which he tried to bribe some Cilician pirate vessels to take him across to Sicily, where he trusted to be able to again rouse the slaves. But the Cilicians took his money and abandoned him; and he then found himself shut off to the north by a deep trench and embankment which Crassus had thrown out across the Bruttian Peninsula. He broke out indeed in spite of this; but a great body of his adherents had been already cut to pieces by Crassus, and he himself fell after a desperate battle near Petilia (B.C. 71). The survivors of the revolted slaves, still numbering many thousands, were scattered over the mountains, where Pompey,—just returned from his campaign against Sertorius in Spain,—pursued and cut them off in detail, boasting that though Crassus had won battles, he had cut up the rebellion by the roots. Six thousand of the slaves who were captured were crucified along the Appian Road. Still isolated bands were in existence in the neighbourhood of Thurii as late as B.C. 60, living a life of brigandage, where they were cut to pieces by Octavius, the father of Augustus.

6. Affairs in the East. Meanwhile some attempts had been made to clear the sea of pirates, and P. Servilius Vatia earned the cognomen of Isauricus by defeating the people of Isauria beyond Mount Taurus in Asia, and added parts of Pamphylia, Pisidia, Isauria, and Cappadocia to the new province of Cilicia (B.C. 78-74). Other generals were strengthening the north frontier of Macedonia, by defeating bordering barbarians, and advancing the Roman arms for the first time to the Danube. But what proved the most important event for Rome was a renewed struggle with Mithridates. This went through two phases, sometimes called the Second and Third Mithridatic wars.

7. **Second Mithridatic War.** When Sulla returned home in B.C. 84, he left L. Licinius Muraena as propraetor of Asia, with L. Lucullus as quaestor. Muraena was eager to distinguish himself by a victory over Mithridates. There was not yet complete peace in his province: some places, such as the island of Mitylene, still held out against the Romans, and as the settlement of Pergamus had been

verbal and not by a written treaty, there was sure to be points of dispute that might be made an excuse for attacking Mithridates. Muraena did in fact find such an excuse in a dispute as to the possession of parts of Cappadocia. He entered that country, pillaged villages and temples, and refused to obey an order of recall sent from the Senate. He sustained a defeat at the hands of Mithridates near Sinope (capital of the Pontic kingdom), and only desisted from the war when Sulla sent Gabinius with positive orders for his return, and with directions to make terms between the kings of Pontus and Cappadocia (B.C. 81).

Mithridates had seemed glad to accept Sulla's orders and to make peace; and till B.C. 74 he lived on fairly good terms with the Roman governors of Asia, who were forbidden by Sulla's law to cross the frontier to attack him, though there was still an outstanding dispute about parts of Cappadocia, and Mithridates was doing his best to prepare for another war.

8. **Third Mithridatic War under Lucullus.** In B.C. 74 a question as to the succession to the throne of Bithynia brought matters to a crisis. Nicomedes, king of Bithynia, died in that year and left his dominions to the Roman people. Whether this was like the will of Attalus, which left the royal property to the Romans, hoping that they would be induced to respect the independence of his people, or not, the Romans determined to treat the whole country as their own, and add it to the province of Asia till further arrangements should be made. As this gave them a district on the Pontus (Black Sea) and Propontis, and would enable them by blockading the Bosporus and Hellespont to ruin the Pontic trade, Mithridates was expected to espouse the cause of the son of Nicomedes. His previous preparations were known at Rome, and it was determined to anticipate all danger by at once sending a

fleet and army. The army was commanded by one consul L. Licinius Lucullus, the navy by the other consul M. Aurelius Cotta (B.C. 73). Thus began a war that lasted seven years. It opened with a disaster to the Roman fleet under Cotta at Chalcedon; and with an attempt to rouse the Greek cities in Asia to reassert their freedom from Roman imposts under the leadership of M. Marius the One-eyed, whom Sertorius had sent with the pretended authority of proconsul of Asia. But on land Lucullus was much more successful. The grand army of Mithridates, amounting to 150,000 men, was wasted in a siege of Cyzicus, and in engagements with Lucullus who came to its relief; and at the end of the year B.C. 73 the king could muster barely 20,000, while a succession of storms had much weakened and damaged his fleet. Next year (B.C. 72) M. Marius was captured; the death of Sertorius deprived Mithridates of the hope of a diversion in his favour by occupying Roman forces in Spain; and the king himself barely escaped from a blockade of Nicomedia. One of his lieutenants also, who had been sent to invade Roman Cilicia, had suffered similar disasters at the hands of Iulius Caesar, who, while studying rhetoric at Rhodes, had raised a force of volunteers and crossed to Asia to meet him. An attempt to send money to bribe the islands of the Aegean Sea was also defeated, and the treasure captured; and the king's garrisons in Galatian towns were expelled by the tetrarch Deiotărus. Altogether, except as to the first success against Cotta, the two years (B.C. 73-72) were most disastrous to Mithridates, and destroyed all his hopes of wresting the province of Asia from the Romans. His only resource was a combination of the great kingdoms of Central Asia—Armenia and Parthia— against the Republic. Tigranes, king of Armenia, however, had his own battles to fight in Syria, and gave him only vain promises; and he again sustained a great defeat at the hands of Lucullus near Cabira (B.C. 71 spring), and flying into Armenia was kept by the king practically a prisoner till B.C. 69; during which time Lucullus carried all before him, as did also the Roman fleet in the Aegean and the Pontus. However, the war was not at an end. Lucullus determined to demand of Tigranes, king of Armenia, that he should hand over Mithridates; and when Tigranes, elated by his victories in Syria, refused, Lucullus, after a year's delay, in the course of which the Pontic capital Sinope was reduced to surrender, advanced upon his new-built capital (Tigranocerta), in the spring of B.C. 69. Thus the Romans were for the first time approaching the country between the Euphrates and Tigris, where they were destined to maintain for so many centuries a struggle against the Parthians. Tigranes was defeated near Tigranocerta, on the 6th of October, B.C. 69, and Lucullus not only got vast booty, but restored to the throne of Syria the expelled Antiochus Asiaticus, who, on being driven out by Tigranes, had appealed to Rome for help, and was now for a short time again allowed to call himself king of Syria. Tigranes was not yet, however, quite conquered. He summoned Mithridates from his confinement, and under his vigorous guidance again collected a large army, which, however, was again defeated by Lucullus (Sept., B.C. 68), near Mount Arsanias, in the Euphrates valley. But Lucullus was now on the high steppes of Central Asia, where the winters were most severe, and his army refused to remain there. He was obliged to come south into Mesopotamia, and, for the winter of B.C. 68-67, was reduced almost to impotence by the mutinous temper of his troops, who were instigated by his legate and brother-in-law P. Clodius to refuse to endure any farther fatigues or expeditions. The result was that Mithridates once more began a series of successful movements, and seemed likely to recover all those parts of his dominions which had been occupied by the Romans. Tigranes also recovered Armenia, on Lucullus moving westward to relieve his lieutenant Triarius, who (like his predecessor Hadrianus) had been defeated by the troops of Mithridates. Lucullus had done great things, but he was now in danger of losing all that he had gained; and just at this juncture ten commissioners arrived, expecting to find a new province (Bithynia and Pontus) ready to be organized, of which M'. Acilius Glabrio, who came at the same time, was to be proconsul, as well as commander against Mithridates. Lucullus therefore felt himself superseded, and his mutinous army acted as though he were so, and for the most part left him. He still, however, remained during the winter of B.C. 67-66 in Galatia, at the head of some troops, which he did not hand over till Pompey arrived in B.C. 66 to take up the command.

9. **Pompey in the Mediterranean and the East,** B.C. 66-63. The rest of the war is intimately connected with the rise of Pompeius Magnus to a high position in the State. Pompey had been consul in B.C. 70 after his return from Spain, in spite of the law of Sulla, since he was neither of the consular age nor had he been quaestor or praetor. In his year of office laws were passed undoing some of Sulla's arrangements. The law preventing tribunes afterwards holding other offices was repealed, and the juries were no longer confined to Senators, but were to be one-third Senators, one-third Equites, and one-third of the order next to the Equites, called *Tribuni aerarii*. This made the stricter Optimates suspect him, and they eagerly opposed a bill brought forward in B.C. 67 by a tribune named A. Gabinius, because they regarded it as certainly pointing to Pompey, whose reputation had been steadily rising.

10. **The Lex Gabinia, and War with Cilician Pirates.** The occasion was this. The Cicilian and other pirates had become a serious danger throughout the Mediterranean. Their numbers and boldness had risen to such a height that commerce was threatened with extinction, and the sea was almost impassable except to large vessels

with armed men on board. They had plundered the coasts of Asia, Greece, Epirus, and Italy itself; had carried off two propraetors with their train, many ladies of high rank, and had even run into the harbours of Caieta and Ostia and set fire to the ships. Every now and then they met with retribution, as when they captured Iulius Caesar on his way to Rhodes and exacted a heavy ransom, which he raised in Greek cities, and then obtained ships, pursued, captured and put them to death at Pergamus. But, as a rule, anything the Romans had done had been either unsuccessful or insufficient. The Balearic Islands (*Maiorca* and *Minorca*) had been taken over as offering them harbourage; P. Servilius Isauricus had destroyed one great nest of them, and, though C. Antonius had failed in Crete, Q. Caecilius Metellus had been more successful there (B.C. 68). Still these were only partial measures; no general plan of repression had ever been set on foot, and the people were feeling the effects of the interruption of commerce in a serious rise in the price of provisions. The law of Gabinius proposed that some one should be appointed with absolute power for three years all over the Mediterranean and fifty miles inland from all coasts, with two hundred ships and unlimited credit on the treasury, with the express purpose of clearing the sea of these pests. All eyes turned at once to Pompey, and, in spite of various methods of opposition, the bill was not only passed, but Pompey was named with an even greater equipment. He was to have twenty-four legates, 120,000 sailors and foot-soldiers, with 500 horse. Pompey justified the confidence of the people. Within a surprisingly small number of months he had accomplished his task; and, during the winter of B.C. 67-66 he resided in a now pacified Cilicia, founding cities and settling the best of the pirates in districts where they could live honestly.

11. **Pompey sent against Mithridates,** B.C. 66. The relief to the Romans and all Italy was great; Pompey's reputation was at its height, and a law proposed by a tribune, C. Manilius, to confer on him the command against Mithridates was eagerly passed, in spite of the opposition of the Optimates in the Senate (B.C. 66). Pompey was again completely and rapidly successful. Mithridates, indeed, when he arrived, was at a very low ebb of his fortunes, in spite of his successes of the previous two years. The loss of the piratical fleets was a severe blow to him; Tigranes, king of Armenia (his son-in-law), was again alienated from him; and his attempt to gain the alliance of the Parthians was frustrated by Pompey whose forces were vastly superior to the king's, while his fleet was guarding all points on the coast from Phoenicia to the Bosporus. Still Mithridates refused submission; and when his troops were cut to pieces in attempting a night retreat, he himself escaped to Armenia, and, finding no chance of support there, marched round the Black Sea to Colchis, intending to enter the dominions of his son, Machares, near the Crimea. Pompey followed him for some distance, wintering on the Khur, and inflicting a defeat on the Albani and Iberes, who commanded the passage over the Caucasus. In the spring (B.C. 65) he proceeded as far as the Phasis; but failing to come up with Mithridates, he left him to be dealt with by the Roman fleet, and returned southward to take over the district between the Euphrates on the east and the Mediterranean on the west, Mounts Amanus and Taurus on the north and the desert of Arabia Petraea on the south, including Palestine. This was now to be formed into a new province under the name of Syria; and Antiochus, whom the Romans had restored to the territory taken from him by Tigranes of Armenia, was to be deposed. It was in the course of this business that Pompey found it necessary to

enter Palestine and capture Jerusalem, in consequence of the disturbance created by the rivalry of the two kings, Hyrcanus III. and Aristobulus, the former of whom had called in the aid of Aretas, king of the Nabataei, in Arabia. The city was delivered to Pompey without a blow; but the temple was obstinately defended, and was only taken after more than two months' siege with much bloodshed on both sides (December B.C. 63).

12. **Death of Mithridates, B.C. 63, and Settlement of Asia.** While engaged in Palestine Pompey learnt that Mithridates was dead. He had reached Panticapaeum (Kertch), had forced his rebellious son Machares to commit suicide, had again collected an army, and even meditated an invasion of Italy by the valley of the Danube and the Brenner. But he was closely blockaded by the Roman fleet; his people were suffering from their crippled trade; and an insurrection, instigated by his one remaining son Pharnaces, compelled him to put an end to his life. After his death there was no more resistance to the Roman arms in Asia, and Pompey was able to make a settlement of Asiatic affairs as he chose. It will be well to notice what this settlement was.

(1) Two new "provinces" were formed:

    (*a*) Bithynia and Pontus, sometimes spoken of by either name, including the country left by the Bithynian king Nicomedes (B.C. 74), with the addition of most of the territory lately held by Mithridates as king of Pontus.

    (*b*) Syria, the district from the upper Euphrates and the Gulf of Issus to Egypt and the Arabian desert, was made a province, the lately restored king Antiochus Asiaticus being wholly deprived of this territory. But the country was too vast and diversified to be all under one administration. The difficulty was got over by leaving numerous cities and their immediate territories "free," *i.e.* not under a Roman magistrate, but with a local government (royal or other) of their own, though paying tribute to Rome. Thus Jerusalem and the Jews generally, thus Tyre and Sidon, remained autonomous though tributary, some of the coast towns being taken from them and added to the Province. Thus Aretas was heavily mulcted and reduced to pay tribute, but was allowed to retain his government in the same way as many other petty princes retained their government, but had to observe the *Pax Romana*. M. Aemilius Scaurus was appointed by Pompey as first governor of this province.

(2) The rest of Asia was left independent indeed, and the larger kingdoms re-established; but their kings were set up for the first time, or restored by Pompey's authority, and really reigned by permission of Rome.

These kingdoms were:

(*a*) Tigranes was restored to Armenia.
(*b*) Cappadocia was secured to Ariobarzanes.
(*c*) Antiochus (not Asiaticus) was confirmed in the kingdom of Seleucia and Commagene.
(*d*) Attalus was made prince of the interior of Paphlagonia.
(*e*) Deiotărus, tetrarch of a large part of Galatia.
(*f*) Aristarchus, king of Colchis.
(*g*) Archelaus, High Priest of Comana (equivalent to king).
(*h*) Pharnaces (son of Mithridates), king of Bosporus: but certain towns were declared free; as Phanagoria (on the Sea of Azov) and Mitylene in Lesbos, which had held out for Mithridates, and had been subdued in B.C. 81.

13. **Pompey's Return to Rome**, B.C. 62. These

arrangements constituted what was called an imperator's *acta*. They held good as long as he had imperium, and provisionally at any rate afterwards; but to be put on a clearly legal footing they had to be "confirmed" by a formal vote of the Senate: and when Pompey returned to Rome in B.C. 62, many thought that he would refuse to disband his army, or lay down his imperium until these *acta* were confirmed; and there was some alarm on all sides as to what he might do. He was coming home with great glory. The sea had been cleared of pirates; two large provinces had been added to the Empire; Asia was pacified, and nearly all the kings in it were reigning by his means or consent; even the Parthians, who were on the Eastern frontier and were so much dreaded, had been forced to surrender what they had taken from Armenia, and had made terms. Pompey also was bringing enormous wealth to enrich the exchequer, and a great number of noble and princely captives to adorn his triumph. With such prestige and such forces he might perhaps play the part of Sulla or Marius, and both parties were uneasy. But Pompey disappointed hopes and fears alike. He disbanded his army as soon as he landed in Italy, and came to Rome to claim his triumph. He did not lay down his imperium, for, if he had done so, he could not have had his triumph. He therefore could not actually enter the city on his arrival late in B.C. 62, but he could meet the Senate outside the Pomoerium in certain temples. He did not triumph till the 28th September, B.C. 61; and we shall find that the question of the confirmation of his *acta* was the cause of much political trouble.

STATUE OF POMPEY.

CHAPTER XVI.

THE BEGINNING OF THE BREAKDOWN OF THE REPUBLIC.

1. *The evils requiring reform in the last period of the Republic*—(1) *Depopulation of Italy and attempts to stop it;* (2) *the misgovernment in the provinces;* (3) *violent party contests in Rome, and the points on which the parties were at variance;* (4) *hostility of the orders.* 2. *The leading men in the state during the revolutionary period: Of the Populares—Caesar, Pompey, Crassus.* 3. *Of the Optimates— Catulus, Lucullus, Cato.* 4. *Cicero, Catiline.* 5. *The conspiracy of Catiline.* 6. *Consequences of the action of Cicero in putting down the Catilinarian conspiracy.*

1. **The Evils requiring Reform in the last period of the Republic,** B.C. 63-31. We have now come to a period in which events led quickly to the breakdown of the Republic, and it will be well to see whether we can point out some of the causes of it. No one cause is sufficient to account for the revolution, and no one man. There were many circumstances which combined to bring it about, and the mistakes or crimes both of those who attacked and of those who defended the constitution alike led up to the final catastrophe. Let us see what the evils in various parts of the empire were which required reform, and then we may pass to the remedies which opposing parties in Rome proposed for them.

(1) *The Depopulation of Italy.* Lands were for the most part held by few men in large estates and worked by slaves.

The free country people had to a great extent migrated to the towns, and especially to Rome, finding no chance of prosperity in the country. Therefore Rome was becoming crowded with a poor and discontented class. This tendency had long existed, but, partly owing to the vicious practice of distributing cheap corn, it had by this time come to a climax. Various attempts had been made to remedy it by using the *ager publicus* for allotments to poor citizens, and thus persuading them to settle in the country. There was still, however, some *ager publicus* left, principally in Campania, once forming the territory of Capua, which was rented to farmers (*aratores*); and also considerable tracts in Etruria confiscated by Sulla, in some of which he had put *possessores*, while in the case of others (for instance, at Volaterrae and Arretium) the law had not been carried out, and the original owners had remained in possession, always however with the terror before them lest some new proposal should be made for dividing it and displacing them.

Here there was one source of political division at Rome. Various tribunes, belonging to the popular party, made proposals from time to time for dealing with the *ager publicus* in such a way as to induce farmers to settle on their properties throughout Italy. But there were too many interests involved. The Optimates looked upon those already in possession as their best supporters and were unwilling to do anything which might alienate them. The division of the Campanian lands also among freeholders meant the loss of the quit-rents (*vectigal*) to the treasury, and the more complete dependence on the tribute of the provinces over which the authority of the Senate was less secure. There was also a great deal of *ager publicus* in the provinces. The sale or enfranchisement of that also was proposed by Rullus in B.C. 63, but was opposed by the Optimates on similar grounds,—fear for the revenue, and fear of disturbances tending to put power in the hands of military leaders and weaken that of the Senate. The question was more acute than usual just now, because Pompey wanted allotments for his veterans and was therefore anxious for some solution of it. We shall see presently that this helped to throw him into the arms of Caesar, who carried a law in B.C. 59 that settled the question of the greater part of the Campanian land for a time.

(2) *The Provinces.* In the provinces there were many grievances which threatened trouble—heavy taxation, malversation on the part of governors and publicani, and insecurity of redress before the law courts. It was commonly said that a provincial governor had to make three fortunes: one to pay the cost of games, public entertainments, and other modes of obtaining office, a second to bribe the jury when tried for malversation, and a third to live on. All these he looked to make out of his province; so that some said that it would be better for the provincials if there was no such thing as trial for malversation—a man would have one less fortune to make. Not only so, but either from the wording of the law or from tradition, an eques could not be tried under the *lex de repetundis*, and the only persons liable were the proconsul, the quaestor, and the legati, if Senators. This monstrous privilege gave the publicani practical immunity at home. Their only restraint came from the proconsul, and him they found means to pacify or overawe. These things were surely making for the dissolution of the Empire. Some stringent reform was necessary; but the interests opposed to such reform were so great, that it would hardly be effected without a break-up of the present hold of the few upon office and power. Yet it would be wrong to think that all provincial governors were dishonest or oppressive. If it had been so, a more wide-spread disaster could hardly have been averted, such as that which overtook the Romans in Asia in B.C. 88. The provinces were, in fact, on the whole peaceful

and fairly prosperous. In B.C. 63 (Pompey having subdued and settled Asia) Cicero was able to say that the Empire was at peace, threatened by no rising in the provinces or acts of hostility from neighbouring princes. The evil effects of the misgovernment were to be felt first of all at Rome itself, where the eagerness for these profitable offices led to fierce party warfare.

(3) *Violent Party Contests at Rome.* We may now turn then to Rome with clearer ideas as to the dangers brewing there. We may see that the two parties—the Optimates and Populares—were sharply divided on many questions: the manner of dealing with the *ager publicus*; the reforms of the law courts, necessary for giving the provinces security for justice; the mode of dealing with the crowds of impoverished men who, living in Rome side by side with immense wealth and luxury, were always ready to be led into disorder; the real opening of office so that it should be within reach of all those legally entitled to it and yet not fall into unworthy hands. At present the higher offices were looked upon as all but the monopoly of a few noble families; and the eagerness for them, combined with the difficulty of securing them, led to violence at elections, and the hiring of regular bands of roughs to break up meetings or keep other candidates and their supporters from appearing.

(4) *Hostility of Equites and the Senate.* Besides these sources of difference there was a feud between the Senate and the Equites. The Equites were the rich middle class, not noble, as in a sense the Senators were, but always liable to become so by election to office making them life-senators. One great cause of jealousy between them was the question of juries. It had been always the custom in *quaestiones* or trials for the jury to consist of senators, till Gaius Gracchus transferred that function to the equites (B.C. 122). Sulla had restored the right to the senators in B.C. 81; but in Pompey's consulship (B.C. 70) a new law ordained that

one-third of the jury should be Senators, one-third Equites, and one-third tribuni aerarii—men whose rateable property came next below that of the Equites. But, though a settlement had been thus made which roughly satisfied both parties, there were other causes of dissension. The farming of the taxes in Asia was in the hands of publicani, who were all Equites. We have seen that the taxes were paid partly in kind and partly in money, and that the companies of publicani, estimating the amount that they would yield, paid a certain sum to the exchequer and made what profit they could. A bad harvest, or an interruption of traffic, would bring them loss, and about this time they had made so bad a bargain that they were threatened with bankruptcy. The body who had the right to relieve them was the Senate; but the Senate hesitated, and consequently there was a strained feeling between the orders. The Equites were looking to the leaders of the Populares as their natural supporters, because the policy of the Populares was to depress the Senate, to consult it as little as possible, and to pass measures through the Comitia over its head.

2. **The Leaders in the State**, B.C. 70-44. With these elements of revolution working, the character and loyalty of the leading men were of the first importance. Would they avail themselves of these thorny questions in order to push themselves forward and get above the law, or would they use their influence to carry or resist reforms within the lines of the constitution? The leading men of whom we ought to have some clear idea were:

(1) *Gaius Iulius Caesar*, B.C. 101-44. Caesar was born in B.C. 100 (or 101) of one of the most illustrious patrician families; yet his aunt was wife to Marius, and from the first he had been closely connected with the popular party. He married a daughter of Cinna, and defied Sulla's order to divorce her. He served his first campaign in operations at Lesbos, which followed Sulla's return from Greece

(B.C. 81–80), and after Sulla's death returned to Rome and gained reputation as an orator by prosecuting some of the opposite party for extortion (B.C. 75). This seems to have directed his attention to oratory as the road by which he was to advance in life; for he went in B.C. 75–74 to study rhetoric in the famous schools of Rhodes. But while he was there, the second Mithridatic war began with another invasion of Asia Minor, and in B.C. 74 he collected troops, crossed over to Asia, and defeated the king's general. He also showed his spirit in dealing with some pirates by whom he was captured on his way to Rhodes and put to ransom (p. 206). But he does not seem as yet to have discovered that his chief ability lay in the direction of military command. He returned to Rome again in B.C. 73, and, giving his support to all the measures of the popular party, began his official career by seeking the usual magistracies. Returning from his quaestorship in farther Spain in B.C. 67, he found that the burning question at Rome was the giving of extraordinary powers to Pompey, first for the piratic, and then for the Mithridatic wars. Caesar had not yet obtained such a position as to make him a rival of Pompey, and he cordially supported him, biding his time till he should have gone through the regular grades of official promotion. As commissioner of the Appian road in B.C. 67, and aedile in B.C. 65, he expended such large sums of his own that he became deeply in debt, and could only hope to stave off bankruptcy by the profits of office. After being praetor in B.C. 62, he was propraetor in farther Spain in B.C. 61–60, and there first won a name as a general, and also (by means that seem to have been oppressive) relieved himself of his load of debt. On his return he claimed a triumph, but his enemies in the Senate contrived to put off the decision as to granting it until he had to choose between entering Rome to make his profession for the consulship, and so giving up his triumph, or waiting outside Rome and so giving up the consulship. He chose the consulship and gave up the triumph; but the Senate had made a deadly enemy of him, just at the same time as they were estranging Pompey by hesitating to confirm his *acta* in the East. It was a dangerous thing to do; for by this time Caesar had shown of what metal he was made, and had by all his political actions definitely taken the lead of the Populares

(2) *Gnaeus Pompeius Magnus*, B.C. 106-48. Pompey was older than Caesar, much less enterprising, and, though perhaps as ambitious, yet much more scrupulous as to the means of gratifying his ambition. He was, in fact, a man to whom success had come so early, and remained so constant, that self-confidence and a high degree of self-esteem had become a second nature to him; and he could not rightly deal with opposition in Rome, because it seemed to him unintelligible and incredible. He must have had great energy and promptitude, for everything he undertook had been done quickly and completely—the crushing of the opposition to Sulla in Sicily and Africa, the sweeping away of the remnants of the gladiatorial rebellion, the clearance of the pirates, the winding up of the Mithridatic war, and the settlement of Asia and Syria. But it must be owned that in the greater part of this work he had been supremely fortunate in the time of his intervention: Crassus had broken the back of the gladiatorial war, Lucullus of the Mithridatic; and in the one instance in which he had to deal with a formidable and unconquered adversary—namely, Sertorius in Spain—he had met with disasters and defeats as well as successes, and owed his final triumph to the knife of the assassin.

(3) *M. Licinius Crassus*, B.C. 115-53. The two leaders, however, strengthened their position by attaching to themselves the richest man of the day, M. Licinius Crassus. He was about nine years older than Pompey, and, like him, had

been of the party of Sulla. He had done good service to Sulla, and was personally brave, as he showed in the war of Spartacus: but he had neither genius for war nor real interest in politics. His life-long passion had been the accumulation of an enormous fortune—the foundation of which he had laid during the Sullan confiscations. He had been Pompey's colleague in his first consulship (B.C. 70), but had been on bad terms with him throughout. Most of the senators owed him money, and he expected the influence thus obtained to be as great as that of Pompey, which was gained by public services. Jealousy of Pompey made it easy perhaps for Caesar to win him over, in spite of the difference in their politics. At any rate, in B.C. 61, he enabled Caesar to go to his province by being security for his debts; and when Caesar returned in B.C. 60 to stand for the consulship, he was induced by him to become reconciled to Pompey: and the three made a coalition, generally called the **First Triumvirate**, which was not a legally established commission, but a private understanding between the three men to support each other. We shall see presently (p. 233) what each of the three proposed to secure by this arrangement. It was continually in danger of breaking up owing to the mutual jealousies of Pompey and Crassus, and, after the death of Crassus, the growing antagonism of Caesar and Pompey soon brought it to an end.

3. **The Leaders of the Optimates.** The party of the Optimates had less need of a leader than the Populares. They were not attacking; they were simply defending privileges and old institutions. They in fact were jealous of any one who possessed superiority of character or genius; for they were a true oligarchy, and dreaded above all things the supremacy of one man who would put all citizens on an equal footing. For a long time office had been almost a matter of course for members of the great families in their turn. It was a kind of birthright which they looked for as

natural and assured. Many of them cared above all things for the ease and luxury which the great wealth thus secured brought them, and could not be induced to take any farther interest in politics, when once they had gone through the routine of the duties which their birth and position imposed on them. They did not understand the times, nor see that a new generation had grown up determined to share in the spoils, or (in the case of the better of them) resolved that power should no longer be so exclusively in the hands of a class which had so often shown itself corrupt or incompetent. They of course understood that there was an opposition party; but they either underrated its strength, or felt too confident in their own to take active measures. The leaders therefore of the Optimates had not, like the leaders of the Populares, a crowd of eager followers at their back. The former had to rouse, the latter to restrain their partisans. These men therefore were neither so conspicuous nor so interesting as the others. (1) **Q. Lutatius Catulus** (about B.C. 120-60) had held the highest offices, had successfully opposed the revolutionary proceedings of Lepidus (B.C. 78-77), had denounced bribers, opposed the laws for giving Pompey extra-constitutional powers, and had for years been the head of a commission for restoring the Capitol. He enjoyed the highest character for honesty, incorruptibility, and consistency. But he was essentially a mediocre man, had no following, and evoked no enthusiasm. (2) **L. Lucullus** (born about B.C. 120, died B.C. 57) had made himself famous by his conduct of the Mithridatic war (B.C. 74-64), had celebrated a triumph, and possessed enormous wealth. But after his return to Rome, he took little part in politics except in an opposition to Pompey's demand for the confirmation of his *acta*, and the personal feeling involved in that took away much of its credit. For the last few years of his life he seems to have withdrawn from public life to enjoy his wealth, or from ill-health. (3) **M. Porcius Cato** (B.C. 95-46), afterwards called Uticencis from the place of his death, was a good deal younger than these two men, but had gained considerable influence in the Senate since his entrance into it as quaestor in B.C. 65, and was the representative of the "stern and unbending" Optimates, who opposed every demand of the popular party, were against every concession, and would listen to no compromise. He modelled himself on the character of his great-grandfather the Censor, professed the Stoic philosophy, and made his life and manners conform to that ideal. His character for inflexible integrity no doubt gave him influence in his own party, but could not atone in the eyes of the other for his obstinate opposition.

There was nothing in these men to win that interest and admiration from the other classes in the State which make popular heroes. They might carry measures in the Senate, but it was Pompey and Caesar to whom the people looked as representing the governing class. Their interests, however, were usually supposed to be antagonistic. Caesar had always belonged to the popular party. Pompey had never clearly shown to which he would attach himself. What he would do when he came back with the prestige of his great successes in the Mediterranean and the East was a matter of much interest and conjecture.

4. **M. Tullius Cicero**, B.C. 106-43. There were two men indeed who, in the absence of both these leaders, occupied for a time an important position in Roman politics. They were the great orator, M. Tullius Cicero (B.C. 106-43) and L. Sergius Catiline. Of the same age as Pompey, Cicero had without any military achievements risen steadily through the regular grades of office on the strength of his talents. He was a "new man," that is, no ancestor of his had held curule office; yet his influence in the law courts was so great that he had gained the usual offices without serious opposition. To the wrong-doing of the

provincial governors he had shown his determination to oppose the weight of his brilliant rhetoric by his prosecution of Verres (p. 195). But the constitution of Rome seemed in his eyes sacred—it was the *libertas*, "the liberty," won by the heroes of the past. He would equally oppose all who put that in danger, whoever they might be. His idea was that it might be recovered and made a reality, if strenuous efforts were made to purify the law courts, to treat the provinces with equity, and induce the best of the nobles to leave their sumptuous villas and fish-ponds and really throw themselves into the business of government. The disunion of the orders (Senators and Equites) seemed to him to stand most in the way of forming a steady phalanx of the "best" men to oppose the forces of disorder and disruption. To secure this union every effort was to be made, every plausible concession granted. But revolution must be resisted at any cost. He therefore joined the Optimates, whom he vainly hoped to rouse to the sense of their danger and the right method of meeting it. But he spoke to deaf ears; nor was he himself sufficiently true to his principles. His voice was often raised in defence of notorious wrongdoers; and the proud Optimates, though glad of his help, were often stung by his speeches, and never quite looked on him as one of themselves.

5. **Catiline's Conspiracy**, B.C. 63. The other man who now gained a temporary prominence was L. Sergius Catilina (about B.C. 108-62). Caesar in B.C. 63 had not yet won his military triumphs in Spain, and as yet had held no higher office than the quaestorship and aedileship. He was to be the leader of the Populares; but he was biding his time, and the hour was not yet come. The extreme wing of the party, however, was not content to wait, and Catiline now came forward as the leader of this section. An aristocrat by birth, though without fortune, he had joined

the party of Sulla, and had, according to common report, been guilty of the worst sort of excesses committed during the proscriptions. The proscription of a brother or brother-in-law, the murder of a wife and son, the corruption of a vestal virgin were all attributed to him. Yet he was praetor in B.C. 68, and propraetor in Africa in the following year, and came back in B.C. 66 to stand for the consulship. But whether it was from the scandals attaching to his name, or because of his want of wealth, he found a strenuous opposition to farther advancement. The consuls elected in B.C. 66 were disqualified for bribery, and when he tried to take their place the influence of the Senate secured the election of the previously rejected candidates; and P. Clodius Pulcher (at that time in the party of the Optimates) was set up to accuse him of extortion in Africa, so as to prevent his being a candidate at the Comitia of B.C. 65. Some other means were found to prevent his candidature in B.C. 64 also, when Cicero and C. Antonius were elected. He was thrown into violent opposition by these measures. In B.C. 65 he was said to have conspired to kill the consuls, although this so-called "first conspiracy" was never investigated, far less proved. But in B.C. 63, Cicero affirms that he was aware from the beginning of his consulship, that a similar conspiracy was again afoot. He declares that throughout the year Catiline was gathering round him a band of desperadoes, that their plan was if possible for Catiline to be elected consul, and then to gratify his followers by offices and every kind of revolutionary legislation—abolition of debts, confiscations, and plunder. The opportunity was thought to be a good one: for one of the consuls, C. Antonius, was believed to favour him; partisans of Catiline were governing Spain and Africa; there were disturbances in Gaul; there were troubles in Etruria, because the "possessors" put in by Sulla had not prospered, and the owners whom they had displaced were eager to get back their lands. Nothing overt, however, seems to have been done until after the elections of B.C. 63. When they were over, and Catiline again defeated, he entered (it is said) on a deliberate plot. The programme was to assassinate Cicero, to fire the city in several places, assault the houses of leading senators, and cause such confusion as to give an invading army every opportunity of capturing Rome. Such an army was now known to be collecting near Faesulae in Etruria (*Florence*) under C. Manlius, an old officer of Sulla, who had been joined by numerous malcontents, either from the city or the ruined landowners on the Sullan allotments (27th October). The plans of Catiline however were even yet mere matters of rumour, or had come to Cicero's ears by the doubtful channel of Fulvia, the mistress of one of the conspirators. However certain Cicero may have felt about them, he had not yet sufficient grounds to justify an arrest. At a meeting of the Senate on the 21st September he had asked Catiline for an explanation. The latter had already been threatened with impeachment by Cato, but now deigned no answer except that he proposed to give the larger party in the State what it most wanted, a leader. Still this did not amount to guilt. Though the Senate passed the usual decree (p. 146) vesting the consul with supreme power, it was in view of the threatened movement of Manlius, against whom also extra military precautions were taken. But on the 5th November a meeting was held at the house of M. Porcius Laeca, at which (according to Cicero's informant) the worst designs had been settled upon in order to welcome and assist Manlius. Cicero secured a guard for his own house, strengthened the city watches, and on the 9th November delivered in the Senate the first speech against Catiline, in which he charged him with his designs and denounced his impudence in appearing in the Senate. The manifest disfavour of the senators so cowed Catiline that, with a brief appeal against a hasty judgment, he quitted the house. That same night he left Rome ostensibly for Marseilles, at which town a man might escape the consequences of impeachment by living in voluntary exile. If Cicero was sure of his guilt, why did he allow him thus to escape? He felt the force of this objection, and in a public speech next morning tried to explain his motives, and promised the people protection.

But though Catiline was gone, the conspiracy was still alive, as was shown by the fact (known at Rome in a few days) that Catiline had not gone to Marseilles, but to the camp of Manlius, and had taken command of it with the usual ensigns of imperium. The Senate at once declared him a public enemy (*hostis*) along with Manlius, ordered the consuls to levy troops, and sent a message to the camp of Manlius offering amnesty to all who should quit it within a certain time. This seems, however, to have had no effect. Adherents were flocking to Faesulae, and the alarm at Rome rose high.

Cicero now struck his great blow. The duty of marching against Manlius was left to his colleague, C. Antonius. His own care was the treason within the city, which was to prepare the way for the invasion. He had learnt (by means of the same spy) the names of those involved, among whom were a praetor and a tribune, Lentulus and L. Bestia. The difficulty was to get proof. This was presently overcome by a rash act of the conspirators themselves. The Allobroges were the most troublesome tribe in the province of Transalpine Gaul, and had frequently caused alarm by revolts, or by threatening revolts. They no doubt had grievances, and at this time their envoys were in Rome to plead for the remission of a heavy money burden. The conspirators were anxious to secure support from the Province, both in the way of approval and in the more tangible shape of auxiliary cavalry; and they offered the envoys that, if they

P

would get their tribe to furnish this support, they would undertake in return to secure the objects for which they were in Rome. The envoys (after some negotiation) consented; prepared to leave Rome carrying despatches to their Senate from the chief conspirators; and undertook to visit Catiline on their way home, to deliver him a letter from Lentulus, and to take his instructions. But reflection caused the cunning barbarians to resolve upon betraying the conspiracy. It was far from certain that, even if the conspirators succeeded, they would be able to do as they promised; and their success was much less likely than their failure. It would pay the Allobroges better to secure present favour by turning informers, than to involve themselves in a movement most likely to fail. They therefore employed Fabius Sanga, their patronus, to inform Cicero of what had been going on. This was exactly what Cicero wanted to complete his case. There might be difference of feeling as between himself and Catiline; there would be no difference of feeling as to men who would use the forces of Gaul against Rome. He bade the envoys keep up the semblance of fidelity to their bargain, and prepare to leave Rome on their way home, carrying the letters with them. They accordingly started, and were promptly arrested on the Milvian Bridge. Cicero (on his authority as consul) summoned to his house all those who were named by the Allobroges; asked them to acknowledge their handwriting and seals; and then handed over the letters unopened to the praetor urbanus (2nd of December). There were four men who had thus committed themselves by writing: P. Cornelius Lentulus, C. Cornelius Cethegus, Statilius, and Gabinius. They were kept under surveillance during the night; and next morning (3rd December), at a meeting of the Senate, the letters were opened and read by the praetor. They were vague enough, and did not bear on their face anything treasonable; that of Lentulus to Catiline being purposely obscure: "*Who I am you will learn from the bearer. See that you play the man and fully realize your present position. Omit no necessary measures: avail yourself of all auxiliaries, even the most humble.*" They were, however, supplemented by the evidence of an informer (Volturcius) and of the Allobroges; and rightly or wrongly the Senate was convinced of the guilt of the accused. They were ordered into custody in the houses of senators, and Lentulus was compelled to abdicate his praetorship. On that evening Cicero delivered his third Catilinarian speech to the people—telling them of this treasonable league with the Allobroges to raise a war in Gaul, and of a store of arms found in the house of Cethegus. He found popular feeling with him, and after spending the 4th in enrolling a guard of Equites for the forum and temple of Concord, he brought the question solemnly before the Senate there on the 5th. It was not a question of guilt that the Senate was asked to decide. That had been already decided. It was asked now to advise the consul what he should do. By the decree passed some time before, he was, according to custom, invested with the power of life and death, if it seemed necessary for the safety of the State. The Senate had no right to order the execution of citizens: it was the consul, in virtue of this decree, who had the right: but he desired to be supported by a resolution of the Senate, and avowed that he was able and willing to carry out whatever it decreed. There was a division of opinion: some were for death, others for lifelong imprisonment and confiscation, others for postponing a decision till Catiline and Manlius had been put down. The second of these proposals was earnestly supported by Caesar, who almost carried the day, when the speech of Cato turned the scale in favour of death. Thereupon Cicero at once had the four men strangled in the Mamertine prison.

The movement at Rome, whatever it was, was crushed.

But the rebel camp of Manlius at Faesulae, with Catiline now in command, was still existing, though the execution of the conspirators at Rome seems to have caused large numbers to withdraw, and Catiline, indeed, had never been able to supply all with arms. There were as many as 20,000 men at one time in or near the camp; but when Catiline, recognizing the extremity of his danger, tried to make his way into Gaul, he seems to have had little more than 3000. They were, however, all desperate men, and when they found themselves debarred from the road to Gaul by the legate and army of C. Antonius, they turned to bay near Pistoria and fought fiercely till nearly all were killed. Catiline himself rushed into the middle of his enemies, and fell fighting furiously to the last.

6. **Consequences of the Action of Cicero.** Perhaps the conspiracy of Catiline seems more important to us than it did to contemporaries, because more than almost any other event it is continually brought before us by Cicero himself, who was extraordinarily proud of his action in thus "saving the Republic," and never ceased to refer to it. Still it was really important, as showing that there was a considerable party in the State ready to go any lengths to secure the reforms which they desired   Great names were freely mentioned in connexion with it: Caesar, Crassus, and the consul C. Antonius were believed to have sympathized if they did not join; and we must remember that one of those executed was a member of the government of the year, Lentulus the praetor. Again, the manner of its suppression was a dangerous precedent. The *senatus consultum ultimum* had been passed before in other cases, and was vaguely held to give the consuls and other magistrates the power of inflicting death if necessary (p. 146). But this was not supported by any law, and the use of it by Cicero was pushing the claim to the extreme point. It would not be forgiven, but might be imitated, by the other side; and at

any rate it was a lesson to the Populares as to the length to which senatorial authority might be pushed. The personal results to Cicero, such as overtook him a few years later, were of little consequence except to himself. But it was distinctly a move in the direction of violence and the neglect of ordinary legal procedure, which were of evil omen for the future.

BUST OF CICERO.

CHAPTER XVII.

THE TRIUMVIRATE.

1. *The political position of Caesar in* B.C. 60.   2. *The political position of Pompey.*   3. *The formation of the first so-called Triumvirate and its purpose.*   4. *Caesar's provinces.*   5. *The province in Gaul beyond the Alps.*   6. *Non-Roman Gaul.*   7. *Connexion of the Romans with the larger Gaul.*   8. *Caesar's measures for protecting his interests during his absence.*   9. *Cicero's exile and recall. P. Clodius, his tribuneship and quarrel with Pompey.*   10. *Cato sent to Cyprus.*   11. *Caesar's nine campaigns in Gaul,* B.C. 58-50: (1) *The Helvetii and Germans;* (2) *the Belgae and Nervii;* (3) *the Veneti;* (4) *German invaders of Gaul. First expedition to Britain;* (5) *Second expedition to Britain. Fall of Sabinus and Cotta;* (6) *the Nervii and Treveri. Invasion of Sicambri;* (7) *Vercingetorix, chief of the Arverni. Sieges of Gergovia and Alesia;* (8) *minor rebellions and measures of organization.*   12. *The end of Caesar's government of Gaul.*

1. **The Political Position of Caesar in** B.C. 60. One effect of the proceedings in the matter of Catiline was to raise the position of Caesar, and cause him to be regarded more distinctly as a leader of the Populares. He was elected pontifex maximus in the March following. Being praetor in B.C. 62, he on several occasions showed his determination to resist any extension of the power of the Senate over the magistrates; and when he went in B.C. 61 as propraetor to Spain, he added to his influence by the military successes which he gained there. When he returned in the summer of B.C. 60, he found matters ripe for a new and more

decisive movement, and he promptly took advantage of the opportunity.

2. **The Political Position of Pompey.** Pompey returned from the East towards the end of B.C. 62. His arrival in Italy had been looked forward to with anxiety by both parties. Both hoped for his support, for he had not shown decisively his adherence to either. He dismissed his army as soon as he landed in Italy, though with promises to the veterans that he would obtain them grants of land. He did not therefore intend to play the part of Sulla or Marius and support himself by arms. He seems indeed to have thought that his services had been so great, that he could be denied nothing. He soon found, however, that the Senate was jealous of him, and that he had to face a determined opposition. When he asked to have his *acta* (that is, his arrangements made during his command in the East) confirmed by one decree of the Senate, his demand was opposed by Lucullus and a large party, who claimed that each particular 'act' should be considered separately. This would take a long time, and Pompey looked upon it as a humiliation and an injury. As to grants of land for his veterans difficulties also were made which would lower his influence with the men. He was therefore on bad terms with the Optimates. But he also failed to please the Populares. There were two questions agitating the city when he returned or shortly after. One was the trial of P. Clodius for sacrilege. Clodius, a dissolute young noble (brother-in-law of Lucullus), had made his way in woman's dress into the house of Caesar (then pontifex maximus), whose wife Pompeia was entertaining ladies engaged in celebrating the mysteries of the Bona Dea, from which males were strictly excluded. His trial was made an occasion of violent party conflict. The bill for his impeachment contained a special clause as to the selection of the jury by the praetor urbanus. This was declared to be a device for tampering with the jury

system, and was violently opposed. Clodius (raised to the position of a kind of popular hero) riotously broke up the assembly for passing the law, and eventually an amended proposal was carried, leaving him a right of challenge, whereby he obtained a jury that he was able to bribe.

The other question was one between the Equites and Senate. The publicani (who were all Equites) had made a bad bargain as to the collection of the taxes in Asia. It was their own fault. The business was looked on as so profitable, that the various companies bid eagerly against each other. As it turned out, they had bidden too highly, and were threatened with bankruptcy; for the taxes fell far short of the sum they had contracted to pay the treasury. The only authority that could relieve them of their bargain was the Senate, which, by a long established convention, had the management of the revenue. Cicero was very anxious that the concession should be made, not because he thought it equitable, but because he thought any quarrel between the orders tended to throw the rich middle class (the Equites) on the side of the enemies of the Senate and the Constitution.

Now in both these cases Pompey failed to conciliate either side. In the case of Clodius he spoke so vaguely of his deference to the Senate, that he offended the Populares without pleasing the Optimates; and in the case of the publicani he held aloof altogether, disappointing the extreme party in the Senate, headed by Cato, without winning the support of the Equites. He therefore was as far off as ever from getting the two measures which he did care for—the confirmation of his *acta*, and the grant of land for his veterans—passed.

3. **Caesar proposes to form a Triumvirate,** B.C. 60. Such was the state of things when Caesar returned from Spain (B.C. 60). He too had a new grievance against the Senate. He demanded a triumph, but if he was to have

one, he must stay outside the walls till the Senate voted it to him; and as he was a candidate for the consulship of B.C. 59, he was obliged to appear in Rome seventeen days before the election in order to make a declaration of his candidature, which was called a *professio*. His enemies in the Senate saw their way to embarrass him. They managed to put off the decision as to the triumph so long, that he was forced to give it up or give up being candidate for the consulship. He decided to give up the triumph, entered Rome, and was elected. But he was determined not to submit to farther opposition. He proposed to Pompey to join him and M. Licinius Crassus (the richest man in Rome) in a sort of committee of three, whose united influence would be sufficient to get all that they wanted from Senate and people. Pompey and Crassus had been on bad terms, and Pompey thought that to the influence of Crassus (to whom a large number of senators were deeply indebted) he owed much of the opposition which he had encountered. Caesar managed however to reconcile them, and succeeded in getting both to support him at his election. The effect was immediately evident. When Caesar became consul (1st Jan., B.C. 59), the measures which both desired were quickly passed. Pompey's *acta* were confirmed, an agrarian law was carried, which not only gave his veterans lands, but settled a large number of needy citizens on the *ager publicus* in Campania. The Equites were conciliated by the publicani being allowed an abatement of a third in their contract for the revenues of Asia, and the population of Rome by a distribution of cheap corn. As his share of the advantages, Caesar was to have a province at the end of his consulship for the unusual period of five instead of one year. This was to be given him by a law, and not (as usual) assigned him by lot under the direction of the Senate. The importance of this we shall see presently. It was also agreed that before long Pompey and Crassus were on their part to hold the consulship again, and each of them also to have a province for five years in the same way. This last was not yet made a subject of legislation; but the other measures were, and they were not passed without some show of force. Pompey, who now married Caesar's daughter Iulia, appeared at the head of an armed force in the Campus, nominally to keep order, but really to overawe the voters; and in the Senate, when Cato persisted in opposition, Caesar ordered his lictors to arrest him, though he presently suggested to the tribunes to release him. Moreover, the opposition of Caesar's colleague Bibulus, who was a supporter of the Optimates, and his attempt to stop Caesar's legislation by announcing bad omens, and declaring that he was 'watching the sky,' were neglected. The Senate, too, was studiously ignored, summoned as seldom as possible, and not consulted as to the laws which were to be brought before the people. This was not *illegal*, for the Senate had no *legal* claim to be consulted as to laws; but it was a breach of immemorial custom, and was the beginning of a great change. In the reformation of crying abuses, the most notable of Caesar's laws in B.C. 59 is that which affected the provinces. The laws *de repetundis* had been so worded, that only the governor himself and those of his staff who were senators could be tried under it. Caesar now carried a law by which any one of the governor's staff, whether senator or eques, could be sued for restitution of money illegally received. This no doubt would be disliked by the equites, but they had to yield something in return for the relief in the matter of the Asiatic revenues.

4. **Caesar's Provinces.** The law for Caesar's five years' rule of a province, from B.C. 58, was proposed by a tribune, P. Vatinius. It overrode a vote of the Senate, which had assigned to the outgoing consuls for their province, Italy, that is, the care of the forests, roads, and other public works in Italy. This would have given him no

military command and no position of political importance: whereas the law of Vatinius gave him for five years the province of Gallia Cisalpina, that is, the whole of North Italy between the Rubicon and the Alps, with Illyricum annexed, and three legions. Gallia Cisalpina, a province since B.C. 181, was not, however, quite like other provinces. It was full of Roman colonies, and all cities south of the Po had the Roman franchise, while the Transpadani had the imperfect franchise called Latinitas. It was more like a part of Italy than a province, and though in the north there were occasional difficulties with Alpine tribes, it was not likely to give occasion at this time to important military operations. It was more likely that Illyricum would do so: for that district, on the east of the Adriatic, including Istria, had never been thoroughly organized. Sometimes it had been put under the governor of Macedonia, sometimes under the governor of Cisalpine Gaul, sometimes had been let alone so long as it paid its tribute. Since it had come under the dominion of Rome, however, in B.C. 228, it had often been disturbed either by internal commotions or attacks from neighbouring barbarians, and therefore Roman magistrates and armies had frequently been there. That Caesar thought it possible that he should have occasion to fight there is shown by the fact that his three legions were stationed at Aquileia, from which they might easily be transported to Illyricum.

5. **The Province in Gaul beyond the Alps.** What actually happened was very different. The real danger that was threatening at the time was from Gaul beyond the Alps, from which rumours of difficulties and commotions had lately been rife. Caesar therefore determined to have the province of Transalpine Gaul added to his others. This would doubtless have been secured him by a law like the others; but the Senate, anxious that their traditional right of assigning provinces should not be wholly ignored, made

a virtue of necessity and assigned it to him, partly influenced also by the hope that he might meet with disasters there which would ruin him. At this time the Roman province across the Alps was confined to the south-eastern district of France, which has in consequence retained the name of Provence. It was bounded on the east by the Alps, on the north by the Rhone from the lake Geneva to Vienne, on the west by the Cevennes and the Upper Garonne, on the south by the Pyrenees and the Mediterranean. Formed in B.C. 118, its importance to Rome was two-fold: it secured the road to Spain, and stood in the way of northern barbarians seeking Italy. In B.C. 105 it had been menaced and in parts occupied by the Cimbri and Teutones, and its most northern tribe, the Allobroges, had more than once given trouble and been in rebellion.

6. **Non-Roman Gaul.** With the rest of Gaul the Romans had dealings, but as yet had exercised no authority beyond the Province. Caesar speaks of it as falling into three divisions: Aquitania in the south-west, from the Pyrenees to the Garonne; Celtica, the great central block of country from the Garonne to the Seine, including western Switzerland; and Belgica, from the Seine to the lower Rhine, thus including northern France, Belgium, and southern Holland. In Aquitania there was an admixture of Iberians from Spain, in the north, of Germans from beyond the Rhine.

7. **Connexion of Rome with the larger Gaul.** In this greater Gaul the Romans as yet had not, as I said, acted as rulers. They had from time to time been asked to interfere between contending tribes, and had adopted the Aedui (between the Loire and Saône) as "friends and allies," which implied an undertaking, more or less vague, to protect them against attack. The great enemies of the Aedui were the Sequăni and Arverni, and in order to crush the Aedui these tribes had asked help from Germany. Thus

there was a prospect of a struggle between German and Roman influence in Gaul. But, since B.C. 100, the Romans had been suffering from troubles at home, and had neglected Gaul, and allowed the German king, Ariovistus, to get a footing there. He had come on the invitation of the Sequani, and as the Romans failed to help the Aedui, in answer to their request, he had forced them to give hostages to the Sequani; but, having got into Gaul, he refused to return, and occupied part of the territory of the very people who had invited him, and was always being joined by fresh immigrations from Germany. The Roman government, far from looking on this as dangerous, had recognized the situation, and acknowledged Ariovistus as "king and ally." This was done while Caesar was consul (B.C. 59), who, therefore, was acquainted with the state of affairs in Gaul, and had been a party to the arrangement.

8. Caesar provides for his Interests at Rome during his Absence. Such were the districts which Caesar was to govern for five years from B.C. 58. Before leaving the city, however, he made arrangements to secure himself from his enemies. Pompey and Crassus were to stay in Rome till B.C. 55 to prevent their attacks. For already there were signs of a resolute opposition: two of the praetors of B.C. 58 consulted the Senate as to prosecuting him for violence during his consulship, and one of the tribunes was only prevented by the veto of his colleagues from doing the same. Moreover, as he afterwards discovered, some of the Optimates sent secretly to tell Ariovistus that his opposition to Caesar would be agreeable to the Senate. It was necessary, therefore, to secure that friends should, as far as possible, hold the chief offices, and declared enemies be got away for a time. It was this that led to the banishment of Cicero and the employment of Cato in Cyprus.

9. Cicero's Exile. The instrument employed for this purpose was P. Clodius Pulcher, who hated Cicero because the latter had given evidence against him in the case of the violated mysteries. Clodius had been quaestor in Sicily in B.C. 60, and in B.C. 59 intended to stand for office again. He was a patrician, and naturally his next step was the aedileship. But a much more convenient and powerful office was that of tribune, who could summon meetings of the tribes and bring in laws. But to be tribune he must be a plebeian, and the only way to become a plebeian was to get adopted into some plebeian family. If a man was still under the *patria potestas* he could be adopted by means of a fictitious sale on the part of his father: but if he was *sui juris* (*i.e.* free from the *patria potestas*), it could only be done by a process called *abrogatio* in the old *Comitia Curiata*, with the sanction of the pontifices, and with the presence of an augur. Caesar as pontifex maximus and Pompey as an augur could therefore, if they chose, at once carry out the required formality or stop it. It was known that one of the objects of Clodius in becoming tribune was to attack Cicero. For some time Pompey and Caesar would not consent; but in the course of B.C. 59 Cicero was speaking in defence of his old colleague C. Antonius (deservedly impeached for his conduct in Macedonia), and in the course of his speech made some allusion to the politics of the day, which (he says) was reported in exaggerated terms to Pompey and Caesar. In three hours the adoption of Clodius was accomplished. Soon afterwards Clodius was elected tribune. He entered upon his office on the 10th December, B.C. 59, and passed several laws aimed at the monopoly of the Optimates,—one to prevent the frequent interruption of *Comitia* by the announcement of evil omens, another to prevent the summary exclusion of members of the Senate by the censors, and a third to legalize certain guilds or *collegia* of workmen, which had been declared illegal by a decree of the Senate, and a fourth for a distribution of cheap corn. Having secured popular favour by these laws, early in B.C. 58 he proposed another law rendering liable to banishment any magistrate who had put citizens to death without trial; and, as soon as it was passed, gave notice of an action against Cicero. It was clear that Cicero's execution of the Catilinarian conspirators brought him under this law. His only resource was to avoid prosecution by going into voluntary exile. Caesar, who liked and admired him personally, had given him more than one chance of honourably leaving Rome. He offered to take him to Gaul as one of his legati, or to give him a place on the commission for assigning lands in Campania, or to grant him a *libera legatio*, as it was called, that is, the privilege of travelling anywhere in the empire with the dignity and rights of an official despatched by the State, though without duties. But Cicero for a long time would not believe that Clodius meant to attack him as tribune, or that he would be allowed to succeed if he did. When he saw that he really meant to do it he appealed to the triumvirs, to the consuls, to every one whom he thought could help him. But no one stirred; and he was forced to anticipate the trial by going into exile. Clodius immediately carried a bill declaring him a public enemy (*hostis*), confiscating his property, and forbidding him "fire and water" (that is, making it unlawful for any one to supply him with the necessaries of life) within 400 miles of Rome. His exile only lasted about sixteen months, for Clodius, growing insolent from success, irritated and insulted Pompey, secretly supported (it was believed) by Crassus, and behaved with such violence that Pompey retired to his house, and refused to appear in the forum as long as Clodius was tribune. He also countenanced the recall of Cicero. The riotous partisans of Clodius frequently interrupted the *Comitia* for passing the law; but it was at length effected in August, B.C. 57.

10. Cato sent to Cyprus. For the time, however, Cicero was removed from Rome. Cato also was got rid of, though in a different way. Clodius secured his nomination on a commission to depose Ptolemy, king of Cyprus, on the pretext that the king had abetted the pirates, and to confiscate his treasures. It was an unjust measure, likely to bring odium on whoever carried it out. But the absence of Cato was secured for some time.

Nor were these the only means Caesar had of keeping up his influence at Rome. The advantage of his province was that however much he might be engaged at a distance in military operations during the summer, he could winter at some such town as Revenna or Lucca, on the southern borders of his province, where he could be visited by his friends, and be almost as if he were at home. Meanwhile he found himself engaged in a task of extraordinary difficulty, but one which was to place him in a position beyond his highest expectations.

11. Caesar's nine Campaigns in Gaul. (1) The Helvetii. Caesar was still outside Rome making his preparations for his province when news came that the Helvetii, that is, the Swiss living between Bâle and Geneva, were migrating in a body to Western Gaul (Aquitania), and meant to pass through the Roman province. For several reasons Caesar determined to prevent this: (1) It would leave a considerable district empty which would be probably filled by Germans or other tribes, who would be troublesome neighbours to the province; (2) it would bring the Helvetii (who had been found dangerous enemies in B.C. 103) close to the western frontier of the province, which was ill defended; (3) the emigrating mass of 300,000 souls was not likely to find fresh settlements without creating some disorders; (4) in passing through the province they would come in contact with the Allobroges, who had always been a disturbing element in the province,

CAESAR'S FIRST CAMPAIGN IN GAUL.

and had been more or less in rebellion four times since B.C. 75. His resolution was quickly taken. In a week he reached Geneva, ordered a levy of auxiliaries in the province, where there was only one legion, broke down the bridge over the Rhone at Geneva (the last town of the province), detained the Helvetii by evasive answers to their request for a passage, and meanwhile strengthened the left bank of the Rhone by an earthwork and foss wherever, for about ten miles from Geneva, it was fordable. The Helvetii, after vainly attempting to force a passage, turned away from the Rhone, and asked and obtained leave to pass through the territory of the Sequani. But this was a much more difficult route; the Jura had to be crossed, and then the river Arar (*Saône*). A vast host of men, women, and children, with their train of waggons, would move slowly. Caesar had time to hurry to North Italy, bring the three legions from Aquileia, raise two fresh ones in Cisalpine Gaul, and yet catch them up before they were all over the Saône. He cut to pieces one of their tribes, the Tigurini, overtook the rest near Bibracte (*Autun*), again defeated them with great slaughter, and forced the survivors (less than a half the original number) to return to their native land, rebuild the towns which they had burned on setting out, and settle down once more in peace.

The Germans. This was the beginning of Caesar's operations in Celtic Gaul, and from it the other campaigns seemed to follow almost inevitably. In the first place, it immediately brought him face to face with Ariovistus and his Germans. The victory over the Helvetii turned the eyes of the Aedui, who had been beaten by Ariovistus, and of the Sequani, part of whose territory Ariovistus was occupying, upon Caesar. He readily undertook to be the champion of Gallic freedom, and immediately demanded a colloquy with Ariovistus. This being refused, he sent an ultimatum: (1) Ariovistus was to bring no more Germans into Gaul; (2) was to abstain from attacking the Aedui; (3) was to give back, and allow the Sequani to give back, Aeduan hostages. But Ariovistus would listen to nothing. He claimed the right of conquest over the Aedui, defied Caesar, and hinted that he was supported in doing so by a powerful party in Rome, which desired his defeat and fall. Caesar determined to act at once. By great exertions he outmarched Ariovistus, and seized Vesontio (*Besançon*) on the Doube; and after some difficulties with his soldiers, who feared the unknown country and the warlike barbarians, he came up with and defeated him between Bâle and Mulhausen. The slaughter was immense, and was rendered more complete by the hostile natives, who cut off stragglers of the German host as they were traversing the thirty-five miles which separated them from the Rhine. Ariovistus himself escaped across the Rhine, but by this victory north-eastern Gaul was cleared of the foreigners, and a powerful band of Suevi, who had reached the Rhine on their way into Gaul, abandoned their intention and returned home. For the first time Roman legions wintered in non-Roman Gaul.

(2) **Second Campaign. Gallia Belgica. The Nervii**, B.C. 57. A direct consequence of this was a movement in Belgica. The Belgae feared an attack, and that the Roman occupation of Gaul would prevent their getting recruits. On hearing of this movement Caesar enrolled fresh legions, which he stationed at Besançon, and after taking the chief towns across the Aisne, and receiving the submission of the Remi, he found himself in presence of the Nervii, on the left bank of the river Sambre, a tributary of the Meuse. They were a very warlike tribe, and his engagement with them was one of the most formidable in the whole war. Their defeat made Caesar master of Belgic Gaul, with the exception of one tribe on the Meuse (the Aduatuci), whose chief town he had next to take. While Caesar was thus

conquering Belgium, his legate, P. Crassus, was subduing the tribes of Normandy and Brittany, and the result of the operations of B.C. 57 was to bring the whole of north-western France, with a considerable part of Belgium, under Roman sway. It was not at once organized as a province, but the tribes had submitted without any terms, and would eventually have to accept whatever constitution Rome gave them.

(3) **Third Campaign**, B.C. 56. **The Veneti**. In his third year Caesar was engaged in the same districts, not so much in making new acquisitions, as in putting down risings in those already acquired. The Venĕti, in Brittany, whose country, intersected by firths, made them a seafaring folk, were destroyed by a fleet which Caesar had caused to be built in the Loire during the winter. The Aquitani were subdued by his legates, and he finished the campaign by conquering the Morini, near Boulogne.

(4) **Fourth Campaign**, B.C. 55. **The Rhine and Britain**. Gaul was now conquered. But his occupation of the northern country brought him face to face with the German tribes, who were crossing the Rhine either for their own advantage or to assist the Belgae. He found a vast host of them (numbering, it is said, 430,000 souls, with women and children) in the plain between the rivers Niess and Meuse, stormed their laager of waggons, and drove them in utter rout towards the Rhine. The greater number perished by the sword or in the river. He then caused a bridge to be built across the Rhine near Bonn, and endeavoured to deter the Germans from venturing again into Gaul, by burning the houses and cutting down the corn of the Sicambri. He, however, only remained eighteen days north of the Rhine. The rest of the season was devoted to an expedition to Britain; because from this island (of which he could get little definite information) he learnt that the Gauls got supplies and other aid. His landing near Deal was stoutly resisted by the natives, and when a storm shattered his ships, they

again attacked his camp with great courage. Caesar was about a month in the island without being able to advance any distance from his place of landing, and towards the end of September returned to Gaul for the winter.

(5) **Fifth Campaign**, B.C. 54. In his fifth year he renewed his attempt on Britain—this time with greater forces, and with high expectations as to the wealth of every sort which he would find there. The civilized and wealthy appearance of Kent had much impressed him. Of the interior he knew nothing; but hoped to find it equally worth subduing. There was a good deal of interest in the expedition felt at Rome, and he was accompanied by a large fleet of trading vessels, whose owners hoped to find a new field of enterprise in the island. But this expedition was little more successful than the last. His ships again suffered from a storm and high tide, and though he advanced as far as St. Albans, crossing the Thames near Brentford, and defeated Cassivelaunus, he got no more satisfaction than a submission of several tribes, who gave hostages and promised tribute. Late in September he again crossed to Gaul, which he found in a state again bordering on insurrection. In the winter of this year, in fact, he met with nearly his only disaster, two of his legates, Sabinus and Cotta, with a legion being cut to pieces on their way to join Q. Cicero, who with another legion was closely besieged in a camp near the modern Charleroi.

(6) **Sixth Campaign**, B.C. 53. **Nervii and Treveri.** But though Caesar succeeded in relieving Cicero, he had to spend the whole winter and the next summer in the country, to again fight the Nervii and Treveri, and other tribes in Belgica, and once more to cross the Rhine, as well as to meet another raid of Sicambri over the Rhine. Finally, late in the year he held a meeting of Gallic tribes, at which the loyal chiefs joined in condemning the rebels, and Caesar might feel that he was again acknowledged as supreme in the north.

(7) **Seventh Campaign,** B.C. 52. This, however, was not quite the end of his troubles in Gaul. In B.C. 52 a rebellion broke out in the south near the province, under Vercingetorix, the chief of the Arverni. In this campaign Caesar failed to take Gergovia (almost his only failure); but after a long siege took Alesia, a fort on a hill between Tonnerre and Dijon, into which Vercingetorix had thrown himself. Vercingetorix eventually surrendered, and was taken to Rome, where he died in prison.

TESTUDO (FROM TRAJAN'S COLUMN).

(8) **Eighth and Ninth Campaigns,** B.C. 51-50. The last two years of Caesar's stay in Gaul, though not entirely free from local rebellions and some severe fighting, were mostly spent in measures meant to conciliate the newly conquered peoples; and in this he was so successful that he left Gaul on the whole content to join the Roman system. This was in truth his great glory. The conquest had cost, it has been reckoned, the lives of nearly a million human beings. It would indeed be melancholy to think that there should be no result from all that slaughter. Whether for

good or ill, however, it had settled that Gaul was to develop as Latin and not German, and to share in the civilization and conversion of the Roman empire.

12. **Caesar's position in Gaul,** B.C. 50. Caesar had been now more than eight years in Gaul. He had been originally appointed for five years, but circumstances which we shall have to study immediately had caused the addition of five years more to his government, which would now end in B.C. 49. He wished to be elected consul for B.C. 48, so that he should only leave his province to take up the consulship, leaving no interval of which his enemies at Rome might take advantage to impeach him. The refusal of the Senate to allow this induced him to quit Gaul and invade Italy, and thus brought on the civil war.

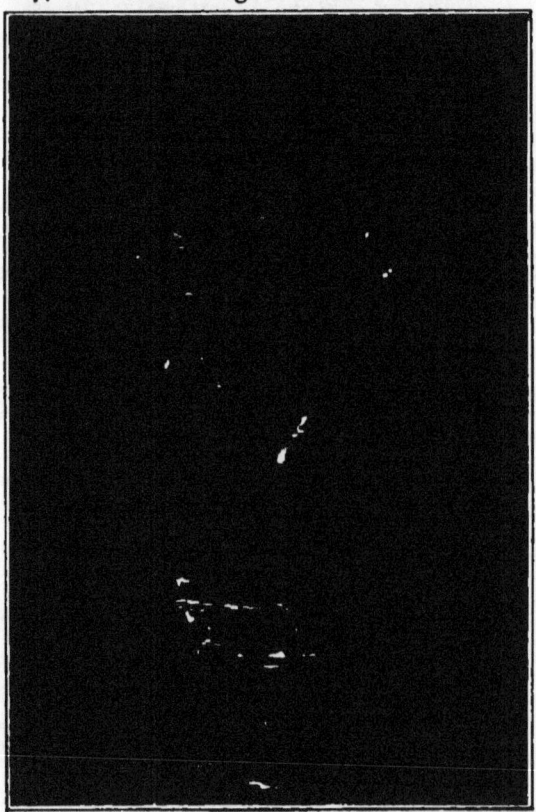

BUST OF I. CAESAR.

CHAPTER XVIII.

THE CIVIL WAR.

1. Gradual estrangement of Pompey from Crassus and Caesar. 2. Pompey praefectus annonae; he wishes to return to the East. 3. The conference at Lucca. 4. The breakdown of the new agreements between the triumvirs. 5. Pompey sole consul. 6. Pompey's laws. 7. Pompey secures a strong position against Caesar. 8. Provocations offered to Caesar. 9. Caesar crosses the Rubicon in January, B.C. 49. *10. Pompey and his party quit Italy. 11. Caesar enters Rome, March,* B.C. 49, *but fails to get himself appointed Dictator. 12. Siege of Marseilles by Caesar. 13. Caesar's war in Spain against Pompey's legates. 14. Caesar as Dictator holds the consular elections, in which he is returned as consul. 15. Caesar follows Pompey into Epirus,* B.C. 48 *(January). 16. Battle of Pharsalia. 17. Flight of Pompey. 18. Murder of Pompey in Egypt. 19. Caesar follows Pompey to Egypt. 20. The Alexandrine war. 21. Caesar dictator and consul; troubles in Rome. 22. The war with Pharnaces in Pontus and battle of Zela* (B.C. 47). *23. The battle of Thapsus* (B.C. 46) *and death of Cato at Utica. Caesar master of the empire.*

1. **Gradual Estrangement of Pompey from Crassus and Caesar.** We have followed Caesar's conquest of Gaul without stopping to notice what was meanwhile going on at Rome. But in fact important changes had taken place there which affected Caesar deeply, and with these he had been kept acquainted; for, as a rule, he left Transalpine Gaul in the winter and visited Cisalpine Gaul or Illyricum to hold the *conventus*, or assizes, and while in the former he was easily visited by friends and supporters,

and thus took part in Roman politics. Now in the first years of Caesar's absence, Pompey had been gradually becoming estranged from Crassus, and in some degree from Caesar too. He thought that Clodius was secretly supported in his attacks upon himself by Crassus, who, after all, was rather Caesar's friend than his own. Finally, when Cicero returned from exile in September, B.C. 57, he came professing boundless gratitude to Pompey, but hinted as openly as he dared that Caesar was his enemy, and did his best to detach Pompey from him.

2. **Pompey as Praefectus Annonae. He wishes for a Command in the East.** In this same year there was a great scarcity of corn at Rome: prices were very high, and a famine was feared. On the proposal of Cicero, soon after his return, Pompey was appointed *praefectus annonae*, or minister for the supply of corn, throughout the empire, with ships and legates, and authority over all ports and corn markets for five years. It gave him a great position and wide authority. He at once went to Sicily, and sent his legates to other corn-growing countries, and in a few months the scarcity at Rome ceased and the price of corn went down. But when Pompey returned to Rome he found the Optimates jealous of him, and was also violently attacked by Clodius. He thought Crassus was at the bottom of this; and, being deeply offended and alarmed, he wished to get away from Rome to the East with an army. Just then Ptolemy Auletes, king of Egypt, was in Rome asking to be restored to his kingdom, from which his people had justly expelled him. He had aided Pompey against the Jews in B.C. 63, and Pompey therefore supported his request and wished to have the task of restoring him. But the Senate was unwilling to send him back to the East, where his name was so powerful; and accordingly a Sibylline oracle was produced forbidding the restoration of Ptolemy by arms. The proposal to appoint Pompey, made by one of

the tribunes, was abandoned, and finding himself attacked by the violence of the popular party and an object of suspicion to the Optimates, he had no resource but to renew the understanding with Caesar and Crassus.

3. **The Conference at Lucca in the Spring of B.C. 56.** Caesar had his own reasons for wishing closer connexion with Pompey. L. Domitius Ahenobarbus, candidate for the consulship of B.C. 55, openly declared that he would as consul secure Caesar's recall and impeachment, and was meanwhile trying to get his laws annulled on the ground that the *obnuntiatio* of Bibulus made them invalid. Cicero was also opposing the execution of his agrarian law. It was time to renew the old agreement for mutual support. In the spring of B.C. 56 Caesar came to Lucca, and there Pompey and Crassus and many of their partisans held a conference with him. The result was a reconciliation of Pompey and Crassus and a new arrangement for the future. Caesar was to have five more years in Gaul, and the right of standing for the consulship of B.C. 48 without returning to Rome to be elected. Pompey and Crassus were to be consuls in B.C. 55, with a five years' provincial government afterwards, Pompey in the two Spains, Crassus in Syria. Thus, when Caesar returned to Rome, he would come straight to the consulship without giving up his imperium for one hour, while Pompey and Crassus also would still be in possession of imperium and armies. These arrangements were immediately carried out. Pompey and Crassus were elected consuls for B.C. 55, though amidst scenes of some violence. The Senate voted not to include the provinces of Gaul and Illyricum among those to be allotted, and a law was proposed by the tribune, C. Trebonius, assigning them to Caesar, as well as the Spains to Pompey and Syria to Crassus.

4. **What overset the new Agreement of the Triumvirs**, B.C. 55-49. Thus the supremacy of the trium-

virs and their mutual understanding seemed restored; and Cicero, thinking that it was useless to struggle farther, and that the Optimates had basely abandoned their own cause, conformed outwardly at least to the state of things, and now thought that the best hope for public security was the maintenance of peace between Pompey and Caesar. Events, however, before long weakened the bonds between them. In the first place, in B.C. 54, Pompey's wife Iulia (Caesar's daughter) died. In the next place, Crassus, who went to Syria at the end of his consulship, fell in B.C. 53 at Carrhae, in a war with the Parthians. The triumvirate therefore was now reduced to a duumvirate. It was a question between Pompey and Caesar; and the Optimates soon came to think that their best course was to back up Pompey and belittle Caesar. Partisan conflicts were increasing in Rome. Clodius on the side of the extreme Populares, Milo in the interests of the Optimates, each with hired bands of ruffians, were continually creating disturbances and breaking up the *Comitia*. They prevented the election of consuls for B.C. 53 until six months of the year were passed; and the same thing happened in the next year. In January of B.C. 52, however, Clodius was murdered in a scuffle with Milo on the Appian road near Bovillae. This gave rise to fresh riots in Rome. The body of Clodius was carried by the mob into the Curia and burnt on a pile of broken branches, in the course of which the Curia caught fire and was destroyed. At length, on the 25th of February, the Senate named an interrex, who returned Pompey as sole consul.

5. **Pompey Sole Consul,** B.C. 52. Pompey wished to be Dictator. But the appointment of a "dictator for suppressing sedition" (*seditionis sedandae causa*) was an antiquated custom, which had not been heard of for many years, and the perversion of the dictatorship by Sulla had rendered the word almost as unpopular as that of king. It would also no doubt have been resented by Caesar and his party. Even

the sole consulship was regarded with suspicion, and the Populares wished to elect Caesar as Pompey's colleague. To avoid that, after six months he named as his colleague Metellus Scipio, whose daughter he had married. For six months, however, he occupied an almost autocratic position in Rome, and was regarded by the Optimates as the saviour of society.

6. **Pompey's Laws.** During these months he passed, or caused to be passed, several laws dealing with the abuses of the time: one as to the selection of jurors, under which Milo was condemned; another *de iure magistratuum*, ordaining that in future consuls and praetors should not go to a province till five years after their consulship or praetorship. The object of this was to prevent intrigues at home for desirable provinces, and to avoid the danger from the long continuance of imperium. This law also enforced the personal appearance of a candidate for the consulship to make his *professio*. Finally, he passed a severe law on bribery. From the provisions of the law as to a five years' interval before taking a province, Pompey was necessarily exempt, for he had been holding the government of the Spains since B.C. 54, and the Senate continued it another five years. According to the agreement at Lucca, Caesar also was to be excepted from this law. There was some oversight, however, in drawing it up, and accordingly the tribune Caelius (at Pompey's suggestion) carried a law expressly excepting Caesar. This was a concession to Caesar's claims, but he had still some reason to be anxious as to the future.

7. **Pompey's strong Position.** By the five additional years of Spanish government granted to Pompey, his imperium would outlast Caesar's consulship by several years. But not only so. That might have been compensated for to Caesar by his having himself another equally important province. But Pompey's position was altogether anoma-

lous. He was proconsul of the Spains, and yet was consul at Rome. Even at the end of his consulship he did not go to Spain, but governed it by means of three legati in command of three consular armies, he himself remaining at Rome (though unable to enter the *pomoerium*), with imperium, and the right of raising legions. This Caesar was forced to see was a measure meant to protect the Senate from coercion on his part, and he felt it to be a menace to himself. Moreover, after the fall of Crassus the Senate resolved to send additional legions with Bibulus, who was to succeed him in Syria, and voted that Caesar should supply one and Pompey the other (B.C. 51). But Pompey had, during the Gallic wars, lent Caesar two legions, and now claimed the return of one; so that in fact Caesar's army was weakened by two legions. Caesar sent them, but by the time they arrived in Italy news came that C. Cassius (who had remained in Syria after the defeat of Crassus, as proquaestor) had defeated the Parthians, and repelled their invasion of Syria. The fresh legions therefore were not wanted, and were first stationed at Capua, and afterwards put into winter quarters in Apulia, where they would be ready for Pompey at any time.

8. **Provocations offered to Caesar.** Caesar's resentment and alarm were farther roused by frequent motions during B.C. 51 and 50 for naming his successor, and forcing him to lay down his command before being elected consul in B.C. 49. Pompey did not exactly encourage these motions, but he temporized,—all along maintaining that he believed Caesar would obey the wishes of the Senate and lay down his imperium before coming to Rome to stand for the consulship. Caesar, however, had been taking his measures with caution. He had made up for the loss of the two legions by fresh levies in Gaul, and had visited the Cisalpine towns in the spring of B.C. 50, partly to canvass them for M. Antonius, who was a candidate

for the augurship, but also to ascertain how far they were ready to support himself. He also won over to his side by large bribes one of the consuls for B.C. 50, L. Aemilius Claudius, and one of the tribunes, C. Curio, a dissolute youth overwhelmed with debt. By this means every attempt in the Senate during B.C. 50 to nominate his successor was frustrated. But Pompey had grown more confident. In the early part of B.C. 50 he had had a bad illness, and his recovery seemed hopeless. This called forth an immense outburst of feeling throughout Italy. Everywhere prayers and sacrifices were offered for his recovery; and Pompey believed that Italy was altogether on his side, that he had only to stamp on the ground to raise soldiers, and that Caesar's own army was really disaffected and ready to join him. The gods had offered—it was afterwards said—to remove him from the evil to come, but the prayers and sacrifices of the Italians preserved him for his doom.

9. **Caesar crosses the Rubicon,** January, B.C. 49. The last attempt to supersede Caesar had been vetoed by Curio (about July, B.C. 50), but the consuls for B.C. 49 —C. Claudius Marcellus and L. Cornelius Lentulus— were both hostile to Caesar, and Curio, going out of office on the 10th December, B.C. 50, immediately joined Caesar at Ravenna with reports of the proceedings. He was sent back to appear in the Senate on the 1st January, B.C. 49, bearing a despatch from Caesar which contained an ultimatum,—his last attempt, as he puts it, to obtain a peaceful settlement, rather than (as Curio advised) to march upon Rome. Curio presented the despatch to the consuls, asking them to read it to the Senate. They at first refused, but were forced to do so by two of the tribunes friendly to Caesar—M. Antonius and Q. Cassius. The offer it contained was that Caesar would lay down his imperium, giving up army and province, if Pompey would do the

same. Of course it may be said that he had no right to bargain with the Senate. But it must be remembered that of the two he was in the more constitutional position. A law had given him his proconsulship till the end of B.C. 49[1]; a law had exempted him from making his *professio*. What the Senate was trying to do was to override a law (what Caesar calls a *beneficium populi*) by a decree of its own; whereas, so far from the Senate having the right to override a law, there was no certain legal basis for the authority of a decree of the Senate itself, even when it was not against a law. Caesar could stand upon his legal rights. But Pompey's position (quite unprecedented) depended upon the authority of the Senate. The Senate had extended his governorship of the Spains by its own authority. The Senate advised or authorized his remaining at Rome in spite of the universal understanding that a proconsul must go to his province and stay there. Accordingly when the senators, on hearing Caesar's despatch, voted with but one dissentient that Caesar should resign his province on a fixed day on pain of being held guilty of treason, and that Pompey need not do the same, the two tribunes (M. Antonius and Q. Cassius) naturally interposed their veto. The effect of this was that the measure was not a decree (*senatus consultum*) but a resolution (*auctoritas*), unless the tribunes could be induced to withdraw their veto. At four succeeding meetings of the Senate [January 2, 5, 6, 7] a violent debate was maintained as to whether the tribunes should be urged to withdraw their veto. On the evening of the 7th they were forcibly expelled, and the *senatus consultum ultimum* passed that "the consuls, praetors, tribunes, and proconsuls (this last to include Pompey) should see that the republic took no harm." The effect of this was held to be that the magistrates named

[1] Strictly till March, but custom always extended the tenure till December.

had for the time despotic power, and all personal rights were suspended (p. 146). Antonius and Cassius fled to Caesar, who was at Ravenna when he heard of what had taken place. It was exactly the pretext which he required. He had but one legion (the 13th) with him, but after haranguing the men, and finding them ready to avenge the violated tribunes, he started for Ariminum, where Antonius and Cassius had already arrived. To reach it he had to cross the Rubicon, the boundary between his province and Italy, which it was illegal for a proconsul of Gaul to pass. It was a momentous decision to make, and afterwards various stories were told of his hesitation, and of omens encouraging him to proceed. He tells us nothing of this himself. He is content with the simple fact that he went to Ariminum. By going there he was in definite hostility to the government. He was an invader, and no longer a mere proconsul. At Ariminum a certain Lucius Caesar (a distant relative), along with one of the praetors, met him with offers of mediation. But it was too late. Caesar would make no farther concession than promising to disband his legions, if Pompey would disband those in Italy also and go to Spain, thus leaving the *Comitia* free. Nor, though he listened and answered with courtesy, did he for a single day refrain from pushing on, and occupying town after town on the way to Brundisium and on the road to Rome across the Apennines. He seized Pisaurum, Fanum, and Ancona, and sent Antonius across the Apennines to secure Arretium, which would bar the advance of Pompeian troops through Etruria; and Curio to occupy Iguvium, commanding the pass over the Apennines towards Rome. He met with no resistance even at Auximum, where Attius Varus was stationed with some newly levied cohorts. The inhabitants insisted on Varus evacuating the town, and opened their gates to Caesar. All this was done before the 18th of January, and the news of his success caused a great panic at Rome.

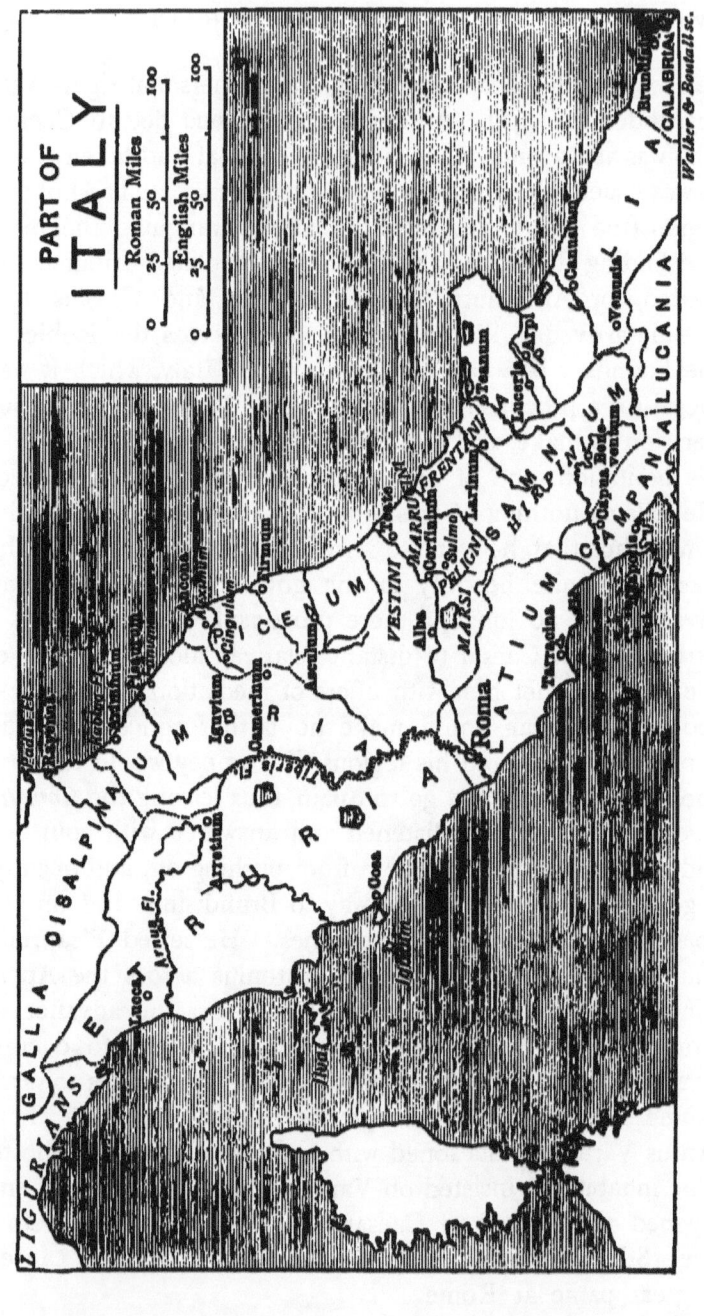

10. **Pompey and his Party quit Italy.** The Pompeian party (as it may now be called) had understood, when they ejected the two tribunes and passed the *senatus consultum ultimum*, that there would be war; and they at once divided Italy and Sicily into districts for defence, and allotted the chief provinces to their supporters, as Syria to Metellus Scipio, and Transalpine Gaul to L. Domitius Ahenobarbus. The raising of troops was the first thing. Caesar had ventured to enter Italy with only one legion (the 13th), because he knew that he would be joined by others before Pompey could get an army on foot. There were only two legions ready for Pompey, those, namely, which had been sent by Caesar for the Parthian war; but they were in winter quarters in Apulia, and would take some time to bring into action. The raising of fresh troops Pompey did not find as easy as he expected, though before he left Italy he had five legions. He seems to have quitted Rome immediately after the meeting of the 7th to raise these troops, leaving the consuls at Rome to arrange for the defence of the city. But the news of Caesar's rapid advance so terrified them, that, without even staying to take the money from the treasury reserve, they hastily quitted Rome on the 18th and joined Pompey, followed by other magistrates and senators, who adhered to the same party. At Teanum Sidicinum, in Campania, Lucius Caesar brought Iulius Caesar's answer; but the consuls and Pompey would only treat on condition of Caesar's withdrawal from the towns already occupied; and Caesar would not withdraw unless Pompey ceased levying troops in Italy, and fixed a day for going to Spain. Both therefore went on. Pompey, however, soon resolved to transfer the war to Greece, where he could be joined by auxiliaries of men and ships from the East. By the 20th of February he was at Brundisium with his five legions. L. Domitius Ahenobarbus had raised two legions and occupied Corfinium, between Caesar and Brun-

disium, but had been obliged by his own troops to surrender to Caesar, who allowed him to go free, but took over his men and arrived at Brundisium on the 8th of March with

THE HARBOUR OF BRUNDISIUM.

six legions and 1000 cavalry. The two consuls with the larger part of the army had already crossed to Dyrrachium, and Pompey with two legions was awaiting the return of the transports. After some fruitless negotiations and an attempt on Caesar's part to block up the harbour, which would have forced Pompey to make terms apart from the main body of his supporters, Pompey and his two legions succeeded in crossing on the night of the 18th of March.

11. **Caesar at Rome**, March, B.C. 49. Caesar had not sufficient ships to follow him, and was besides obliged to secure the corn-growing countries in the west, especially Sicily and Sardinia; for as Pompey was gathering ships in the east, from Alexandria to Byzantium, he would be able to starve out Italy if the west was also in the hands of his partisans. He at once sent a legion under Q. Valerius to Sardinia, and arranged for C. Curio to go to Sicily, which was being held by Cato for the Pompeians. He himself went to Rome with six legions at the end of March. His object was to put himself in some constitutional position. The only way seemed to get himself nominated Dictator, which would give him supreme authority for the next six months, during which he could hold the elections and get returned consul for the next year. But the highest officer left at Rome was the praetor M. Aemilius Lepidus, and though he adhered to Caesar, he had scruples as to the validity of any nomination of his. The old practice was for one of the consuls to name a dictator, and Cicero, whom he consulted, told him that a praetor could not name a dictator or hold consular elections. What remained of the Senate at Rome gave Caesar's legates in Sicily and Sardinia some authority, which would enable them to act with a show of legality; but the constitutional question as to his dictatorship gave rise to so much fruitless wrangling, that Caesar would not wait for a decree.

12. **Caesar at Marseilles.** He left Lepidus in charge of Rome, M. Antonius (tribune) in charge of Italy, and hastened to Transalpine Gaul, where Ahenobarbus (whom he had released at Corfinium), having collected a fleet at Cosa in Etruria, and manned it with his own tenants, was

going to the province allotted him by the Senate. Arrived at Marseilles (a *libera civitas* in alliance with Rome), Caesar was refused admission into the town. But when Ahenobarbus sailed into the harbour, he was not only admitted, but acknowledged as commandant. The people of Marseilles thus formally adopted the Pompeian side in the quarrel. Caesar made up his mind that he must take the town, and in order to do so must have ships. In thirty days from the felling of the timber, twelve ships of war were built at Arles and put under the command of Decimus Brutus, while towers and *vineae* were constructed, and the siege on the land side entrusted to C. Trebonius.

13. **Caesar in Spain**, June-August, B.C. 49. But the main object was Spain, which he dared not leave behind him in possession of Pompeians. In Spain there were three legates of Pompey (still proconsul), L. Afranius, M. Petreius, M. Terentius Varro. The two first of these had joined forces and were stationed at Ilerda (*Lerida*) to resist an invasion from the north. Caesar, though delayed himself at Marseilles, had sent on C. Fabius by way of Perpignan and Barcelona, early in May; but when he himself followed in June, he found Fabius shut up in a narrow district between the rivers Sicoris and Cinca, which joins the Sicoris south of Ilerda. Both rivers were flooded, and their bridges broken down; while the provisions of the district were exhausted. Caesar repaired the bridges and relieved Fabius, but shortly afterwards the bridges were again broken down by floods, Afranius and Petreius holding the only sound one near Ilerda. Thus Caesar was himself shut up in the same narrow fork of country, unable to obtain provisions, which his enemies could do by means of their bridge. He was in great peril, and exaggerated reports of his defeat reached Rome, where the town house of Afranius was thronged with visits of congratulation, and many who had been hesitating as to joining Pompey crossed over to Dyrrachium,

XVIII. SURRENDER OF POMPEY'S ARMIES IN SPAIN.

among them M. Cicero, who embarked on the 11th of June. But the situation suddenly changed. A long train of provisions from Gaul had been stopped by the flooded Sicoris. Caesar managed to get a legion across in coracles constructed on the model of those he had seen in Britain; and his men being thus on both sides of the river, the bridge was quickly repaired, and the provisions secured. Afranius and Petreius endeavoured to retire south of the Ebro, but were outmarched by Caesar, and had to choose between fighting and surrender. Their soldiers were reluctant to fight, and fraternized with Caesar's men, and after some toilsome marches, harassed by Caesar's cavalry, they submitted, and were allowed to quit Spain unharmed. They both afterwards joined Pompey in Greece, and perished later on in Africa. The third of Pompey's legates, the learned M. Terentius Varro, who was governing southern Spain, called Baetica, though he loyally tried to keep faith with Pompey, found that the feeling throughout the province was so entirely for Caesar that he was obliged to submit. Caesar then returned to Marseilles, which, at the beginning of October, surrendered. Ahenobarbus escaped, but all arms, engines of war, and money were given up to Caesar. Thus in the course of the summer of B.C. 49, Caesar had secured Spain and Gaul, while his legates Valerius and Curio had occupied Sardinia and Sicily (Cato making no attempt to maintain himself in the latter). The one failure had been in Africa, whither Curio went after taking over Sicily. P. Attius Varus had taken possession of the province after leaving Auximum and, backed up by Iuba, king of Numidia, had defeated and killed Curio.

14. **Caesar Consul.** Caesar's success in Spain had smoothed the constitutional difficulty at Rome. On his way back to Marseilles he heard that a *lex* had enabled Lepidus to nominate him Dictator for holding the elections (*comitiis habendis*). This had not been done for many years,

because, since B.C. 212, it had been the custom of the consuls not to go out on foreign services till after the elections had been held, and since the time of Sulla, the consuls, as a rule, did not quit Rome till their year of office was over. But in earlier times there were many precedents. The irregularity in this case was that he was named by a praetor; but anything was possible by a law properly passed in the *Comitia*. Caesar returned to Rome, held the election, and was returned as consul with P. Servilius Vatia. He stayed there only eleven days, finding time, however, to carry two laws—one for the relief of debtors who, owing to the revolution, had been forced to sell property at panic prices, and another for the bestowal of the franchise on the Transpadani. Then, leaving Antony to secure the recall of exiles condemned in courts overawed, as alleged, by Pompey's troops, he hurried to Brundisium, where he had appointed his legions to muster.

15. **Caesar follows Pompey into Epirus**, B.C. 48. Caesar set sail on the 4th of January; but Pompey's large fleet, drawn from various nations and under the supreme command of Bibulus, protected the coast of Epirus. Caesar was obliged to run ashore wherever he could. He eventually landed somewhat south of Oricum, and was readily welcomed there and at Apollonia, from which the Pompeian officers were forced to retire. But he failed in an attempted dash upon Dyrrachium, where Pompey had his magazines. Caesar was, in fact, in considerable danger. Though he held the coast in the district of Apollonia, Pompey's fleet swept the sea and prevented him from landing supplies or the rest of his troops from Italy. It was not till the spring that Antony arrived at Lissus (about thirty miles north of Dyrrachium) with four legions and 800 cavalry. But though Caesar, in spite of Pompey's attempt to hinder him, effected a junction with Antony, he could do little. He constructed, indeed, lines of circumvallation round those of Pompey,

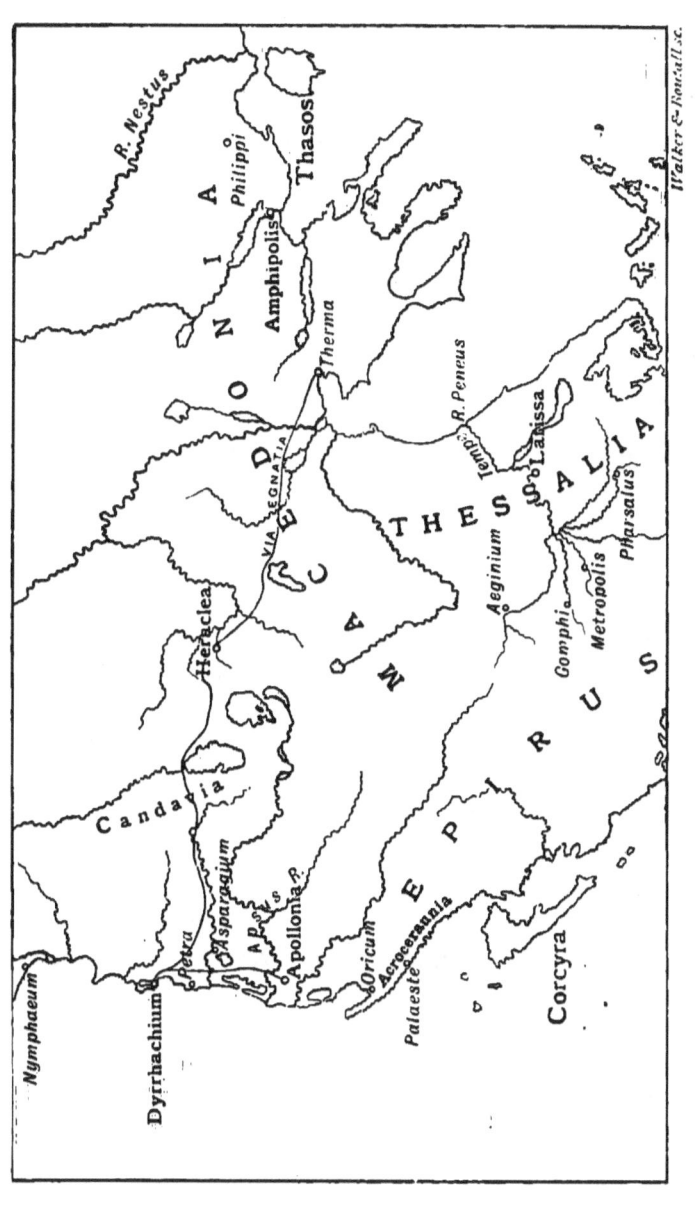

extending to a circuit of fifteen miles; but Pompey, having command of the sea, could get provisions for his men in abundance, though his horses suffered from want of forage, while Caesar's men were reduced to great straits. Moreover Caesar's lines were not complete; there was a weak point at the southern extremity near the sea, of which Pompey was informed by two Gallic deserters, and towards the end of May he successfully pierced them. Caesar fortified another camp hard by: but after meeting with a fresh disaster in attacking a Pompeian legion, he resolved on retiring upon Apollonia, and thence into Thessaly. He had sent his legate, Domitius Calvinus, to intercept reinforcements which Metellus Scipio (Pompey's father-in-law) was bringing from the province of Syria along the Egnatian road: and Caesar hoped to find Calvinus and take up a better position in the interior where Pompey would be separated from his fleet. He retired by a route south of the Egnatian road, and was joined by Calvinus at Aeginium, who had made his way over the mountains from that road, where he was in danger of being caught between two armies—by Metellus Scipio coming up the road from the east, and Pompey going down the road from the west. Both Caesar and Pompey were now marching in the same direction, though on parallel lines. They converged in Thessaly. For Pompey, after meeting Metellus Scipio with the reinforcements, left the Egnatian road, passed through the vale of Tempe to Larissa, and thence by Scotussa across the river Enipeus, within about four miles of Caesar in the district of Pharsalus.

16. **Battle of Pharsalia.** Pompey would still have preferred to avoid a battle. Caesar had no fleet to speak of, while Pompey's ships could sail round the coasts of Greece and bring him supplies. The decision rested with him, for Caesar would scarcely have ventured to attack with an army less than half that of his rival's. But Pompey yielded to his followers, who were elated with the retreat of Caesar and the

reinforcements brought by Metellus Scipio. They were eager to get back to Rome and enjoy the fruits of their victory—offices, confiscations, and other advantages. The battle which ensued on the 29th of June [9th August in the unreformed calendar] was a deathblow to their hopes. It was an example of the superiority of the Roman infantry, when well trained and experienced, over an army which, though greatly superior in numbers, was composed of mixed races, and depended mainly on its cavalry. In Pompey's army there were Asiatics, Greeks, Jews, Armenians, Arabians, Galatians, and Cappadocians. He had seven thousand cavalry against Caesar's one thousand. His legions, however, were mostly levies of the previous year, who did not turn out to be a match for Caesar's veterans. Pompey trusted to his superiority in cavalry to outflank Caesar's line, and charge it on the rear. But though his cavalry did repulse that of Caesar, it was in turn repulsed by Caesar's reserve, or fourth line, and fled in confusion. Pompey kept his infantry on their ground to receive Caesar's charge without going to meet it, and this again proved disadvantageous. The ardour of a line in full advance overbore the dead resistance of men waiting stolidly for an attack. But Pompey had given up all hope when he saw the failure of his cavalry. He hurried back to the camp, gave some directions for its defence, and then retired to his tent.

17. **Flight of Pompey.** Before long Caesar was leading his men to attack the camp, and Pompey was galloping out of the rear gate to Larissa. There he was joined by a few followers, and, without staying for rest, hurried on to the river, where he obtained a boat and reached the coast. Here he found a corn vessel ready to start, bound for Amphipolis. He only stayed one night there (apparently without landing), and went on to Lesbos, where his wife and younger son were with his friend Theophanes. After

two days' stay at Lesbos, he procured a few more vessels, and proceeded on his voyage down the Asiatic coast. At Attaleia in Pamphylia he was joined by about sixty Senators, and collected some ships and men. At Cyprus he found the first signs of his failing influence, for he was informed that the people of Antioch (on the opposite coast) were putting their town in a state of defence to prevent his landing. The same had happened to other fugitives of his party at Rhodes, and it became an anxious question to what country he could go with safety. He seems to have thought of Orodes, king of Parthia, to whom earlier in the year he had offered some concessions in Syria. Finally, however, he decided upon Egypt.

18. **Assassination of Pompey in Egypt.** The sovereigns of Egypt were then Ptolemy XII. (a boy of thirteen) and his sister and wife Cleopatra. They were the children of Ptolemy Auletes, whose cause Pompey had supported in Rome. On the death of Auletes (B.C. 51) he had left the kingdom to these two jointly; but the ministers or guardians of Ptolemy, the eunuch Pothinus and the rhetorician Theodotus of Chios, had contrived to expel Cleopatra, who had fled to Syria, collected forces, and was now endeavouring to recover her share in the kingdom. To resist her Ptolemy was at Pelusium (on the eastern mouth of the Nile) with an army commanded by Achillas. There were Roman troops also at Alexandria left by Gabinius in B.C. 57-6, and some of them seem to have been with the king's army. When Pompey's messenger arrived asking shelter, the royal council was divided in opinion, but eventually decided that it would not be prudent either to receive or to let him go. To murder him would be safest—"dead men do not bite." The deed was entrusted to Septimius, a military Tribune, who had once served under Pompey, and Salvius a centurion. A boat was sent out with Achillas on board, who greeted Pompey respectfully and invited him to come on shore.

Amidst the agonized anxiety of wife and friends Pompey stepped into the boat, took his place in the stern, and recognized and addressed Septimius as an old comrade. He was only answered however by a somewhat surly nod, and when, as he was stepping out of the boat, he felt the sword of Septimius at his back, he hastily drew the folds of his toga over his face and fell without a struggle. His head was cut off and his body left on the sand, until his faithful freedman Philip (who with one slave and two centurions had accompanied him) found the fragments of a stranded boat, with which he made a rude funeral pyre and burned the body. Pompey was an honest, but not a great man. He wished to be supreme at Rome, but yet to maintain the constitution—two things which were incompatible. He never really liked or trusted the Optimates, yet he allowed himself to be used by them for their own purposes. He had a great military reputation, and considerable military talents, but he let the incompetent nobles in his camp overrule him. As a politician he was neither so able nor so unscrupulous as Caesar, and had no great scheme of policy to carry out as Caesar had. As usually happens, the man that knew his own mind won in the end.

19. **Caesar pursues Pompey and arrives at Alexandria.** The victory of Pharsalia was very important. Caesar had lost comparatively few men in the battle, variously stated at 200 and 1200, with about 30 centurions, whereas of Pompey's army 6000 Roman corpses were lying on the field of battle, and still more of his auxiliaries. Yet the party was not beaten. The great fleet was still in the hands of Pompeians. It was stationed at Corcyra at the time of the battle, and when the news of it arrived, Cato, who had been left in charge of the camp at Dyrrachium, joined the fleet, as did Cicero and others. Pompey's elder son Gnaeus was also on board, and, though the Egyptian contingent had deserted, there was still a powerful armament. It was at last

resolved (in spite of the opposition of Cicero and others) to go to the province of Africa, where they expected to be joined by Pompey and Metellus Scipio, and where the Pompeian Attius Varus was still proconsul. Meanwhile Caesar was pressing on in pursuit of Pompey with one legion and some cavalry, leaving orders for another legion to follow, which overtook him on the Hellespont. Somewhere near Antioch, on his way through Asia, he was met by C. Cassius with a fleet of Cilician, Syrian, and Phoenician ships. Cassius submitted, it seems without a struggle and took service under Caesar, who, guessing Pompey's destination when he heard that he had been seen at Cyprus, arrived at Alexandria on the fifth of October, about ten days after Pompey's murder, of which he found men ready to assure him by presenting him with Pompey's signet ring and displaying the murdered man's head.

20. **The Alexandrine War.** Caesar stayed in Egypt till the spring of the following year, B.C. 47. Italy was entrusted to Antony with the remainder of his victorious army. Caesar would no doubt have to fight the surviving Pompeians in Africa; but for this it was necessary to strengthen his fleet and to have control of the naval powers, Egypt, Phoenicia, and Rhodes. Finding a civil war in Egypt, between Ptolemy XII. and his sister Cleopatra, he determined to intervene. His landing with lictors and fasces was resented at Alexandria, because it implied an assertion of Roman authority there; and the riots were so serious, that he sent for reinforcements from Asia, and summoned Ptolemy and Cleopatra to Alexandria to submit their dispute to him. Cleopatra is said to have won his favour by her charms, and he decided that she was to reign jointly with her brother. But this did not suit Ptolemy's minister Pothinus. He instigated Achillas and the army at Pelusium to resist and to advance on Alexandria. Caesar therefore was being besieged in Alexandria while ostensibly supporting the sovereigns of Egypt. He

had not enough troops to defend the city, and he retired to Pharos, which was connected with it by a drawbridge. Here he waited for farther help coming from Asia; but meanwhile he sent envoys in Ptolemy's name to Achillas, and when they were ill-treated by the secret instigation of Pothinus, he put Pothinus to death. Achillas being master of Alexandria set up Arsinoe, Cleopatra's sister, as queen; who, however, soon quarrelled with him and put him to death. Towards the end of the year Ptolemy persuaded Caesar to allow him to go to Alexandria and negotiate with Arsinoe's government. Instead of doing so he joined the enemy, and sought to reduce Caesar by cutting off his convoys of provisions at sea. But in March (B.C. 47) an army arrived at Pelusium under Mithridates of Pergamus, whom Caesar had commissioned to raise forces in Syria and Phoenicia. Ptolemy marched out to meet him: but Caesar went to his support, stormed Ptolemy's camp, and drove him into flight. In his attempt to escape he was drowned, 27th March [6th Feb.]. Shortly afterwards Alexandria surrendered, Cleopatra was made queen with a husband in the shape of another brother, a young boy, who as Ptolemy XIII. reigned with her nominally for a little more than three years, when she put him to death (B.C. 43). Egypt was thus secured.

21. **Caesar Dictator and Consul. Troubles at Rome.** Meanwhile at Rome Caesar had been named Dictator for a year, with the power (though not the office) of a tribune for life, and the right of being consul for five years. Nevertheless things had not gone smoothly at Rome. During the year B.C. 48 trouble had been caused by M. Caelius, a praetor, who had sought to gain favour with the mob by granting debtors better terms than Caesar's law had given them. He had been eventually driven from Rome, and had attempted to join Milo, who was in arms in South Italy to secure his recall from

exile, and there both perished. Other troubles were caused by the profligate P. Cornelius Dolabella, who (like Clodius) got himself adopted into a Plebeian gens and elected tribune, that he might get more consideration for himself; for he was overburdened with debt, and had not got what he hoped from the revolution. Antony as the Dictator's *magister equitum* was the highest authority in the absence of Caesar, but he seemed unable to suppress the party fights and disorders that now arose, and had himself to go to Brundisium to quell a military riot. If we may believe Cicero, he not only wasted time in coarse debauchery, but was enriching himself by confiscations in a way that brought Caesar's displeasure upon him.

22. **The War with Pharnaces in Pontus and Battle of Zela**, B.C. 47. Caesar's presence at Rome therefore was much needed. Yet he determined first to settle Asia. He travelled and did business with extraordinary speed. Three days at Antioch, four at Tarsus, three at Comana sufficed to settle Syria, Cilicia, and Cappadocia. But one of the little wars in which their wide empire was always involving the Romans awaited him in Pontus. Pompey had left Pharnaces, son of Mithridates, king of Bosporus, in B.C. 63. He was now trying to recover some of his father's old dominions south of the Black Sea, which were at this time part of a Roman province, and also some territories in Armenia assigned by Pompey to Deiotărus, tetrarch of Galatia. Deiotarus had fought on Pompey's side at Pharsalia, and had escaped in the same ship. But he tried to make up for that by acting as an obedient vassal of Rome, and begged the help of Domitius Calvinus, Caesar's legate in Asia. Pharnaces, while pretending that he was willing to submit his cause to Caesar's arbitration, nevertheless continued his raids, and inflicted a defeat on the combined forces of Domitius and Deiotarus, and boasted of having recovered his father's kingdom. Caesar now hastened to

Pontus in person. On the 28th of July he met Deiotarus, whom he treated with scant favour, in spite of his humble submission and endeavours to atone for assistance given to Pompey. He deprived him of the greater part of his territories, though he allowed him to retain the title of king, and forced him to hand over some troops which he had trained in the fashion of a Roman legion. Next day he entered Pontus and answered envoys who met him from Pharnaces by ordering him to quit that country, restore certain publicani whom he had seized, and all property taken from allies of Rome. When Pharnaces, pretending obedience, yet shuffled and delayed, he advanced swiftly upon his position on a hill a few miles from Zela, defeated him, stormed his camp, and forced him to fly the country. It was this rapid and decisive victory that Caesar is said to have announced in his despatch to the Senate in three words, *Veni, vidi, vici* [June, B.C. 47].

23. **The Battle of Thapsus**, April, B.C. 46. Caesar was back in Rome by August, B.C. 47: but though his presence was so much needed there he only stayed about three months. By the end of October he was on his way to Africa to put down the surviving Pompeian leaders. They had had more than a year to recover and collect their forces. There was a considerable army commanded by Pompey's father-in-law, Metellus Scipio, and supported by Iuba, king of Mauretania, and a strong fleet under the command of Attius Varus; while Cato was occupying Utica. Caesar was inferior in numbers, and the enemy's fleet harassed him by cutting off his transports. Still he took a number of towns and strongholds without much resistance, and having been reinforced about January, B.C. 46, was strong enough to give Scipio battle whenever he could get the chance. This chance came early in February. As he was advancing to attack Thapsus, Scipio and Iuba, who had been following him, got into such a position that they were forced

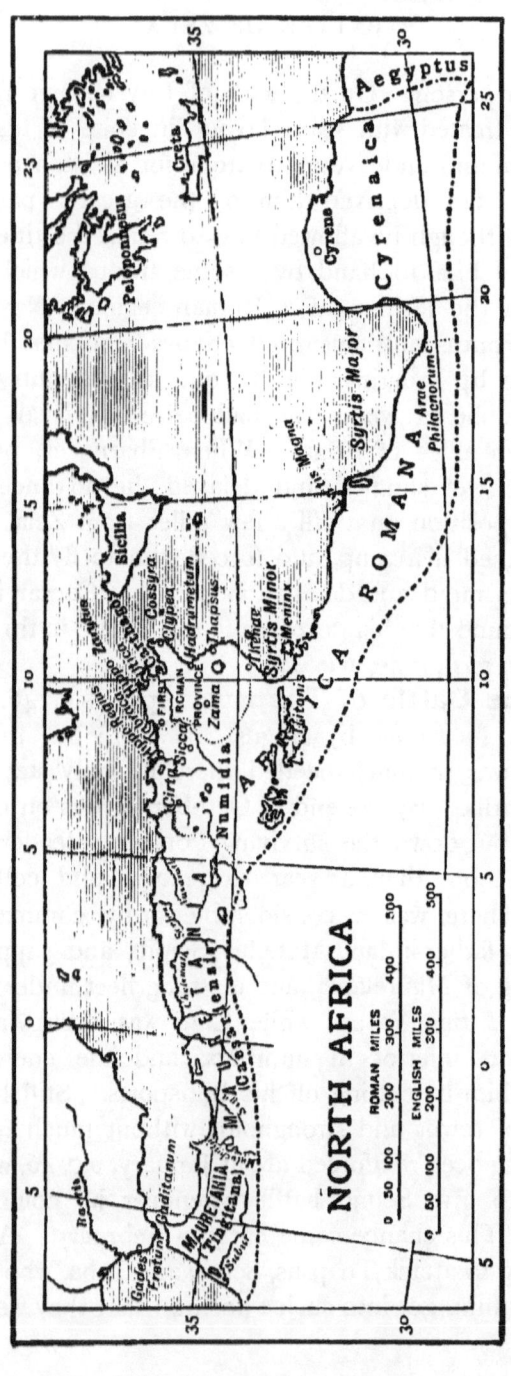

to fight. They were beaten completely and with immense loss, and Caesar, leaving the assault on Thapsus to a legate, advanced himself to attack Cato in Utica. Cato, though a resolute, not to say obstinate, politician, seems to have been a faint-hearted soldier. Two years before he had yielded Sicily to Curio without a blow, and now on Caesar's approach he at once gave up all for lost. Yet he had the courage to die, and to die cheerfully. After conversing calmly on philosophy to a company of his friends, and commending his family to the care of Lucius Caesar, he retired to his bedroom and fell on his sword. The wound was not mortal, and was dressed; but when left alone he tore off the bandages and expired. The other leaders either made their peace with Caesar or perished in various ways. Iuba and Petreius are said to have killed each other; Faustus Sulla and Afranius fell in a military riot. Scipio tried to join Gnaeus and Sextus Pompeius who had gone to Spain, but was overtaken by Caesar's ships and threw himself into the sea. Thus resistance in Africa was crushed, and Numidia made a Roman province. Two months after the battle Caesar embarked for Italy, and arrived in Rome towards the end of May, practically master of the Empire, although he had been nominally only consul with a colleague like any other consul, M. Aemilius Lepidus.

CHAPTER XIX.

FROM THE BATTLE OF THAPSUS TO THE BATTLE OF PHILIPPI (B.C. 46-42).

1. *Caesar's administration from* B.C. 46. 2. *The war with the sons of Pompey in Spain; battle of Munda,* B.C. 45. 3. *Consequences of the battle of Munda.* 4. *Caesar's reforms and projects in the last year of his life.* 5. *Causes of the conspiracy against Caesar.* 6. *The members of the conspiracy.* 7. *The assassination of Caesar.* 8. *The effects of the assassination of Caesar; the conduct of Antony.* 9. *C. Octavianus comes to Rome.* 10. *The war of Mutina,* B.C. 44-3. 11. *Octavianus returns to Rome and is elected consul.* 12. *Octavianus breaks with the Optimates; the Triumvirate.* 13. *The proscriptions; death of Cicero.* 14. *Defeat of Brutus and Cassius at Philippi* (B.C. 42). 15. *Second division of the Empire between the Triumvirs.*

1. **Caesar's Laws and Reforms.** Before Caesar's return to Rome in July, B.C. 46, he had been declared Dictator for ten years (from 1st January, B.C. 45), and invested with censorial powers under the title of *praefectus morum*. He was in all but name an absolute king. He celebrated four triumphs, over Gaul, Egypt, Pontus, and Numidia, thus avoiding all mention of a civil war. It was quite against precedent to celebrate a triumph over fellow citizens, and therefore these triumphs were nominally over Ptolemy in Egypt, Pharnaces in Pontus, Iuba in Numidia. Yet the truth could not be thus obscured, and these processions must have been bitterly offensive to many. Caesar now

spent rather more than six months in Rome, and carried out a number of very useful reforms. The first was that of the calendar. The Roman year, since its settlement traditionally referred to king Numa, had consisted of 12 lunar months or 355 days (more accurately 354 days 8 hours 48 minutes 36 seconds). The solar year consists of 365 days 5 hours 48 minutes 51½ seconds. The error, therefore, was between 10 and 11 days every year. The pontifices from time to time intercalated 27 days after the 23rd of February. But this was not enough, and the error had accumulated till it reached 90 days. That is to say, in a given year about this time, if there were no days intercalated, the calendar was three months in advance, and an event said to happen on 25th July would really have happened about the 25th of May. This often led to great inconveniences. The festivals meant to be in the summer would fall in the spring, those meant to be in the spring would fall in the winter, and so on. Caesar consulted the best mathematicians; and a month of 23 days having been intercalated in February, another of 67 days was inserted between the last day of November and first of December. So that this "last year of disorder" consisted of 445 days, and the first of January, B.C. 45, was brought to its true place in the solar year. Other reforms were meant to prevent farther revolutions and restore prosperity. Mindful perhaps of what he himself had been able to do, he passed a law confining the tenure of praetorian provinces to one, and consular provinces to two years. Another law prevented Senators from residing more than three years outside Italy; and another compelled owners of sheep-runs to have at least a third of their shepherds free men. To purify the law courts he abolished the third decuria of jurors (the *tribuni aerarii*), so that juries should be entirely composed of Senators and Equites. The liberal arts were encouraged by giving the franchise to their professors living in Rome;

and a remedy was sought for poverty and overcrowding by projects of colonization, in Carthage, Corinth, and Gaul.

2. **The War against the Sons of Pompey in Spain** (B.C. 45). From these peaceful employments he was forced once more to take the field. The two sons of Pompey, Gnaeus and Sextus, had taken refuge in the south of Spain. There they found the name of Caesar unpopular on account of the ill-conduct of a governor sent by him to the province. They quickly collected thirteen legions, and were joined by the leaders of the army in Africa who had escaped after Thapsus. With these troops they defeated C. Didius, whom Caesar had sent against them, and it became necessary for him to go there in person. He left Rome on the 3rd of December, B.C. 46, and was back again early in the following September. Though many Spanish tribes were in arms, taking advantage of the Roman dissensions to return to their old habits of brigandage, yet it was not a Spanish war, *i.e.* a war with Spaniards. The two armies were almost wholly Roman; and the Pompeian army was filled with veterans who would fight desperately, because, having served against Caesar before, and having been granted their lives, they could have no hope of farther mercy. Caesar's troops were also veterans exasperated at having to fight again in a civil war. There was likely, therefore, to be little quarter given; and in fact the slaughter was more ruthless than in any part of the civil war. After several minor successes Gnaeus Pompeius pitched his camp in a plain near **Munda**, and there Caesar forced him to give battle (17th March). The struggle was fierce and desperate, and the loss great on both sides. Caesar, however, was completely victorious. Gnaeus Pompeius escaped to the sea only to fall a month later when landing to take water; but his brother Sextus survived, and remained at the head of a formidable naval force for many years afterwards.

3. **Consequences of the Battle of Munda.** Though Sextus Pompeius was thus still left with a large fleet, the battle of Munda secured Southern Spain for the time (the North had not been seriously disturbed), and cleared off the greater part of the Pompeian officers who had survived the battles of Pharsalia and Thapsus. But its most striking effect at the moment was shown at Rome. Rumours of Caesar's defeat had at one time been rife there, and some symptoms of a rising opposition had appeared. But the news of Munda changed all that. Every kind of honour was voted to him: a *supplicatio* for fifty days; the dictatorship for life; the right of being consul for the next ten years; the entire control of the treasury; and complete military authority by the title of *Imperator* for himself and his children. When he returned to Rome, therefore, in September he was in fact in all but name an absolute king; and some even proposed that he should have that title, at any rate in the provinces.

4. **New Reforms of Caesar,** B.C. 45-44. Caesar made a good use of this position during the few months of life that remained to him, both by enforcing the laws already passed, and by passing new ones. He formed also great schemes for improving and enlarging Rome; for draining the lower parts of the town by diverting the river into a canal, and thus including part of the Vatican district within the pomoerium; for erecting new buildings, a forum, a curia, a theatre, and several temples. A great public library was to be collected, and the best jurists were to codify the laws. Outside the city also vast works were to be set on foot; a great canal was to drain the Pomptine Marshes; an artificial emissary was to prevent the flooding of the lacus Fucinus; a great harbour was to be constructed at Ostia; a new road constructed across the Apennines to the shore of the Adriatic; and numerous colonies to be planted, besides those actually settled at Corinth and

Carthage, in various parts of the Empire, in Gaul, Illyricum, Egypt, Syria, and Pontus. Many of these things were actually begun, but his assassination on the 15th of March put a stop to most and delayed all.

5. **The Causes of the Conspiracy against Caesar.** There were many reasons which might cause a plot against Caesar's life among the nobles of Rome. However well he might conduct the government, it was the government of an absolute monarch. Offices depended no longer on popular favour or (as they had generally done before) on family arrangements. Though the form of election was still gone through, Caesar issued letters of recommendation which were practically commands. His dictatorship gave him complete control over other magistrates. He filled up the Senate with friends and partisans of his own of all ranks, sometimes from the provinces, and sometimes from the sons of freedmen, so that there were about nine hundred names on the roll. This was too large a body to be effective or influential; and he himself set the example of treating it with scant respect. Then, too, the triumph after the war in Spain was plainly over fellow citizens, there could be no disguise as to that: and the proposal to give him the title of *rex* aroused the most deeply seated prejudices of the citizens. The story is well known how as he was watching the Lupercalia, the ancient festival celebrated on the Palatine (15th Feb.), Antony in the semi-nude state of one of the Luperci, taking advantage of the license of the festival, attempted three times to place a gold crown on Caesar's head. Caesar indeed, observing the feelings of the people, thrice rejected it, and finally ordered it to be dedicated in the Capitol to the only king —Iupiter; but the incident had its effect. Again, as he was once entering the city, some officious partisans addressed him as *rex*, and were answered by him that they were mistaken, he was not Rex (a well-known surname of a Roman family) but

Caesar. Still he was sensitive as to opposition to this title, and when two of the tribunes pulled off some crowns with which his statues had been secretly adorned, and arrested some leaders of the mob, he showed his displeasure by causing them to be suspended from their office. Moreover he seemed to be establishing a dynasty. His great-nephew, C. Octavius—afterwards Augustus—was now eighteen, had joined his great-uncle after the battle of Munda in Spain, and had been treated in all ways as his heir, and as a prince who was to take up the position when he died. It does not seem that he actually adopted him in his lifetime (that was done by his will), but he treated him in a way that showed what he meant to do. All these things, though they perhaps did not render him unpopular with the lower orders, were deeply offensive to the nobles, who could also reckon on some points both in his policy and conduct likely to prejudice him with the people,—such as his restricting the number of those entitled to cheap corn, and his habit of rather ostentatiously showing want of interest in the theatre and circus by reading and answering his correspondence while sitting there. Finally, like all revolutionary leaders, he was surrounded by many men of bad character whom he was constrained to employ.

6. **The Members of the Conspiracy.** However this may be, certain persons were industriously working up a plot. In our time it would perhaps have been done by securing the co-operation of the press, and paying for frequent paragraphs of detraction. In Rome it was done by scattering 'libels,' or written sentences, about the streets and Forum, and writing them on walls. They were mostly in the form of appeals to M. Brutus to justify his name and assumed descent from the Brutus who expelled the kings, and from Ahala who killed a would-be tyrant. The leaders in the conspiracy were M. Iunius

Brutus, who was praetor urbanus, and C. Cassius Longinus, also a praetor, and married to a half-sister of Brutus. Both had fought on Pompey's side, and had been spared by Caesar, and not only pardoned but promoted to office under his direction. To M. Brutus Caesar had been specially indulgent from affection to his mother. He had arranged that at the end of their praetorship Brutus was to govern Macedonia, Cassius Syria. It would seem that no two men could have more to lose by his death. Another was Decimus Brutus, who had served under Caesar in Gaul and in the civil war, had been since in high command in Gaul, had been specially honoured in the triumph of B.C. 45, and, as it afterwards appeared, was entered in Caesar's will as 'second heir,' *i.e.* to succeed in default of the heir. He, too, was a praetor in B.C. 44, had the command of troops in Cisalpine Gaul, and was nominated to the consulship of B.C. 42. We do not know, considering these facts, why he should have turned against his benefactor, except that he had married the daughter of a leading Pompeian, and may have been influenced by family connexions. C. Trebonius was another who was under similar obligations to Caesar. He had been praetor, commander in Spain, consul, and was nominated to the province of Asia for B.C. 44. And so with others, though in a less degree. There must have been something in Caesar's character that alienated friends: we must allow something also for a genuine feeling that he was an enemy to freedom and the constitution.

7. **The Assassination.** About seventy were privy to the plot, which, therefore, could hardly have been so well concealed had it not been carried out promptly. Even as it was, it seems to have oozed out in some directions, and Caesar had several warnings. A soothsayer had bidden him beware of the Ides of March; his wife had evil dreams; and so many evil omens of various sorts were

reported to him, that he resolved not to go to the Senate house on the 15th. This delay alarmed the conspirators, who were afraid that they had been betrayed. Decimus Brutus undertook the treacherous task of inducing him to break his resolution. He came to his house and appealed to his pride not to let it be said that he failed to appear in the Senate from superstitious fears and fanciful causes. Caesar was convinced and rose to go about eleven in the morning. As he crossed the hall of his house his bust or statue fell and broke in pieces, perhaps thrown down by some friendly hand to warn him. As he walked along the street the crowd pressed round him with petitions, and one man with special eagerness thrust a paper in his hand, begging him to read it at once, as it concerned him deeply. But he either did not hear or did not understand, and gave it with others to his attendant. He entered the Senate, and having taken his seat, was at once surrounded by the conspirators, who pretended to be backing a petition of L. Tillius Cimber desiring his brother's recall. When he turned away, annoyed at their persistence, Cimber clutched his toga. This was the signal agreed upon. Casca struck him with his dagger, which he had concealed in the case used for carrying the writing stilus, and thereupon the others drew their daggers also and plunged them into his body. He at first tried to defend himself; but when he saw M. Brutus among his enemies, for whom he had had such great affection, he cried, "You too, my son!" and drawing his robe over his face, fell pierced by more than twenty wounds. The conspirators had struck with such violence and haste that more than one of their own number was wounded. The other senators, after a pause of horror, rushed out of the house spreading the news far and wide through the city.

8. **The Effects of the Assassination of Caesar.** Whatever private motives the conspirators may have had

for hating Caesar, there were some of them (and especially M. Brutus) who believed that they were doing a good service to the state. Caesar had made himself practically king. The old republican government and liberty would again be restored by getting rid of him. Cicero who was present, though not privy to the plot, loudly applauded the assassins, and professed to believe that a tyrant had righteously been removed and liberty recovered. Let us see why this did not turn out to be the case. Parties at Rome were too deeply divided to allow the removal of one man to make peace. The leaders in the state had all powerful followings, and were determined to secure their own interests, and not to give up any of the offices, governments, or profitable employments which they had obtained from Caesar. These they were prepared to defend by arms if necessary, and their professed loyalty to the constitution, by which they justified the murder of Caesar, would not make them obedient to the Senate if it ordered any change in these things. All were in haste to take possession of what they regarded as their rights, and paid little attention to any votes of the Senate which went against their wishes. The chief magistrate after Caesar's death was Marcus Antonius, the consul, for of course the Dictatorship ended with the death of the Dictator. He was at first alarmed for his own safety, and made some terms with the assassins. But presently, when he found what a warm reception his speech (*laudatio*) at the public funeral of Caesar met with from the populace, he plucked up courage; and inducing the Senate to confirm all the *acta* of Caesar, he got possession of his papers, and of a large sum of money which he had left in the treasury, and did what he chose. Some of the conspirators who had been named to provinces soon went off to them; but M. Brutus and C. Cassius, being praetors, ought not to have left Rome till the end of the year. They found, however, that the people were so angry with them that they dared not stay, and had to retire to Antium. M. Brutus, we saw, had been named for the province of Macedonia, and Cassius for that of Syria for B.C. 43; but when Antony found how unpopular they were, he induced the Senate to change this, and vote Macedonia to his own brother Gaius, and Syria to Dolabella, who had become consul since Caesar's death.[1] This they were determined to resist, and having collected troops and ships went off to take possession of their provinces. Therefore there was a certainty of civil war in the East. In the West there was also every chance of it. In Spain and Sicily Sextus Pompeius was in command of a large army and fleet, and was ready to join whichever party would grant him the best terms; while Decimus Brutus had taken possession (in virtue of Caesar's nomination) of Gallia Cisalpina, which Antony desired for himself.

9. **Octavianus comes to Rome.** Presently this state of things was further complicated by the arrival in Rome (in May) of Caesar's great-nephew and heir, the young C. Octavius, who, being adopted in Caesar's will, was now called **Gaius Iulius Caesar Octavianus**, afterwards the Emperor Augustus. Both sides wished to get his support, and Cicero for some time thought that he had secured him on the side of the Optimates, because he quarrelled with Antony about his uncle's inheritance, and because Antony objected to his being elected Tribune. He was only eighteen years old, but had already impressed many people by his firm and cautious character. His first object, which he carefully concealed, was to avenge his great-

---

[1] P. Cornelius Dolabella had been promised the consulship when Caesar left Rome for the Parthian war. He had actually been elected, but Antony (who objected to him) had declared the omens unfavourable, and so it was a question whether he was legally consul. However, as soon as Caesar was killed, he assumed the office, Antony not feeling strong enough to resist him.

uncle by punishing his assassins; but he also was determined that Antony should not have everything his own way and become alone supreme in the State. He was resolved at least to share in his power. He therefore at first seemed to take part with the Optimates, who disliked and mistrusted Antony, and was even believed to have plotted his assassination; and when Antony towards the end of the year brought over to Italy some legions, which had been stationed in Macedonia, in order to enforce his claim on Gallia Cisalpina against Decimus Brutus, Octavian retaliated by raising a legion among the veterans settled by his great-uncle in Campania. He was presently joined by two of the legions from Macedonia, which deserted Antony, and towards the end of B.C. 44, started for Cisalpine Gaul to prevent Antony from taking possession of that province.

10. **War of Mutina**, B.C. 43. This led to a war round Mutina (the modern *Modena*), in which Decimus Brutus was being besieged by Antony. The Senate eagerly adopted the measures of Octavian, voted him the rank of propraetor and then of proconsul, and sent the two consuls of B.C. 43, Gaius Vibius Pansa and Aulus Hirtius, to take part in opposing Antony, who, after various negotiations with the Senate, was declared a public enemy. The decisive battle in this campaign was fought at a place called Forum Gallorum (*Castel Franco*) on the 15th of April, followed by an attack on Antony's camp on the 16th. But in these two battles both the consuls were mortally wounded; and Antony was able to march off towards the West over a pass that brought him to the coast near Savona and thence to Gallia Transalpina.

11. **Octavian returns to Rome and is elected Consul.** The Optimates were greatly rejoiced at this success; but it soon turned out that they had no cause to be glad. When Antony marched towards the Riviera,

Decimus Brutus broke out from Mutina and followed him for some way, but was too late to catch him, and Antony reached the Province in safety, having been reinforced by another legion brought across the North of Italy by one of the praetors, P. Ventidius Bassus. Moreover Octavian now showed that, though he had meant to resist Antony, he would not help Decimus Brutus, one of his great-uncle's murderers. His legions supported him in this, and refused to march in pursuit of Antony. Instead of doing this, he sent to Rome demanding to be elected consul: and when difficulties were made about it, he started for Rome at the head of his army, and entered the city in August almost as a conqueror. He was immediately elected consul with his cousin Q. Pedius, whom he caused to bring in a law for the trial of all assassins of Iulius.

12. **The Triumvirate: M. Lepidus, M. Antonius, C. Octavianus.** But this was not all. Octavian had come to Rome resolved to break entirely with the Optimates. The Senate, in which they were the superior party, had shown that they meant to disown him. They were encouraged by the success of Cassius in Syria, who had driven Dolabella to commit suicide, and had taken possession of the province; and of M. Brutus who had taken over Macedonia and captured Gaius Antonius. Sextus Pompeius had also declared for them and had been appointed commander-in-chief of the fleet; and the governor of Africa, Cornificius, was going to send soldiers from his province to Rome. The Senate had therefore ventured to refuse Octavian's request for a triumph and the consulship. Accordingly, before setting out for Rome with his three legions, he had sent a conciliatory message to Antony, and meant, if it should seem to suit his policy, to come to terms with him. Now that he was at Rome with his army at his back, the Senate was forced to do everything he wished. The decree declaring Antony a public enemy was

reversed; Octavian himself was granted extraordinary powers, and was named commander, not only of his own legions, but also of those serving with Decimus Brutus. He therefore set off again in September to Cisalpine Gaul to attack Decimus, who, however, was already a fugitive without an army. He had made his way into Cisalpine Gaul, trusting to be joined by L. Munatius Plancus, the governor of Celtic Gaul. But not only had Plancus joined Antony, but so also had M. Lepidus, governor of Narbonensis and Upper Spain. Being, therefore, abandoned by his army, Decimus Brutus attempted to reach Ravenna, and thence cross to M. Brutus in Macedonia. From this, however, he was cut off by Octavian's advance. Turning westward, again he tried to reach the Rhine, but was stopped in Gaul and, on Antony's orders, was put to death by a chief of the Sequani. Antony had now the support of three armies,—his own and those of Lepidus and Plancus,—and it remained to see whether he would come to terms with Octavian. If he did, they would be able to do as they chose at Rome, and the Senate would be quite helpless. The three commanders, Octavian, Antony, and Lepidus met on a small island in a tributary of the Po near Mutina, and made an arrangement for dividing the government of the whole Empire between them. They were themselves to be elected *tresviri reipublicae constituendae* for five years, that is, " a commission of three for settling the republic." The ordinary magistrates were to be appointed, but the triumvirs were at once to name them for the whole five years, and were to exercise absolute powers everywhere over them. It was in fact to be a sort of Dictatorship in commission. Besides these general powers they were each to have superintendence of a special part of the Empire. Lepidus, with three legions, was to have Gallia Narbonensis and Spain; Antony, all the rest of Gaul, with four legions; Octavianus, Africa, Sardinia, Sicily, and other islands, with three legions. Antony and Octavian undertook to crush Brutus and Cassius in the East,—Octavian having the additional task of contending with Sextus Pompeius,—while Lepidus took temporary charge of Rome.

13. **The Proscriptions.** These arrangements were openly announced to the army. But there was also a secret clause inserted, whereby they agreed to put to death certain leading men in the party of the Optimates. The murderers of Caesar were of course to go; they were by this time already condemned under the law of Pedius. But there were others; and each of the three put down names particularly odious to them. Thus Antony entered the name of Cicero and his brother and nephew. Antony allowed Lepidus to put his uncle Lucius Caesar on the list, in return for inserting the name of Lepidus's own brother. The first list thus made up consisted of seventeen names, and orders were sent at once to Rome for their execution. Thus early in December the great orator Cicero was overtaken by a detachment of soldiers near his villa at Formiae and executed, his brother and nephew having been previously put to death at Rome. When the Triumvirs returned to Rome other lists were put up in the Forum (*proscripti*), so that in the end between two and three thousand persons were 'proscribed.' A good many of them escaped, at any rate for the present, by joining Brutus and Cassius in the East, or Sext. Pompeius in Sicily; and we know of several who escaped altogether. But it seems that about 150 senators and a large number of Equites (perhaps a thousand) were actually put to death.

14. **Defeat of Brutus and Cassius at Philippi**, B.C. 42. The triumvirs entered on their office on the 1st of January, B.C. 42. But they did not all three stay long at Rome. There was much to do before they were masters of the Empire. At Rome there had been a kind of commercial panic and other troubles. But when these matters had been to a certain extent put right, Lepidus was left in charge

of the city, while Antony went to get ready an army against Brutus and Cassius in the East, and Octavian to attack Sext. Pompeius in Sicily. For as long as the command of the sea was in the hands of their enemies they would have great difficulty in getting troops across, or securing supplies for their army. Besides, as Rome depended very largely on corn from Africa, Egypt, Sicily, and Sardinia, there was great danger of the city being starved out if Pompeius and other exiles had ships in various parts of the Mediterranean. Octavian did not meet with great success in his contest with Sext. Pompeius this spring, and Antony was for some time prevented crossing from Brundisium by another fleet under Cn. Domitius Ahenobarbus, who had escaped from the proscription. About August, however, Octavian and Antony joining forces managed to get to Apollonia, and thence marched across Macedonia by the great road, called the *via Egnatia*, and found Brutus and Cassius (who had also joined forces) posted strongly at Philippi, opposite the island of Thasos. They were much better off than their opponents because they had a large fleet to bring them provisions, while the army of Antony and Octavian had to rely on the country for supplies, which were already running short. At the end of October and the beginning of November, however, two battles, at an interval of about a fortnight, settled the question. In the first Cassius was defeated by Antony, Octavian by Brutus. But Cassius, thinking that Brutus had been defeated, killed himself rather than become a prisoner. A fortnight later Brutus was defeated by Antony and Octavian together, and finding his officers unwilling to continue the struggle, put an end to his own life also. Many of the leaders were put to death after the battle, but some escaped, and some, with the majority of the legions, submitted to the triumvirs and were taken into their service. Among the survivors was the poet Horace, who had joined Brutus at Athens. In after years he made more than one half-playful, half-sad allusion in his Odes to his disaster and his escape.

15. **The Empire again Divided,** November, B.C. 42. The great result of this fighting was that the two most powerful men in the Empire were now Antony and Octavian (or as we will henceforth call him, Caesar). They determined, therefore, to divide the government of it between themselves once more, this time taking in the East as well as the West. Italy was to be common to both as the head of the Empire, and a common recruiting ground. Antony was to take all the Gauls and Africa, Caesar Spain and Numidia. Lepidus was suspected of having intrigued with Sextus Pompeius: if that turned out to be the case he was to have nothing, if not, Antony agreed to let him have Africa, while he himself meanwhile went to Asia to put down opposition there and to collect money, while Caesar again undertook the war with Sext. Pompeius. They then separated; Antony went to Asia, Caesar returned to Rome. They seldom met again in friendship, and we shall next have to see how this arrangement soon broke down, was renewed on different terms, and ended at last in the complete supremacy of Caesar.

CHAPTER XX.

THE DISSOLUTION OF THE TRIUMVIRATE AND THE BEGINNING OF MONARCHY.

1. *The state of Italy after the battles at Philippi.* 2. *The quarrel between Caesar and L. Antonius.* 3. *The siege of Perusia and destruction of the opposition.* 4. *New compact between Antony and Caesar at Brundisium.* 5. *Peace of Misenum with Sextus Pompeius.* 6. *The rise of Caesar's influence.* 7. *Antony in the East from* B.C. 39 *to* B.C. 32; *his connexion with Cleopatra.* 8. *The immediate causes of quarrel between Caesar and Antony.* 9. *Both sides prepare for war.* 10. *War proclaimed against Cleopatra.* 11. *The battle of Actium (2nd Sept.,* B.C. 31). 12. *Results of the battle of Actium.* 13. *Death of Antony and Cleopatra.*

1. **State of Italy after the Battle of Philippi**, B.C. 42-40. With the exception of one brief visit Antony was never in Rome again after the victories at Philippi, but was wholly engrossed in the government of the East or the pleasures of Egypt. We shall have presently to say something of what he did there. Let us first follow the events which made Caesar supreme in the West, and rendered inevitable a contest between him and Antony for the rule of the whole Empire. At first, however, his authority was not undisputed even in the West. There were two survivors of the civil war strong enough to threaten the peace and prosperity of Italy: one was Gnaeus Domitius Ahenobarbus, who had commanded a fleet in the interests of Brutus and Cassius, and had defeated the triumvirs' admiral

off Brundisium on the very day of the battle of Philippi. He was still in command of sixty ships, and was threatening the eastern shores of Italy and the commerce with the East; while Sext. Pompeius was still unsubdued on the West, and held Sicily and Sardinia, and could hamper the corn trade and threaten Rome with famine.

2. **The Quarrel between Caesar and L. Antonius.** Besides this Caesar found violent opposition nearer home. He returned slowly from Macedonia, being attacked by one of his many illnesses. At Rome he found Lucius Antonius (brother of Marcus) consul, having just celebrated a triumph for some insignificant success in Gaul. Aided by his brother's wife Fulvia, a woman of masculine character, he set himself to thwart Caesar in the interests of his brother. He refused to hand over the legions which Caesar claimed in virtue of his agreement with Marcus, and promoted the discontent among the veteran soldiers to whom Caesar had to assign lands, and also among those from whom those lands were taken, pretending that he did not act fairly as between his own soldiers and those of Antony, and that he was making unnecessary confiscations when he had other means of satisfying the legions. It was all the easier to stir up strife because there was great financial distress at the time, owing to the heavy rise in the price of food, caused by the fleets of Ahenobarbus and Sext. Pompeius infesting the shores. After some months of bickering the breach between the two became hopeless, and Caesar repudiated the young daughter of Fulvia betrothed to him in B.C. 43. He and Lucius Antonius both collected troops. Caesar laid siege to Nursia, in the territory of the Sabines, and to Sentinum in Umbria, both of which commanded the line of the Flaminian road to the north, and recalled Salvidienus Rufus whom he had sent to Spain with troops. L. Antonius induced the Senate to appoint him Imperator for a war in which no enemy was named,

and started from Rome, just before Caesar returned thither, to prevent the approach of Salvidienus. But by this time Sentinum had been taken and Nursia had surrendered, and Caesar's friend Agrippa occupied Sutrium, on the other northern road, the *via Cassia*. L. Antonius, finding himself cut off from any advance towards Gaul, turned aside to Perusia, which was a strongly fortified town, and there he and Fulvia entrenched themselves.

3. **Siege of Perusia**, B.C. 41–40. Caesar, Agrippa, and Salvidienus followed and concentrated all their forces on the siege of Perusia, which held out till March, B.C. 40, when hunger forced the garrison to surrender. Fulvia and L. Antonius were allowed to depart unharmed, but a large number of senators and Equites were put to death, and the party of the Optimates opposed to Caesar never recovered from the losses sustained. As the result of this contest Caesar was left supreme in the West; for Lepidus, who was nominally in charge of Rome as the third Triumvir, had shown neither courage nor decision during these troubles, and never exercised any influence again.

4. **New Compact between Antony and Caesar**, B.C. 40. Caesar now began to be looked upon as the best guarantee for peace and plenty at Rome. For Gn. Domitius Ahenobarbus, finding that he was so successful, ceased to infest the shores of Italy with his fleet, and sailed away to join Antony. The only danger now was from Sext. Pompeius, and both Antony and Caesar wished to come to some terms with him if possible. With a view to doing so, Caesar this year (40) married Scribonia, aunt to Sextus's wife, though many years older than himself. But Antony, when he heard of what had been happening in Italy, was afraid that he would soon lose all power too. He had been living in Alexandria for the last year, fascinated by the charms of Cleopatra, Queen of Egypt, who had met him at Tarsus, and in the whirl of pleasure and dissipation had not attended much to business.

The Parthians invaded Syria in April, B.C. 40, but he left the war with them to his legates, and came to Greece on pretence that his help was needed against Sext. Pompeius in Sicily. But though when his wife Fulvia came to meet him from Perusia, he repudiated her policy and treated her with great unkindness, he yet made up his mind to reduce Caesar's power. His mother Iulia had taken refuge with Sextus Pompeius, and now came to visit him with a proposal that he should unite with Pompeius against Caesar. Antony accepted the suggestion, and, in conjunction with Ahenobarbus and Pompeius, began making descents upon the coasts of South Italy. There seemed therefore every prospect of a new and terrible civil war. This, however, was averted by the diplomacy of Caesar's minister, Maecenas, and Antony's legate, Asinius Pollio. A peace was negotiated, known as the peace of Brundisium, in the autumn of B.C. 40. By this arrangement a partition of the Roman Empire between the triumvirs was made for the third time. All east of the Adriatic (except Illyricum) was to be under Antony, all west of it under Caesar. Africa (that is, the Roman province so called) was to be under Lepidus. Antony was to undertake the war with the Parthians, Caesar to deal with Sext. Pompeius. Fulvia having lately died in Greece, Antony was to confirm this pacification by marrying Octavia, Caesar's sister, who had lately been left a widow by Marcellus. The principal partisans of Antony were provided for in other ways—Ahenobarbus was sent to Bithynia, Asinius Pollio to conduct a war against the Parthini in Illyricum, and Ventidius Bassus was to have the Parthian war.

5. **Peace of Misenum with Sextus Pompeius**. This was followed a few months later, in the early part of B.C. 39, by a treaty with Sext. Pompeius made at Misenum, where he was visited on board his vessel by Antony and Caesar. By this treaty he was to receive a compensation in money for his father's confiscated property, was

to retain a fleet, with the government of Sardinia, Corsica, Sicily, and Achaia (*i.e.* Peloponnesus), and to be consul in B.C. 35. In return for this he was to cease all interruptions to the corn trade. Antony and his wife Octavia then departed to Greece, from which he was to direct the Parthian war. Caesar returned to Rome, where his daughter Iulia (the only child he ever had) was born. On the very day of her birth he divorced his wife Scribonia, partly because he no longer cared to have any personal connexion with Sext. Pompeius, and partly because he was in love with Livia, whom he married early in B.C. 38.

6. **The Rise of Caesar's Influence**, B.C. 38 to B.C. 32. In the six years that followed these transactions, Caesar steadily grew in popularity and power at Rome, while Antony constantly lost credit there. Let us see how this came about. In the first place Caesar was in Italy and often in Rome itself, and therefore what he did was seen and known; while Antony was far away in the East, and what he was doing was only known by report and did not gain in the reporting. In the next place the dangers Caesar had to meet were dangers which directly affected Rome, while Parthian invasions of Syria, or Roman invasions of Mesopotamia did not seem to matter nearly so much. Every one felt the rise of prices, and renewed depredations of Sext. Pompeius were sending them up again almost to the famine point. And this was partly the fault of Antony. Sextus Pompeius complained that Antony had not kept the terms of the peace of Misenum fairly, and had handed over the Peloponnese to him only after thoroughly exhausting the means of the cities in it. He therefore began again his descents upon the coasts of Italy. To ward off this danger would give a man the highest place in the affections of the citizens; and this Caesar now set himself to do.

It took nearly three years (B.C. 38-36), and he met with disasters as well as successes in doing it; but at length in

B.C. 36 Sext. Pompeius was finally defeated, mainly by Caesar's friend Agrippa, and fled to Asia, where next year he was put to death by Antony's orders. But this was not the only service done by Caesar or his legates to the peace of the western world. Gaul was pacified by Agrippa in B.C. 38-7. Illyricum, in which Pollio, acting as Antony's legate in B.C. 39, had earned a triumph, was afterwards taken over by Caesar himself, and farther reduced under his own leadership in B.C. 35-6, and under that of Agrippa in B.C. 34. In this same year Valerius Messalla was sent by him to subdue the Salassi, who blocked the passage over the Alps by the Val d'Aosta. All these achievements were of great service to Rome; they relieved Roman commerce, and an immediate abatement of taxation took place. Moreover, after the defeat of Sext. Pompeius, Caesar established control in Sicily and in Africa by depriving Lepidus of his office of triumvir, when being summoned to Sicily to help against Sext. Pompeius he had tried to annex the government of that island. Caesar himself was rewarded by the Senate with honours which seemed to predict his future sovereignty. His person was declared sacred, he was allowed to wear always the triumphal robes, a public residence was assigned to him on the Palatine, and in the Senate he occupied the bench of the tribunes.

7. **Antony in the East from** B.C. 39 to B.C. 32. Meanwhile Antony, though he still had partisans in Rome, was steadily declining in influence there. After his marriage with Octavia he lived for two years in Greece, only once coming for a short time to Brundisium when asked to help against Sext. Pompeius. The Parthians were indeed repulsed from Syria in 39-38 by his legate Ventidius Bassus, while Cilicia and Palestine were secured by Pompaedius Silo and C. Sosius, for which Antony had the formal credit at home. But in B.C. 36 he met with disasters when invading Parthia: and in B.C. 34, though he invaded Armenia and

captured its king, he acted with such treachery that he was commonly considered to have disgraced the Roman name. Any advantage too which he had gained was lost in B.C. 33, when he made another fruitless expedition as far as the Araxes; and the Parthians overran Media and Armenia. But what ruined his credit perhaps as much as anything was the fact that after two years of marriage with Octavia, who more than once had reconciled him with her brother, he sent her back to Rome on the pretence of the dangers of the Parthian war, and returned to Queen Cleopatra at Alexandria. In the intervals of his expeditions he lived with her as his wife in great splendour and luxury. Public opinion was outraged by the idea of a Roman Imperator attending upon a foreign Queen, and at Roman soldiers acting as though under her orders. Moreover, for the children born of their union various countries in the East were assigned as kingdoms, and the belief was current at Rome (promoted by Caesar's partisans) that Antony and Cleopatra meant to establish a great empire in the East independent of Rome, or one which might eventually embrace the Roman Empire itself, the centre being Alexandria instead of Rome.

8. **The Immediate Causes of Quarrel between Caesar and Antony.** The triumvirate had been renewed in B.C. 37 for a second term of five years, *i.e.* to 31st December, B.C. 33. Since that time one of the three, Lepidus, had been deposed, and it remained to be seen which of the two remaining members of that commission was to become supreme. We have seen that, as far as feeling at Rome went, the tide was steadily setting in the direction of Caesar. Antony was quite aware of this, and attempted to win the support of the Senate and republican party by acting in a constitutional manner. He sent an account of his proceedings and arrangements in the East, his *acta* as they were called, and desired that they might be

regularly confirmed by the Senate. He also intimated that he did not desire the renewal of the triumvirate at the end of B.C. 33. His object was to deprive Caesar of the position, while he would himself still have *imperium* in the East, and be so strong that the Senate would not have courage or means to deprive him of it. He hoped also thus to be able to point to his own conduct as more constitutional than that of Caesar, who he felt sure would not willingly give up his power at the same time. But all this failed in its design. His *acta* were of such a nature that the Senate would have probably in any case refused its approbation except under compulsion; and with Caesar present to support the other side it was certain to do so.

The causes of quarrel between the two triumvirs were always increasing. Antony complained that Caesar had exceeded his powers in deposing Lepidus, in taking over the government of the islands once controlled by Sextus Pompeius, as well as Africa, and in enlisting soldiers for himself without sending, according to their agreement, half of the levies to him. Caesar for his part complained that Antony had no right to be in Egypt, which was not a Roman province; that his execution of Sext. Pompeius was illegal; that his treachery to the king of Armenia was a disgrace to Rome; that his connexion with Cleopatra and his acknowledging Caesarion (a son of Cleopatra, of whom Iulius Caesar was supposed to be the father) as a legitimate son of Iulius was a degradation of his office and a menace to himself.

9. **Both Sides prepare for War.** The quarrel came to a head in B.C. 32. The consuls of that year—Gnaeus Domitius Ahenobarbus and C. Sosius—were partisans of Antony. They endeavoured to conceal the most unpopular part of his proceedings, and on the 1st of January, B.C. 32, Sosius delivered a speech in his favour. But at the next meeting Caesar made a reply to this of such a nature that both

consuls left Rome to join Antony, who on being informed of what had occurred made up his mind that he must fight. He set about collecting troops and ships at the island of Samos, and came as far as Corcyra (*Corfu*) on his way to make a descent upon the coasts of Italy. But Caesar too had been active in preparations. The sea was guarded by his ships, and Antony found that he must wait for reinforcements, which he had summoned from all parts of the Empire over which his influence extended. He himself remained at Patrae, while his fleet was in the Ambracian Gulf, and his land forces encamped near the promontory of Actium.

10. **War Proclaimed against Cleopatra**, B.C. 32. There was now civil war; but as usual with the Romans it was disguised. The preparations made by Antony at Samos had been regarded as a hostile demonstration of Cleopatra, and war was accordingly decreed against her. It was well understood, however, to be against Antony. He was designated consul for B.C. 31; but by publishing his will,— in which Caesarion was acknowledged as son of Iulius, and his own children by Cleopatra were put in possession of large territories,—Caesar had produced such an impression against Antony, that the Senate prevented his entering upon the office and deprived him of imperium. They did not actually proclaim him a 'hostis'; but as in the case of other leaders of a *tumultus*, they offered indemnity to all who would quit him before a fixed day,—thus treating him practically as a public enemy.

11. **The Battle of Actium**, 2nd September, B.C. 31. In the first half of B.C. 31 both sides were engaged in mustering their forces. To the aid of Antony came many princes from Asia, and Cleopatra herself accompanied the fleet from Egypt. The collection of so large a force from so many and such distant regions occupied several months, and meanwhile Antony kept himself safe in the Ambracian Gulf, and

THE BATTLE OF ACTIUM.

no operations of importance went on, except that Agrippa in Caesar's interests attacked various points on the Greek coasts, partly to prevent assistance being sent to Antony, and partly in the hope of drawing him from his safe harbourage at Ambracia. Caesar's land forces had crossed from Brundisium (probably to Apollonia), and advanced to attack Antony from the north. He fixed the head-quarters of his fleet at the Sweet Harbour (mouth of the Acheron); and when he found himself not attacked there, moved farther down and occupied the promontory opposite Actium, on which afterwards Nicopolis was built. Skirmishes between the cavalry of the two sides resulted generally in favour of Caesar's troops, and Antony abandoned the northern side of the Strait into the Ambracian Gulf, confining his soldiers to the southern promontory of Actium. The battle that followed was brought about by a movement made on the part of Antony in obedience to the earnest advice of Cleopatra. She was eager to go back to Alexandria, where they would be on their own ground and could, she thought, sufficiently protect themselves from attack. At Actium they were in the position of invaders, against whom the Western parts of the Empire would surely combine. After some hesitation Antony consented. Early on the 2nd of September his fleet began issuing through the straits from the Ambracian Gulf, intending to sail away south. But Caesar had been informed of the movement, and his ships were waiting for them outside. It was a wet day and the sea was rough. Caesar's ships were smaller than those of Antony, and, though only half as numerous (250 to 500), were more manageable in the heavy surf. They could reverse their course promptly and return to the charge, or, after pouring in a volley of darts upon some great galley, could retreat out of shot. Antony's ships were many of them of great size and were furnished with grappling irons, effective if the cast succeeded, but apt to damage the vessel or cause fatal delay if it failed. The battle raged all the afternoon without decisive result. But Cleopatra, whose ship was on the southern wing of the fleet, was in a state of great excitement and terror, and, unable to bear the suspense, gave the signal for the retreat of her ships. Antony saw the movement but not the signal, and, fancying that it was the beginning of a general panic, followed the flying squadron. But though the contagion of flight spread fast among his fleet, a number of vessels still continued the fight long after nightfall, when many were blazing from the firebrands thrown upon them. Caesar spent the night on board ship, and tried to save the crews of the burning vessels. His victory was complete. Next day Antony's land forces either surrendered at once, or trying to make their way home through Macedonia were followed and forced to submit.

12. **Results of the Battle of Actium.** The results of this battle were most important. There was little hope of Antony being able to make a stand again. His Eastern allies would not venture to send him any more help. Even Cleopatra soon showed that she was willing to betray him in hope of getting good terms for herself. The whole of the forces of the West, as well as of Greece and Macedonia, were at Caesar's disposal. He would only have to appear in Asia Minor to secure the obedience of the Asiatic provinces, and the ready alliance of the princes and sovereigns reigning near the frontiers, generally by the permission or under the protection of Rome. Besides this, Caesar's position relatively to that of his rival was infinitely improved. Antony was now a fugitive and a rebel, without that shadow of a legal position which the presence of consuls and a good many Senators had given him in the previous year. Part of the victorious fleet was in pursuit of him, and it would soon appear whether or not his position in Egypt would save him.

13. **Death of Antony and Cleopatra, and complete Supremacy of Caesar**, B.C. 30. Caesar did

not go at once to Egypt, but spent the winter in Asia and Samos, preparing to finish the war by attacking Cleopatra and Antony in Egypt. Antony had tried to get together another army. There were three legions under Q. Pinarius Scarpus in charge of Africa, which he had himself placed there. He first tried to get these: but Pinarius put his messengers to death, and declined all help. Then he tried to make preparations in case of need for a retreat to the far East, and meanwhile both he and Cleopatra sent messages and presents to Caesar, hoping either to conciliate him or to blind him to their real plans. But they were disappointed in all their devices. The ships, which they were preparing to assist their flight in the Red Sea, were burnt by the Arabs at the instigation of the governor of Syria; the princes and states in Asia refused all help; while some gladiators who were in training at Cyzicus and did attempt to join him, were stopped on their march. His messages, the mission of his son Antyllus with money and presents, the surrender of one of the murderers of Iulius, —all failed to draw an answer from Caesar, who, however, kept up secret communications in an apparently friendly spirit with Cleopatra, whom he hoped to detach from Antony and to induce to put herself in his power. In the early part of B.C. 30 Antony found himself on the point of being attacked on two sides; at Paraetonium by C. Cornelius Gallus, who had taken over the army of Scarpus, and at Pelusium by Caesar himself. He made an attempt to beat back Gallus, but failing in this, hastily marched back to Pelusium. A slight success over some of Caesar's men, who were wearied with their voyage and march, induced him to risk a general engagement. He was decisively beaten, and after a vain attempt to escape by sea, gave up all hope and stabbed himself with his dagger. The wound was not immediately mortal, and he caused himself to be carried to the Mausoleum, where Cleopatra had taken refuge, and there died in her arms. Caesar at once occupied Alexandria, and caused Cleopatra to be brought to the palace. She vainly tried her fascinations on him; and when she found that she could move neither his love nor his pity, and that he intended to take her to Rome to adorn his triumph, she eluded the vigilance of her guards and put an end to her life, as it was currently reported, by the bite of an asp conveyed to her in a basket of fruit.

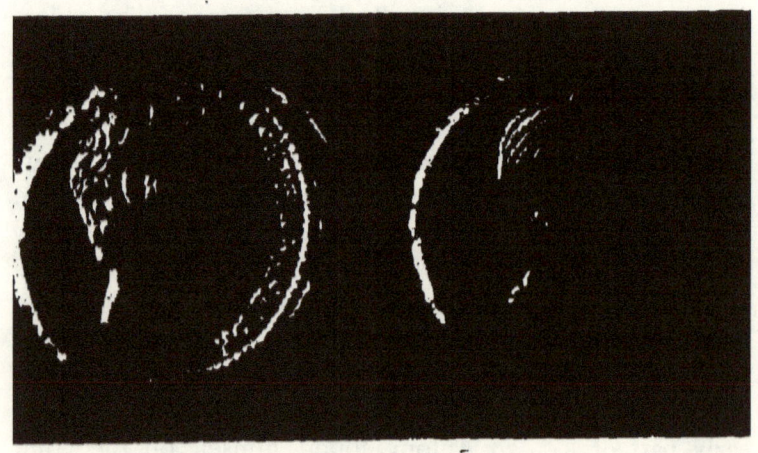

M. ANTONIUS AND CLEOPATRA.

CHAPTER XXI.

THE PRINCIPATE OF AUGUSTUS, B.C. 30 TO A.D. 14.

> 1. *Caesar (Augustus) practically a monarch, but with republican titles.* 2. *The Roman Empire as it was under Augustus.* 3. *The wars of Augustus—in Spain; near the Alps; on the Rhine and Danube; in Illyricum and Pannonia; in the East.* 4. *Why the Empire was from time to time extended.* 5. *Britain not part of the Empire under Augustus.* 6. *Augustus as a restorer and social reformer.* 7. *Augustus as a Legislator.* 8. *The friends and ministers of Augustus.* 9. *The family of Augustus and the succession.* 10. *The last days and death of Augustus.* 11. *Poets and historians of the time of Augustus.* 12. *General review of what Augustus had to do and how he did it.*

1. **Caesar practically a Monarch, but with Republican Titles.** The defeat and death of Antony left Caesar virtually supreme in the Empire. There was no one now who had sufficient influence or following to withstand him. The obsequious Senate hastened to vote him all kinds of honours, and he felt so secure of his position at Rome that he stayed another year in the East to settle affairs there. The most important of the powers conferred on him was the *tribunicia potestas* for life. The tribunes had the right of staying all proceedings of the other magistrates by their veto, of preventing a valid decree of the Senate being passed, of summoning and consulting the Senate, of proposing laws in the *Comitia*, and of giving assistance to any citizen who appealed to

them against a magistrate's sentence. Now, the old rule still held good that a patrician could not be a tribune, and Caesar both by a special act in his uncle's life-time and by his adoption into the *gens Iulia*, was a patrician. He could not therefore be a tribune, but he was to have all the rights and powers of a tribune, and not for one year only, like the other tribunes, but for life. One of the privileges of this office, that which rendered his person sacred, had already been voted to him in B.C. 36, and was of course included in the *tribunicia potestas* now decreed to him. He had also the right of being elected every year as one of the consuls; he was to have a casting vote in all criminal trials, and his name was to be mentioned in all public prayers and private libations. Next year (B.C. 29) after celebrating three triumphs—for his campaigns in Illyricum, for his victory at Actium, and for the capture of Alexandria—he caused the temple of Ianus to be closed as a sign of the restoration of peace, which had only been twice done before in the whole history of Rome, and set about various reforms in the Senate and State, as well as a restoration of public buildings. Next year (B.C. 28) when he and Agrippa as consuls held the census, he was entered on the roll of the Senators as *Princeps Senatus*,—a position of great dignity though it did not add to his powers. Thus in Rome he was, under the old republican titles, absorbing the various parts of government, and taking rank as head of the State. In the next year (B.C. 27) the first great step was taken to give him formally the same authority throughout the Empire, though he represented it as in fact a "restoration of the republic." This was done by making a new arrangement as to the provinces. Caesar, or (as he was henceforth called) Augustus, was head of the army; that seemed to have been all along acknowledged as the result of the imperium which he held as triumvir and had never laid down. Now in some of the provinces there were no legions, only a small number of soldiers forming a body-guard to the governor, or performing police duties. In these provinces governors were as of old to be allotted by the Senate from ex-consuls or ex-praetors, with the general title and powers of proconsuls. In others, where a certain number of legions was always stationed, Augustus was to have supreme authority. Instead of proconsuls they were to be governed by his deputies with the rank of praetor (*legati pro praetore*), who were named by him for such time as he chose, and were answerable directly to him. He had what was called proconsular authority (*imperium proconsulare*) in these provinces, and their governors were his deputies or *legati*.[1] But though his supreme authority was thus nominally confined to the imperial provinces, he in fact exercised it in the others also; for when he chose he could control the allotment of governors by his other powers, and in all he appointed a *procurator*, who had charge of the collection and disposal of the tribute, and was answerable directly to him. The next step taken, in B.C. 23, recognized this by making his *imperium proconsulare* superior (*maius*) to that of the governors of all provinces alike. He was therefore now actually first in all departments of the State, and is henceforth called *Princeps*, or Head of the State. This particular title was not, like the others, definitely conferred on him, or at least we do not know of any law or decree of the Senate doing so; nor did it, like the old republican titles, give him definite powers. Nevertheless it was a recognized designation, meaning that in whatever functions he per-

---

[1] The original imperial provinces were: (1) All Spain except Baetica (*i.e.* Tarraconensis and Lusitania). (2) All the Gauls (Narbonensis, Lugdunensis, Aquitania, Belgica with the Germanies when occupied). (3) Syria (Phoenicia and coele-Syria). (4) Cilicia. (5) Cyprus. (6) Egypt. Afterwards he gave back Narbonensis and Cyprus to the Senate, but took over Dalmatia (Pannonia and Noricum), and Sardinia for a time. All subsequently added provinces were imperial,—Galatia, Moesia, Alpes Maritimae, Alpes Cottiae, Alpes Penninae.

formed he took precedence of all colleagues, and practically could perform them as he chose. The proconsular power was not, as of old, forfeited by entering the city. He could exercise it at all times and in all places. It was not therefore necessary for him to be consul, and he did not take the consulship again till B.C. 5. His most important civil power was the *tribunician*, and after B.C. 23 he counts the years of his reign, starting from the 25th of June in that year, and reckoning the years of his *tribunicia potestas*.

2. **The Roman Empire under Augustus.** The Empire as Augustus found it in B.C. 30 did not differ much from what it had been at the death of his great-uncle in B.C. 44. Nor did he add very greatly to it in the course of his long reign. During the civil wars in fact two of the provinces, Cilicia and Syria, were at times almost separated from the Empire; and though Mauretania was added as a province in B.C. 33 on the death of its king, it was restored in B.C. 25 to king Iuba. In the same year a new province of Galatia and Lycaonia was formed (B.C. 25), and some years later (the exact date is not known, but before B.C. 6) Moesia, answering to the modern Servia and Bulgaria, was also reduced to the form of a province, as a barrier of the Empire on the Danube. Moreover, when Augustus reorganized Gaul (B.C. 16-14) in four provinces—Narbonensis, Aquitania, Lugdunensis, Belgica—two districts along the Lower Rhine, called Germania Superior and Germania Inferior were also occupied and partly organized, while some minor provinces were also organized, as we shall see, in the Alpine regions. Lastly Egypt, after the death of Cleopatra (B.C. 30), was also taken over as a province. It was, however, in a special position. Partly because of its importance as a corn growing country, and partly because of the seditious character of the Alexandrians, it was attached in a special manner to the

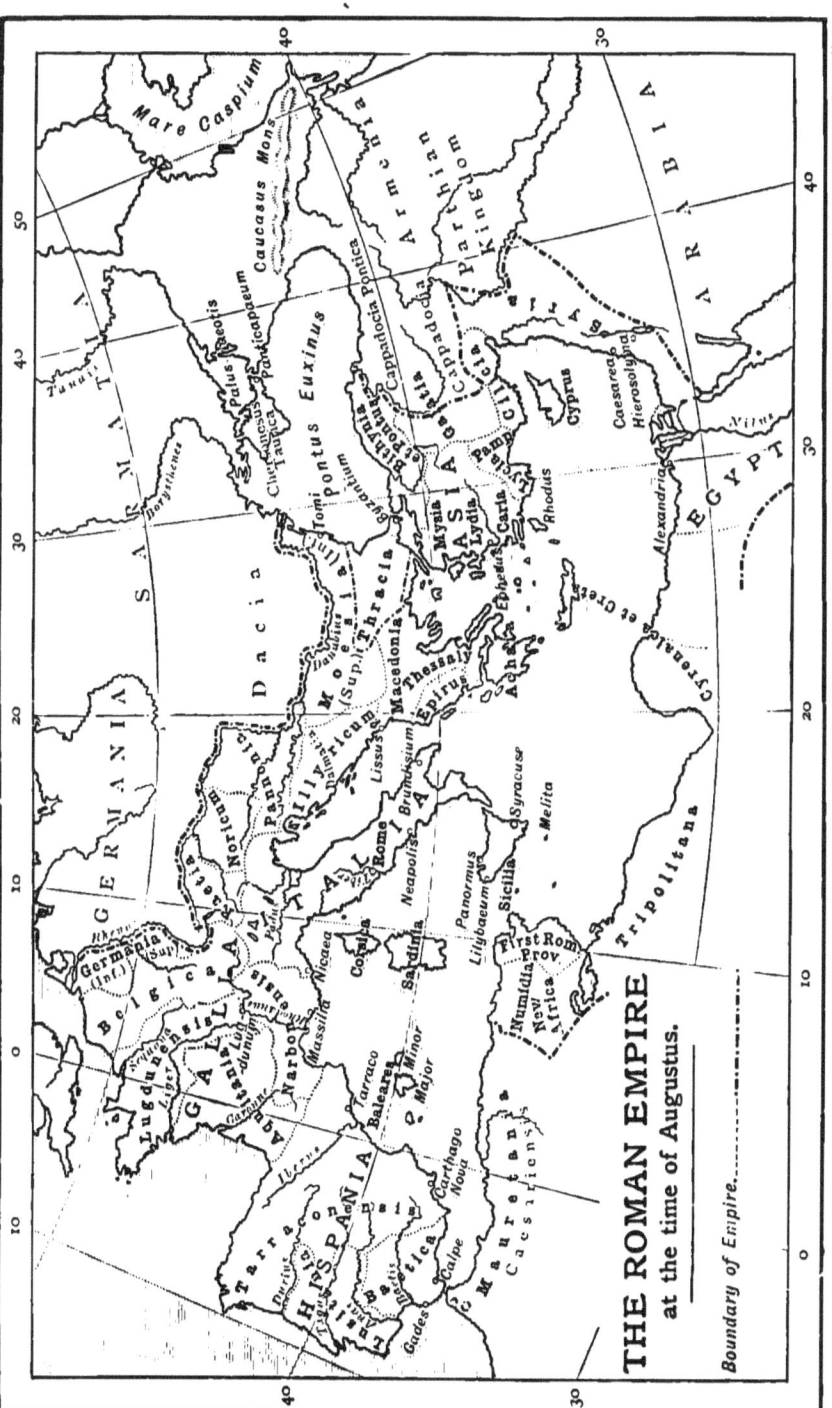

Emperor, who took both the revenues of the domain lands and the taxes into his own treasury (*fiscus*), and administered it by a *praefectus* with three legions, an office confined to men not of Senatorial rank. In fact no Senator was allowed to go there without license from the Emperor. Augustus, then, during his reign strengthened the Empire on the Rhine and the Danube, and secured a great source of corn supply for Italy by adding the new province of Egypt, but otherwise did not extend its limits. For a time, indeed, the part of Germany which lies between the Rhine and the Elbe was in Roman hands. But an attempt to strictly enforce the tribute in it brought about the greatest disaster of the reign, and after the fall of Varus (A.D. 9), the Rhine became once more the boundary of the Empire.

3. **The Wars of Augustus.** But though Augustus made no great addition to the number of Roman provinces, he had in his own person, or in that of his legates, to undertake many wars, either to suppress risings in the provinces themselves, or to defend their frontiers from neighbouring barbarians. The only war in which after B.C. 30 he was personally engaged was that against the Cantabri, the fierce and warlike highlanders of N.W. Spain, who were a terror to the province of Tarraconensis. He went on an expedition against them in B.C. 25, which did not prove very successful, and it was not till B.C. 19 that his great minister Agrippa finally subdued them. But the Empire was chiefly vulnerable on the north-west along the Rhine and the Danube, and in the east along the Euphrates. We have seen how much the Romans dreaded the Parthians, and their invasion of the province of Syria. Crassus had lost his army and his life in fighting them in B.C. 53, and though his quaestor C. Cassius repulsed them two years afterwards, Antony, or his lieutenants, was constantly engaged with them between B.C. 38 and his

death. It was one of the triumphs of Augustus, on which the poets are most eager to dwell, that during his reign danger from the Parthians was avoided, and that they not only respected the territory of the Empire, but sought his favour by restoring the standards and trophies which they had taken from Crassus and Antony. In return Augustus gave an undertaking to abstain from entering Mesopotamia, while he retained a kind of overlordship in Armenia. There were, however, some warlike expeditions in the east during his reign, such as the invasion of Arabia in B.C. 24, under Aelius Gallus; some skirmishing with Parthian invaders of Armenia, under his grandson Gaius in A.D. 2-3; and a war with Queen Candace of Aethiopia in B.C. 22, under Gaius Petronius. But by far the most important military affairs were those in the north-west, both in the Alpine regions on the northern frontier of Italy, and farther north still along the Lower Rhine and Danube. The struggle with the barbarians in these districts lasted with intervals from about B.C. 17 to the end of the life of Augustus. He did not command himself in the wars needful for protecting the frontiers, though for nearly three years he remained in Gaul (B.C. 16-14) or in north Italy to direct operations or to settle terms with the tribes. But he was served by a number of very able commanders, especially his two stepsons, Tiberius (afterwards Emperor) and Drusus, who in B.C. 15-14 conquered the Rhaeti (in the Eastern or Tridentine Alps), while in the west three new districts were organized more or less completely as provinces: (1) First, one under the name of the Maritime Alps, along the River Var, and including the modern Savoy and Nice; (2) secondly, Alpes Cottiae, in what is now north Italy, with capital Susa; (3) and, thirdly, Alpes Penninae, the Swiss valley of the Rhone, Canton du Valois. Having thus secured north Italy, Drusus was sent to the northern part of Belgica

(Holland), where along the Lower Rhine, on the left bank as far up as Cologne, two districts were marked out as requiring the presence of armies, and called Germania Superior and Germania Inferior. For some purposes they belonged to the province of Belgica, but at any rate from a military point of view they were separate provinces. In B.C. 16 some German tribes (Sicambri, Usipetes, Tencteri) had defeated a Roman army under M. Lollius. This disaster brought Augustus into Gaul. For a time, either by show of force or by his negotiations, the German tribes on the right bank of the Rhine were kept quiet, and when Augustus returned to Rome at the beginning of B.C. 14 he is said to have pacified Spain, Gaul, and Germany. But very soon the Germans moved again, and in B.C. 13-10 Drusus fought with and defeated the Frisii, Chauci, Sicambri, Chatti, and Cherusci, while Tiberius was engaged in subduing the Dalmatians and Pannonians. Roman power was thus extended beyond the Rhine to the Elbe. Drusus died by an accident in B.C. 9: but until the great disaster of P. Quintilius Varus, Roman Germany, in somewhat loose fashion, extended to the Elbe. Before that disaster, from about 1 A.D., there were frequent and dangerous movements in Germany, in which Tiberius was again engaged (A.D. 4-5); and after the defeat of Varus (A.D. 9) the Roman frontier was again pushed back to the Rhine. At his death, therefore, Augustus left the Empire much as he found it in regard to extent, and felt very strongly that it was as large as could be properly defended or administered. His last charge to his successors was, to be content with it as it was.

4. **Why the Empire was from time to time extended.** Such a policy however is not capable of being precisely carried out. Where there is a long frontier closely watched by hostile tribes, always ready to seize any opportunity of making raids across it, there will always

seem some necessity for occupying territory so as to push the enemy farther and farther away. Therefore we find succeeding emperors engaged both on the Rhine and Danube, as well as on the Euphrates, in military expeditions or in organizing new provinces. But in spite of such efforts it was after all across the Rhine and the Danube that the nations were to come who were destined to break up the Roman Empire and to renew it again in a different fashion; and from far away in the centre of Asia came other hordes who later still were to do the same for the eastern half of the Empire. This does not come within the limits of our history; but it is interesting to mark that Augustus had to struggle with the same dangers as his successors for many centuries after his death, the same dangers which eventually proved fatal.

5. **Britain not taken by Augustus.** Our own country cannot be reckoned as part of the Roman Empire during his life-time. Iulius Caesar had imposed tribute on some British tribes in B.C. 54; but we never hear of it being paid, or of Roman officers going to the island. We do know, however, that certain British princes visited the court of Augustus, and we may presume that it was either in reference to this tribute, or in order to invoke his interference in local disputes. Augustus did once at least seriously intend to go to Britain, but troubles in Gaul prevented him, and the idea was never carried out. It was not till the reign of Claudius (A.D. 41-54) that there was a province of Britain.

6. **Augustus as a Restorer and Social Reformer.** But in spite of these wars the reign of Augustus was on the whole a peaceful one. After Actium he was, during the course of his long reign, absent from Italy at different times, about twelve years in all. The rest of the forty-five years he spent in or near Rome, and took great pains in establishing the government of the country and city,

in legislation, and in reforms of all sorts. The city was divided into fourteen regions, and 265 parishes (*vici*), for various purposes of local government; a police force (*cohortes urbanae*) was organized to keep order; a regular fire-brigade was established in consequence of the frequent fires which occurred; great pains were taken to clean the bed of the Tiber and to keep up the embankment against floods, regular commissioners being appointed for the purpose. He encouraged both by his influence and example the restoration of decayed temples, and the erection of theatres and public buildings. He built a new and very splendid forum, in addition to the completion of that begun by Iulius, and was able with truth to make the famous boast that he had found Rome brick and left it marble. Much also was done to make Italy safe and well ordered. He himself superintended the repair and maintenance of the great North Road (*via Flaminia*) with its bridges and stations, and induced other rich men, especially those who earned triumphs, to do the same in regard to other roads as well as public buildings in the city. He divided Italy into eleven regions, apparently for police purposes, though we are not distinctly told the object or result of this division; he restored and re-peopled many of the old *coloniae* and *municipia* which had suffered in the civil wars, and he tried to encourage the citizens to return to their farming and other country pursuits. He maintained fleets at Ravenna on the east, at Misenum on the west coast, and a third at Forum Iulii (*Fréjus*) in Gaul, to protect commerce from piracy, and to maintain the safety of the shores. He established a system of posts along the great roads in Italy and the rest of the Empire, that there might be a ready means of communication with the capital; and in many of the provinces he established towns with the rank of colonies or *municipia*, whose citizens had either the full Roman franchise or the partial franchises called

Latinitas. He worked with the object in view of knitting this whole vast Empire as nearly as possible together as one body, while maintaining at the same time many of the privileges of Italy, and making the citizenship a reward of loyalty, and its withdrawal a punishment for violence or disloyalty.

7. **Augustus as a Legislator.** While thus working for the whole Empire, its safety and happiness, Augustus was not unmindful of the mischiefs which were prevalent at Rome itself, and had contributed largely to the fall of the constitution. He wished the Senate still to have high dignity and power, and he took great pains to remove from it unworthy men, and to compel suitable persons to serve in the old republican offices, which were still maintained, and which gave an *entrée* to it. He had a great dislike to an idle aristocracy, enjoying wealth and rank, and doing nothing for the State. Many of the old families, finding that they could no longer look forward to amassing great fortunes by uncontrolled government of the provinces, tried to shirk the offices at Rome which used to lead to such appointments, as only causing useless expense. Especially a seat in the Senate, which was no longer necessary for high employment in the provinces, since the Emperor selected whom he chose, seemed less and less desirable to many. To counteract this Augustus always treated the Senate with studied respect, constantly brought matters of State before it, and gave it influence by referring to its control the trial of malversation in the provinces and cases of high treason; while persons of a certain rank, if their means fell short, received presents from him to enable them to maintain their dignity as Senators. At the same time he took care to support the privileges and dignity of the next *ordo* in the State, the rich middle class, or Equestrian order, from which was drawn not only new members of the Senate but a large part of the officers

employed by him in the provinces. While trying thus to make the wealthier classes conscious of their duties to the State, he attempted also to raise the standard of morality and to encourage family life. Severe penalties were imposed on adultery, stricter regulations made as to divorce, and marriage was encouraged by the granting of special privileges and exemptions to married men and the fathers of children; while those who remained unmarried beyond a certain time were not only taxed more heavily than before, but were unable to take more than half of any legacy or property left them. Augustus was also a restorer of religion. It is always difficult to say how far a man of that age believed the popular theology. Probably Augustus regarded it with a kind of indulgent scepticism, as incapable of being proved or disproved. But he believed in Divine Providence in some form, and was apparently convinced that it was for the good of the State that old rituals and observances should be maintained. He therefore diligently restored temples, and prided himself on reviving ancient ceremonies. He was not foolish enough to regard himself as divine, yet (with some reluctance) he allowed temples in some provinces to be erected to the "genius of Rome and Caesar." The fact was that he believed in himself and his mission, and by the convenient assumption that each man had a "genius,"—a kind of divine presence specially attached to himself, and hardly distinguishable from himself,—such worship could be paid without flagrant absurdity according to the feelings of the time.

8. **The Friends and Ministers of Augustus.** One of the secrets of the success of Augustus was that, unlike his great-uncle, he had the faculty of attaching friends to himself who remained faithful. His principal ministers during a large part of his reign were the men who, being about his own age, had been the friends of his boyhood.

The most important of these was **M. Vipsanius Agrippa**. He was born in the same year as Augustus; was with him at Apollonia in B.C. 44; helped him in the siege of Perusia, and in his struggles with Antony; put down risings in Gaul (B.C. 38); was the chief agent in the defeat of Sext. Pompeius in B.C. 35; commanded the army for him in Illyricum (B.C. 35), and the fleet at Actium (B.C. 32-1); crushed the Cantabrians (B.C. 25-19); and did a great deal to put down risings in the East

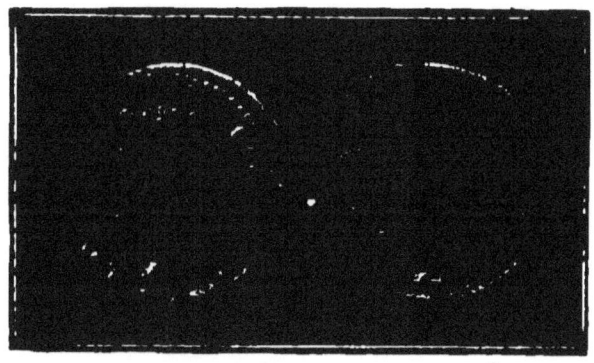

M. VIPSANIUS AGRIPPA

(B.C. 17-13). In fact, till his death in B.C. 12 he continually served the Emperor with complete fidelity and brilliant success. He was indeed marked out at one time as his successor, being married to his niece Marcella, and afterwards to his daughter Iulia; yet when Augustus designated his nephew Marcellus as his heir, Agrippa, though he was naturally disappointed, and retired for a time from Rome, yet never faltered in his loyalty. Never Emperor had a greater or more faithful servant. He was not only a successful general, but he supported his master's views in all respects, and expended immense sums (at his wish) on public buildings and improvements in Rome. Another friend, who also served Augustus faithfully to the end, was **C. Cilnius Maecenas.** Unlike Agrippa he was not a military hero. He was a luxurious valetudinarian, who avoided office or conspicuous positions. Nevertheless to his sagacity and fidelity Augustus owed much of his own success. He trusted him entirely in times of difficulty, even allowing him to use his signet ring at Rome when he was absent; and though towards the end of his life (he died in B.C. 8) some coldness rose between them, Maecenas never swerved in his fidelity. Only two of Augustus' friends—Salvidienus Rufus and Cornelius Gallus—committed acts of disloyalty against him which entailed fatal consequences. His selection of military commanders seems (with the exception of Varus) to have been successful, and his two stepsons, Tiberius and Drusus, both showed themselves men of energy and excellent soldiers. He was curiously fortunate in almost everything he undertook or had done for him. Even his survival to seventy-seven may be regarded as a stroke of good fortune, for his health had been feeble from boyhood, and he had at frequent intervals severe, and what threatened to be fatal, illnesses. His first real wife Scribonia was much older than himself, and he had married her for political reasons. Immediately after the birth of his only child Iulia, he divorced her, and almost at once married **Livia**, whom he caused Tiberius Nero to divorce. But even this, which to our ideas seems an unpromising beginning, turned out to his happiness. Livia retained his devoted attachment and respect to the end:—"Good-bye, never forget our married life"—were the last words of the dying Emperor; his last conscious action was to kiss her lips.

9. **The Family of Augustus and the Succession.** Though Augustus was happy in his marriage, he was not fortunate in regard to the family from which his successor should come. The position of the *Princeps* was

indeed in no sense hereditary. When Augustus died the various offices which he held, and which combined made him *Princeps*, would be vacant, and there was no known way of conferring them upon one man except by the ordinary forms of election, by a lex, or by votes of the Senate. Still as he went on holding these offices, and making the position of *Princeps* more and more a recognized and official one, it seemed to be taken for granted that one of his family would succeed him. But as one after another of these died this became impossible. As observed above, Augustus never had but one child—Iulia : his wife Livia brought him no children. But by Roman law adopted sons took the same rights as real sons. It was always open therefore for Caesar to put one of his relations or any one else in this position. At first, then, he looked out for a successor among the descendants of his sister Octavia, to whom he was much attached. Now Octavia was twice married. By her first husband, C. Claudius Marcellus, she had a son and two daughters. This son (the young Marcellus of Vergil) was early promoted by Augustus, with the avowed intention of making him his heir. He died, however, in B.C. 23. Octavia married a second time in B.C. 37 M. Antonius, by whom she had two daughters. For a time it was from the descendants of these that a successor was looked for, and, in point of fact, after one intervening reign, the imperial family was carried on by their descendants. But after B.C. 21 this idea was abandoned for another. In that year Agrippa, who was married to Octavia's daughter Marcella, at the wish of Augustus divorced her and married the Emperor's own daughter Iulia. Within three years he had two sons born of her, Gaius in B.C. 20, Lucius in B.C. 17. In this latter year Augustus adopted both these boys, and had them educated with an avowed view to the succession. They grew up to manhood, and filled some of the magistracies; and one after the other had the title of *princeps iuventutis*. But in A.D. 2 Lucius Caesar died at Marseilles, and Gaius Caesar in A.D. 4 of a slight wound in Asia. Agrippa himself died in B.C. 12. After his death Iulia bore a posthumous son, but he was said to be of a feeble and vicious disposition, and though Augustus adopted him in A.D. 4, on the death of Gaius, he shortly afterwards repudiated him. There were not wanting people who said that the deaths of Gaius and Lucius, and the rejection of Agrippa Postumus, were the work of Livia, who wished her son Tiberius to be the successor. At any rate Augustus was now reduced to this measure. Tiberius was of an unpopular and reserved disposition, but Augustus, though he knew his faults, seems to have been attached to him. He adopted him in A.D. 4, at the same time as Agrippa Postumus, and after Agrippa's rejection Tiberius was treated as the heir and successor. He received *Tribunicia potestas* along with his adoptive father for ten years in A.D. 4, that he might be possessed of one of the most important functions of the *Princeps* in case of Augustus's death; and, in order to still farther provide for the succession, Augustus required him to adopt Germanicus, son of his dead brother Drusus, though he had a son of his own. From this time Tiberius was the undisputed successor. While the Emperor's adopted sons Gaius and Lucius were alive he had retired to Rhodes and lived there in sullen retirement; but from this time forth he takes his place, and is only absent from Italy when commanding in Germany or Illyricum.

10. **Death of Augustus.** The later years of Augustus were saddened by the losses in his family, and by the military disasters across the Rhine. The destruction of Varus is said to have affected him in an extraordinary manner; and though the exertions of Tiberius and his nephew Germanicus did something to repair the disaster,

there was good reason for anxiety as to the safety of the Empire on the Rhine frontier. Nevertheless he retained considerable vigour and cheerfulness to the last year of his life. The end came in the course of a tour through the pleasant scenes of the Campania coast. He accompanied his adopted son and heir, Tiberius, as far as Beneventum on his way to Brundisium, from which he was going on an expedition to Illyricum. Having bidden him good-bye, Augustus was going slowly back to Rome, halting at Naples, where he attended some Greek games, and joined cheerfully in a banquet that followed them. But at Astura he had caught a chill, now followed by symptoms of dysentery. Tiberius was hurriedly sent for to return, but found the Emperor dead. He had reached Nola and the house in which his father had died fifty-four years before. Finding himself dying, he admitted his friends to a last interview, asking them with a half-sad, half-playful humour whether "he had played the farce of life well," quoting the familiar *plaudite*, which ended Latin plays. And when they had left the room, as he was asking for news of one of his family who had been ill, he suddenly felt that death had come, and as he tried to utter a last word of affection to Livia, and once more kiss her lips, he expired (19th August, A.D. 14). His will had been made the year before, and deposited with the Vestal Virgins, and with it two other rolls, one containing an account of the business of the Empire, the other a statement drawn up by himself of his own achievements from the moment when the assassination of Iulius called him into public life. He wished this to be inscribed on columns in Rome, and in different parts of the Empire. Fortunately one copy was written on the walls of a temple at Ancyra in Galatia, in Greek and Latin, the greater part of which is legible to this day, and tells us at any rate what Augustus believed himself to have accomplished.

11. **Poets and Historians of the time of Augustus**: It is common to speak of the age of Augustus as the golden age of Latin Literature, and indeed most of the authors whose works have survived, and are considered to display the highest standard of Latin style, not only lived in his reign, but were patronized and encouraged by him, and often lived in intimacy with him. But after all those that have survived are few. The greatest of Roman writers, M. Tullius Cicero, was put to death in B.C. 43, when Augustus was only twenty years old, and can hardly be reckoned as belonging to this age, though he knew and corresponded with the young Octavian. There were histories of various kinds written during this period that have been lost, such as the History of the Civil Wars to the death of Iulius, by C. Asinius Pollio, and a continuation of it by Messala. There was too a great history of Macedonia by Pompeius Trogus, of which we have an epitome or abbreviation by Iustinus. A very learned man named Terentius Varro, a contemporary of Cicero, lived till B.C. 28, and one of his works on Agriculture has survived, as well as part of another on the Latin Language. But the great historian who lived at this period, and of whose work we have most, was **Titus Livius**. He was born in B.C. 59, about three years after Augustus, at or near Padua; he died in A.D. 17, also three years after him. He wrote a great History of Rome in 140 books from the foundation to B.C. 9, and though the earlier parts are perhaps fanciful and pretend to more certainty than was possible to obtain, the style is beautiful, and there is an evident intention of being honest. In the later books (which are unfortunately lost) he told the story of his own age, and in his account of the Civil War took so much the anti-Caesarean side that Augustus used laughingly to call him the Pompeian. It is to the credit of the Emperor that he supported and patronized him in spite of this.

THE POETS.

However, it was the poets that lived in the time of Augustus that have been the great glory of the period, and who enjoyed both the favour and munificence of Augustus. There were many poets who had a considerable reputation in their day, but those whose fame has proved lasting are Vergil, Horace, Tibullus, and Propertius. Of these the greatest name is that of **P. Vergilius Maro**, who was born in B.C. 70, and died in B.C. 19, being thus about seven years older than Augustus. He was born near Mantua, and suffered from the confiscations carried out in B.C. 41-40, though by the influence of Asinius Pollio he got his lands back. It was while on a visit to Rome on this business that he seems to have been introduced to Augustus, with whom he always remained in high favour, as well as with his great minister Maecenas. Vergil was not only a delightful poet who celebrated the charms of country life and the beauties of Italy, but he became a representative of his age and country. His greatest poem, the *Aeneid*, is a national epic meant to glorify the origin and destiny of Rome, and incidentally the descent and high mission of Augustus. It keeps permanently alive not only the spirit of the age but the highest view of Roman history.

Q. Horatius Flaccus (B.C. 65-8), equally delightful as a poet, is on quite a different footing. His Odes were the first really successful attempts on a considerable scale to introduce lyrical poetry into Latin literature; but he too made them the means of celebrating heroic legends and great heroes of Roman history, besides preserving the feelings of admiration and reverence with which the Roman world of his day regarded Augustus and his family. His Satires and Epistles sometimes show us the lighter side of social life, sometimes touch rather superficially on the Greek philosophy, which served the sceptical age as a kind of religion or code of morals. **Aulus Tibullus** (B.C. 59-18) wrote mostly love songs or the praises of quiet life.

He too had his patron among the great men of Augustus' court, M. Valerius Messalla, whom he accompanied in his expedition to Gaul. **Sex. Aurelius Propertius** was another of the poets patronized by Maecenas, and more or less connected with the court. He was considerably younger than those mentioned above (though the dates of his birth and death are uncertain), and never so popular as a poet. He, however, helped to glorify Augustus and make his reign famous. Lastly, **P. Ovidius Naso,** born in B.C. 43 at Sulmo, came of a well-to-do equestrian family, and was intended by his father for a political and official career. But his bent for poetry and for a life of leisure and freedom, or perhaps frivolity, was too strong, and he declined to stand for any office that would bring him into the Senate. He does not seem to have belonged to the Maecenas set, though he knew Propertius and some others who did, and had heard Horace recite his poems, which he only did in private society. He was only on the fringe of this inner circle, and probably was never admitted to close intimacy with Augustus, although his *Fasti* are said to have been undertaken by the Emperor's wish. Yet he lived with men of high rank, and his third wife was a daughter of Fabius Maximus and intimate with relations of Augustus and Livia. He is almost the only instance of severity on the part of Augustus to a literary man as such. In A.D. 8 he was suddenly banished, and forced to live the remainder of his days at Tomi on the Black Sea, about forty miles south of the Danube, and on the extreme verge of the Empire, where he remained till his death in A.D. 18. The cause of his banishment is not really known. It was unlike Augustus to punish a poet for his work—mere personal satire he laughed at, as he could afford to do; and though the reason given was the immorality of Ovid's verse, that would justly have applied to many other writers of the day. The most common theory is that he knew something as to the misconduct of the Emperor's granddaughter Iulia, who was banished in the same year. So far as Augustus employed or influenced the employment of his muse, it was again, as in the case of Vergil, employed in stirring up interest in Roman religion and the great history of Rome. The *Fasti* or Calendar, with its days marked by great events, gave him the opportunity of dilating on Roman heroes, as well as on the chief points in the career of Augustus himself, and thus he became a national as well as a court poet.

One of the points in the character of Augustus drawn by Suetonius was his support of men of genius, and a true picture of his court cannot be conceived without taking into consideration this group of literary men which surrounded him and to whom he often gave lavishly. They repaid him by making his praises known far and wide, quite outbalancing the few who wrote against him. It is a great thing for a man's fame both in his life-time and after his death to have the good word of poets and men of letters. It was one of the misfortunes of Iulius Caesar that he had most of such men against him. Augustus neglected no means of making his government liked and his person revered.

12. **What Augustus had to do and how he did it.** The reign of Augustus may be reckoned as extending from B.C. 30 to A.D. 14, forty-four years, during which he was ceaselessly employed in defending or ruling the Empire. The general result of his government was without doubt to increase the happiness of the world. We must remember what the Roman Empire was. It consisted of a vast number of different nations, not at one in origin, habits, or language. At the census of B.C. 28 the number of full citizens returned was little more than four millions. That must have been scarcely a tenth

of the inhabitants of the Empire. Therefore Augustus had to govern a large dominion in which only a tenth of the inhabitants had political rights, or in the political sense, freedom. He did it in a way which made men on the whole happier and more contented. How was this? Partly, no doubt, it was the effect of the previous harshness of the Republic. There had been a time when in south-eastern Europe and in Asia numberless communities, many of them quite small, cared for nothing so much as political independence, the right of conducting their own affairs, and making wars or alliances as they chose. The severe rule of the Republic had crushed that spirit. Men were content now with being allowed to manage nothing more than municipal business, if only they had protection from violence and oppression, and could pursue their trades, cultivate their farms, and grow rich by merchandise without being ill-used by imperial magistrates or harried and robbed by barbarians or pirates. Now it was just this security which Augustus gave them. He took care that the magistrates sent out to govern did not oppress or rob the people, he kept the sea free from pirates, and defended the countries bordered by dangerous barbarians. The *pax Romana* was enforced everywhere; and yet in quiet provinces there was no great army to exhaust or overawe the people. No wonder then, that after generations of oppression, or miseries from civil and border wars, these peoples were inclined to regard Augustus as a *praesens Deus*—almost a god of peace and security. The same sentiments prevailed in Italy. "Oh, best guardian of the race of Romulus," writes Horace when Augustus had been three years absent, "return! . . . your country calls for you with vows and prayer . . . for when you are here the ox plods up and down the fields in safety; Ceres and bounteous blessing cheer our farms; our sailors speed o'er seas infested by no pirate; credit is kept unspotted; crime is checked; family life purified; none fears the invasion of Parthian or German ... each man closes a peaceful day on his native hills, trains his vines to the widowed trees, and home returning, light of heart, quaffs his wine and blesses you as his god!" It was this sentiment, though not expressed always in such lyrical terms, that made the success of Augustus. He was at home and abroad the pledge of peace and security. Accordingly, though there were still many who in theory preferred the old Republican form of government (which, indeed, Augustus professed to maintain), there were never in all this long reign any plots or conspiracies of importance against his person. The few that did occur he could afford to treat with magnanimity and wise leniency. Augustus was a great statesman. Within certain limits he could endure opposition without feeling angry with opponents or treating them harshly. Yet he could be severe at times, for he loved justice and order, and thought loyalty to his government was a moral duty. His tastes and habits were simple. He disliked display and pomp, long banquets, and much wine. Perhaps he was, as some said, cold-blooded and deficient in enthusiasm. Yet his family affections were warm and constant; he seldom lost a friend; he liked to have children about him; enjoyed the company of men of letters, and was courteous and gay in society. His health was always delicate, and it is not impossible that he may have been really sincere in his twice expressed wish to retire from his position and restore the republican machinery to full working order. But whether he was sincere or no, the thing was plainly impossible. Disorder and party spirit were only put to sleep, they were not dead. The restraining hand once off, the eager rivalry for office and plunder was ready to begin again. The Senate could not secure the loyalty of legions and their commanders;

nor could the rabble of Rome, idle, needy, and venal, be trusted to select magistrates who should afterwards, without training or high character, have a prescriptive right to govern provinces and command armies, without a supreme master to recall or punish them. Augustus was not the first or the last man who has found himself bound to a task, which he could not avoid if he would, and which has ended in becoming so much a part of himself that he would not lay it aside even if he could.

REMAINS OF THE ROSTRA OF IULIUS.

INDEX.

Abydos, siege of, 120.
Acarnania, 121.
Achaean League, the, 88, 114, 121, 133.
Acheron, R., 299.
Achillas, 266.
Acilius Glabrio, M', in Greece, 123, 124, 133. Governor of Bithynia and Pontus, 205.
Acrocorinthus, 113, 121, 122.
Actium, battle of, 194, 298-300, 315.
Adherbal, 157.
Aediles, 37, 38, 73.
Aedui, 241, 242.
Aeginium, 264.
Aegusae, battle of, 82.
Aemilius Claudius, L., 50.
Aemilius Lepidus, M., revolt of, 197.
Aemilius Lepidus, M. (Triumvir), 259, 261, 273, 285-287, 289, 292, 293, 295.
Aemilius Papus, Q., 163.
Aemilius Paulus, L., at Cannae, 102.
Aemilius Paulus, L. (in Liguria), 127.
Aemilius Scaurus, M., 127.
Aemilius Scaurus, M. (first Governor of Syria), 209.
Aenaria, 169.
Aeneas of Troy, 7.
Aequians, the, 5, 31, 32.
Aes Corinthiacum, 133.

Aesernia, 57, 65.
Aesis, R., 40.
Aesium, 57.
Aethiopia, 309.
Aetolian League, the, 88, 114, 121; war with, 122-126.
Afranius, L., 260, 273.
Africa, province of, 193, 293, 301.
Agathocles of Syracuse, 60.
Ager publicus, 36, 53, 89, 144, 213.
Agger Servii, 14.
Agrigentum, 108.
Agrippa, *see* Vipsanius.
Agrippa Postumus, 318.
Ahala, C. Servilius, 40, 279.
Alba Fucentia, 57.
Alba Longa, 7, 31; destruction of, 12; war with, 21.
Alban Mount, the, 8.
Albani (Asia), 207.
Alesia, 245.
Alexander, king of the Molossi, 60.
Alexander, Macedonian Pretender, 132.
Alexandria, 266; Caesar at, 267-269, 302.
Algidus, Mt., 31.
Allobroges, 225, 226.
Alps, the, 2, 3, 97, 98; Alpine provinces: Cottiae, Maritimae, Penninae, 309.
Alsium, 57.
Amānus, Mt., 207.
Ambracia, 125, 126.

INDEX.

Ambrones, 159.
Amphipolis, 265.
Amulius, 7.
Anagnia, 61.
Ancona, 255.
Ancus Marcius, 12.
Ancyra, inscription at, 319.
Andriscus, 132.
Annius Milo, P., 250, 269, 270.
Antioch, 268, 270.
Antiochus the Great, king of Syria, 120; war with, 122-124.
Antiochus Epiphanes, 130.
Antiochus Asiaticus, 204.
Antiochus, king of Commagene, 209.
Antium, 32, 55, 171.
Antonius, C. (brother of the Triumvir), 283.
Antonius, C. (Cicero's colleague), 223, 225, 238.
Antonius, C. (Creticus), 206.
Antonius, L. (brother of the Triumvir), 291, 292.
Antonius, M. (the Orator), 171.
Antonius, M. (the Triumvir), 252-254, 259, 262, 270, 282, 284, 285, 292, 293, 296-302, 317.
Anxur, 55.
Aous, R., gorge of the, 120.
Apennines, the, 2, 255, 277.
Apollonia, 120, 262, 315.
Appian Way, the, 50, 54, 171, 201, 217, 250.
Appuleius Saturninus, L., 163.
Apuani, the, 127.
Apuli, the, 4, 59.
Apulia, Roman protectorate in, 50, 53.
Aquae Statiellae, 127; Aquae Sextiae, 155, 159, 169
Aquileia, 58, 126.
Aquilius, M', 143, 179.
Aquitania, 236, 306.
Arabia Petraea, 39, 207.
Arar, R., 24.
Aratores, 213.
Archelaus (officer of Mithridates), 180.
Archelaus of Comana, 209.

Archimedes, 107.
Ardea, 16, 25, 32, 55.
Argos, 122, 133.
Ariminum, 57, 101, 255.
Ariovistus, 237, 241, 242.
Aristarchus, king of Colchis, 209.
Aristobulus, 208.
Aristonicus, 175.
Armenia, 179, 203, 209, 295, 296, 309.
Army, the Roman, at first a temporary militia, 19; first paid, 35; organization at the time of Punic wars, 68; changes in, made by Marius, 162.
Arpi, 101.
Arsanias, Mt., 204.
Arsinoe, 269.
Arverni, 245.
Ascanius, 7.
Asculum, battle of, 63; revolt at, 65, 66.
Asia, 124, 125; province of, 147, 148, 154, 175, 180, 193, 300; taxes in, 216, 232.
Asia (Upper), settlement of, by Pompey, 209.
Asinius Pollio, C., 293, 320.
Astura, 46.
Athens, 88, 120, 134; Sulla's siege of, 181.
Athesis, R., 156.
Atilius Regulus, M., 81.
Atilius Regulus, C., 97.
Attaleia, in Pamphylia, 266.
Attalus I., king of Pergamus, 114, 120.
Attalus III., king of Pergamus, 147, 174.
Attius Varus, P., 255, 261, 268, 271.
Augustus, with Iulius in Spain, 279; in Rome after the assassination, 283; Consul, 284; joins Antony, 286, 287; his rising influence, 294, 295; his Principate, 303-326; his restorations and laws, 311-314; his death, 318.
Aurelius Cotta, M., 203.

INDEX.   329

Aurelius Propertius, Sext., 322.
Aurunci, the, 5.
Auximum, 58, 255, 261.
Aventine, the, 11, 153.

Baetis, R., Baetica, 108, 261.
Balearic Isles, 156.
Belgica, 236, 242, 243, 306.
Beneventum, battle of, 64; colony at, 57, 65.
Bibulus, M., 234, 249, 252, 262.
Bithynia, 174, 202, 208.
Bocchus, king of Mauretania, 158.
Boeotia, 123, 134, 181.
Boii, the, 59, 86, 97, 126.
Bona Dea, 231.
Bononia, 57, 126, 127.
Bovianum, 166.
Bovillae, 250.
Bribery, laws against, 131.
Britain, Caesar's first invasion of, 243, 244; second invasion, 244; intercourse with Augustus, 311.
Brundisium, 57, 173, 256, 258; peace of, 293.
Bruttium, 4; Bruttii, punishment of the, 116.
Brutus, *see* Iunius.
Brutus, Decimus, 260, 280, 284, 286.
Buxentum, 57.

Cabira (Galatia), 203.
Caecilius Metellus, Q. (Cos. B.C. 147), 133.
Caecilius Metellus, Q. (in Iugurthine war), 157, 163, 170, 171. Creticus, 206.
Caelius, M., 251, 269.
Caenina, 11.
Caere, 47.
Caesar, *see* Iulius and Augustus.
Caesar, Gaius, 317, 318.
Caesar, Lucius, 317, 318.
Caesarion, 297.
Calatia, 50.
Calendar, reforms in the, 11, 175.
Cales, 49, 55.
Camillus, M. Furius, 34, 41, 42, 45.

Campania, invaded by Samnites, 51; Hannibal in, 104; colonies in, 117; public land in, 153, 213, 233.
Campus Martius, the, 13.
Candace, 309.
Cannae, battle of, 102-105.
Cantabri, 308, 315.
Canuleius, C., 39.
Capite censi, 23, 162.
Capitolinus, Mons, 9-11; Iuppiter, 16.
Cappadocia, 174, 176, 201, 202, 209.
Capua, 50; siege of, 104, 105; *see also* 151, 170, 200, 252.
Caria, 123.
Carseoli, 57.
Carthage, commerce of, 2; early treaty with, 19; power of, in Sicily, 63, 64; rivalry of, with Rome, 66; constitution of, 74, 75; compared with Rome, 75, 76; first war with, 76, 77; mercenary war at, 84; second war with, 92-113; destruction of, 133-137; colony in (Iunonia), 151, 152; Marius at, 189; Caesar's colony in, 278.
Carthage, New (Carthagena), 95, 109, 110.
Casinum, 55.
Cassius, Longinus, C., 252, 268, 280, 283, 285, 288, 308.
Cassius, Longinus, L., 156.
Cassius, Q., 253, 254.
Cassius, Spurius, 31, 38.
Cassivelaunus, 244.
Castor and Pollux, 31.
Castrum Novum, 57.
Catilina, *see* Sergius.
Cato, *see* Porcius.
Caucasus, Mt., 207.
Caudine Forks, the, 49.
Celtiberians, the, 137.
Censorship, the, 39, 71.
Centuriae, 22, 90, 91; *Comitia Centuriata*, 118, 187.
Cephisus, R., 181.
Cercina, 169.

INDEX

Ceres, 26.
Chaeronea, battle of, 181.
Chalcis, 113, 121-123.
Chauci, 310.
Chersonesus Taurica, 178; Thracian, 122.
Cicero, *see* Tullius.
Cilicia, 175, 179, 193, 201, 203, 206, 295, 306.
Cilnius Maecenas, C., 293, 316.
Cimbri, the, 156, 159, 160.
Ciminian Forest, the, 44.
Cinca, R., 260.
Cincinnatus, 32, 40.
Cineas, 63.
Cinna, *see* Cornelius.
Circeii, 16, 32, 55, 168.
Circus Maximus, 9.
Cirta, 157.
Civitates foederatae, 49, 66, 83, 117, 160, 191.
Claudius, Appius, father-in-law of Tib. Gracchus, 147.
Claudius, Appius (legate of Sulla), 170.
Claudius Caecus, Appius, 54, 63, 90.
Claudius Marcellus, C., 253.
Claudius Marcellus, C. (husband and son of Octavia), 317.
Claudius Marcellus, M., 104, 105; his siege of Syracuse, 107, 108; his death, 105.
Claudius Nero, C., 106, 107.
Cleopatra, 266, 268, 292, 296, 298-302, 306.
Cloaca maxima, 13.
Clodius Pulcher, Publ., 204, 223; his sacrilege, 231; procures Cicero's exile, 237, 238; murdered by Milo, 250.
Cloelia, 30.
Clusium, 29, 40, 184.
Coelius, Mons, 9, 11, 12.
Collatia, 13.
Colleges, the sacred, 188.
Colline gate, the battles at the, 17, 184.
Colonies, 43, 55-58, 65, 117.
Columna rostrata, 80.

Comana, 270.
Comitia Curiata, 20, 23, 238; *Comitia Tributa*, 38, 54, 90, 91, 118, 187; *see also* Centuriae.
Conquisitores, 68.
Consuls originally called praetors, 25, 71.
Corcyra, 87, 114.
Corfinium, 257.
Corinth, burning of, 133, 134; colony at, 278.
Coriolanus, 32.
Corn, price of, 63; distributions of, 38, 151, 154, 197, 279.
Cornelia, mother of the Gracchi, 144.
Cornelii, persons enfranchised by Sulla, 188.
Cornelius Cethegus, C., 226.
Cornelius Cinna, L., 170, 181, 216.
Cornelius Dolabella, P., 270, 285.
Cornelius Gallus, C., 301.
Cornelius Lentulus, L., 253.
Cornelius Lentulus, P., 226.
Cornelius Scipio, P., father of Africanus, 97, 108.
Cornelius Scipio, Gn., brother of preceding, 108.
Cornelius Scipio Africanus, P., 109-113.
Cornelius Scipio Asiaticus, L., 124.
Cornelius Scipio Africanus, P. (Aemilianus), 137, 138, 147.
Cornelius Scipio Nasica, P., 126; (his son), 147.
Cornelius Sulla, L., 158, 166, 167; in Greece, 180-183; his advance upon Rome, 183; his dictatorship and legislation, 185-189; *see also* 215.
Cornificius, Q., 285.
Corsica, 80, 83, 85, 86, 193.
Cosa, 57, 65, 259.
Country life, 119.
Crassius, *see* Licinius.
Crĕmĕra, R., 32.
Cremona, 57, 86, 97, 117.
Crete, 193.
Crimea, the, 207.

INDEX. 331

Critolaus, 133.
Croton, 57.
Cures, 11.
Curiae, 20, 23; *Curio*, 27.
Curiatii and Horatii, 21.
Curio, C., 253, 259, 261.
Curius Dentatus, 52, 64.
Curules Magistratus, 71.
Cyclades, the, 120.
Cynoscephalae, battle of, 121.
Cyrene, 193.
Cyzicus, 203, 301.

Danube, R., 306, 309.
Decemvirs, the, 38, 39; decemviri sacrorum, 54.
Decius Mus, P., 47, 48.
Deiotărus, 203, 270.
Delium, 123.
Delos, 180.
Demetrias, 113, 121-123.
Demetrius of Pharos, 87.
Dertona, 58.
Diaeus, 133.
Diana, temple of, 16.
Dictatorship, the, 25, 73; of Sulla, 185; of Caesar, 261, 274.
Didius, C., 276.
Domitius Ahenobarbus, L. (Praetor B.C. 96), 143.
Domitius Ahenobarbus, L. (Cos. B.C. 54), 257, 259, 261.
Domitius Ahenobarbus, Cn., 288, 290, 292, 293, 297.
Domitius Calvinus, 264.
Drepana, 82.
Drusus, step-son of Augustus, 309.
Duilius, C., 80.
Duoviri (of a colony), 44; *duoviri navales*, 70.
Dyrrachium, 132, 260, 262.

Ebro, R., 95, 108, 261.
Ecnomus, battle of, 80, 81.
Egypt, 120, 130, 266, 297, 301; province of, 306-308.
Elateia, 181.
Elea, 78.
Empire, extent of in B.C. 146, 138; at the death of Sulla, 190; in time of Augustus, 306; partition of by Triumvirs, 286, 287, 289, 293.
Emporiae, 95.
Enipeus, R., 129.
Ennius, Q., 119.
Epicydes, 107.
Epirus, reduced to subjection, 129.
Eporedia, 58.
Equites, 23, 148, 154; quarrel with Senate, 213, 233.
Ergastula, 142.
Eryx, Mt., 82.
Etruria, Sulla's colonists in, 223.
Etruscans, the, 4, 8, 13, 29, 44, 52; religion of, 23.
Euboea, 120, 134.
Eumenes, king of Pergamus, 129.
Eunus, 142.
Euphrates, 207, 308.
Evander, 7.

Fabii, fall of the, 32-34.
Fabius, C., 260.
Fabius Maximus Cunctator, Q., 96, 101, 102.
Fabius Sanga, 226.
Fabrateria (Fregellae), 58, 151.
Fabricius Luscinus, C., 63.
Faesulae, 100, 224, 225.
Fanum, 255.
Feronia, fair at, 12.
Fidenae, 11, 34.
Fimbria, C. (legate of Valerius Flaccus), 183.
Firmum, 57, 65.
Flamen, 27.
Flaminius, C., 87, 100, 101.
Flavius, Cn., 54, 55.
Flora, 26.
Forum boarium, 19.
Forum Gallorum, 284.
Forum Iulii, 312.
Fregellae, 49, 55, 61.
Fregenae, 57.
Frentani, 66.
Frisii, 210.
Fucinus, lacus, 277.
Fulvia betrays the Catiline conspiracy, 224.

Fulvia, wife of Antony, 291-293.
Fulvius Flaccus, M., 153.
Fulvius Nobilior, M., 125.
Furies, grove of the, 153.

Gabinius (a Catilinian conspirator), 226.
Gabinius, Aulus, 202, 205, 266.
Gabino cinctu, 8.
Galatia, 125, 203, 205, 276, 306.
Gallia Celtica, 236.
Gallia Cisalpina, 3; Togata, 126, 127; Caesar in, 235.
Gallia Transalpina, the province in, 155, 235-237; lands in, 163; Caesar in, 240-246.
Gallus, Aelius, 309.
Gallus, Cornelius, 316.
Gaul, four provinces in, 306.
Gauls burn Rome, 40, 41; wars with, 44, 45, 86, 87; join Hannibal, 98, 101; cease to help Hannibal, 107.
Gaurus, Mt., 46.
Gelo of Syracuse, 38.
Gentes, 20.
Gergovia, 245.
Germania, superior and inferior, 306, 310.
Germanicus, 318.
Germans, 237, 241-243, 310.
Gladiators, 200.
Gracchus, *see* Sempronius.
Graviscae, 58.
Great Plains, battle in the, 112.
Greece, 2, 89; Macedonian supremacy in, 114; treatment of, by Rome, 130, 134, 193; Greek towns in Italy supply ships, 78; Greek influence in Rome, 89, 119; Greek States in league with Rome against Macedonia, 115; Greek cities in Asia, 123.

Hadria, 57.
Halycus, R., 76, 79.
Hamilcar Barca, 82, 93, 94.
Hannibal, 93; elected commander in Spain, 95; his oath, 96; his march to Italy, 97, 98; his victories in Italy, 99, 100; in South Italy, 101-104; in Asia, 123, 124.
Hanno at Messana, 78.
Hasdrubal, brother-in-law of Hannibal, 95.
Hasdrubal, brother of Hannibal, 106, 107, 109.
Hastati, 68.
Helvetii, the, 240, 241.
Heraclea, battle of, 61.
Hercte, Mt., 82.
Hercules, 19.
Hermaeum, 81.
Hernici, the, 5, 16, 38.
Hiempsal, 157, 169.
Hiero of Syracuse, 78, 79, 107.
Hieronymus, 107.
Hills, the seven, 14.
Hippocrates, 107.
Hirtius, Aulus, 284.
Homer, 7.
Horatii, the, 21.
Horatius Cocles, 29.
Horatius Flaccus, Q., 288, 321.
Hortensius (legate of Sulla), 18.
Hyrcanus, 208.

Ilerda, 260.
Ilipa in Spain, battle of, 110.
Illyricum, 87, 114, 129, 193, 235, 295.
Imperium, 71.
Indibilis, 110.
Ingauni, 127.
Insubres, 86, 126.
Interamna Lirinas, 55.
Interrex, 20.
Isaurians, the, 201.
Isthmian Games, proclamation at, 121, 122.
Italia, extension of name, 2-4; bad state of, in the 2nd century B.C., 143; amalgamated with Roman State, 191; depopulation of, 212, 213.
Italians and the citizenship, 147, 152.
Italica (Corfinium), 165, 166.
Italus, King, 4.

INDEX. 333

Ianiculum, 10, 29, 153, 171.
Ianus, 26; temple of, closed, 86, 304.
Ierusalem, capture of, by Pompey, 208.
Iews, the, 131, 209.
Iovis, 26.
Iuba, 261, 271, 273.
Iudicia, 149, 205, 215.
Iugurtha, 138, 156, 157.
Iulia, wife of Marius, 138.
Iulia, wife of Pompey, 234, 250.
Iulia, mother of Antony, 293.
Iulia, daughter of Augustus, 294, 315, 317; granddaughter, 323.
Iulius Caesar, L. (Cos. B.C. 90), 166.
Iulius Caesar, L. (his son), 255, 257, 278.
Iulius Caesar, C. (Dictator), 190, 203, 216, 218; advises against executing the Catiline conspirators, 226; pontifex maximus, 230; his provinces, 234, 235; his campaigns, in Gaul, 240-6; crosses the Rubicon, 253, 254; besieges Marseilles, 260; defeats Pompey's legates in Spain, 260, 261; Dictator and Consul, 261, 262; in Epirus, 262, 263; defeats Pompey in Pharsalia, 264, 265; in Egypt, 267-270; settles Asia, 270, 271; Dictator, 269, 274; in Africa, 271-273; his reforms, 274-278; in Spain, 276, 277; death, 280, 281.
Iunius Brutus, M. (first consul), 30.
Iunius Brutus, M. (father of the assassin of Caesar), 197.
Iunius Brutus, M., 279, 280, 281, 283, 288.
Iunius Norbanus, C., 183.
Iunius Silvanus, M., 156.
Iuno, temple of, 41.
Iuppiter Capitolinus, temple of, 13, 16.
Ius conubii, ius honorum, 38.
Iustinus, 320.

Khur, R., 207.
Kings, the seven, 10-16; expulsion of, 16, 23.

Labicum, 32.
Lacinian promontory, 60, 105, 107.
Lade, battle of, 120.
Laelius, C., 112.
Lamia, 123.
Larissa, 121, 264, 265.
Latifundia, 119.
Latin League, the, 5, 12, 16, 28, 29, 30, 31; dissolved, 46, 47.
Latinitas, 166, 235.
Latinus, king, 7.
Latium vetus, 5, 16.
Lavinium, 7.
Lesbos, 216, 265.
Lex Calpurnia de repetundis, 131; Canuleia, 39; Rupilia, 143; Iulia (B.C. 90), 166; Papiria Plautia, 166; Pompcia, 166; Gabinia, 205; Manilia, 207; Vatinia, 235.
Liber, 26.
Licinian rogations, 53.
Licinius Crassus, L., 164.
Licinius Crassus, M., 200, 218, 219, 233, 248, 249, 250, 308, 309.
Licinius Lucullus, L., 203, 220.
Licinius Muraena, 201.
Ligurians, the, 86, 107, 117, 126, 127.
Lilybaeum, 81, 111.
Lingones, 41.
Liparae Insulae, 83.
Liris, R., 7.
Lissus, 262.
Liternum, 57.
Livia, wife of Augustus, 294, 316.
Livius Andronicus, 89, 119.
Livius Drusus, M. (the elder), 152; (the younger), 164.
Livius Macatus, M., 105.
Livius, M. (Cos. B.C. 207), 106.
Livius, Titus, 320.
Locri Epizypherii, 78.
Lollius, M., 310.
Lucani, the, 4, 59, 68, 165.
Lucania, protectorate in, 50.

INDEX.

Lucca, 58, 126, 127; conference at, 249.
Luceria, 55.
Lucretia, 25.
Lucullus, *see* Licinius.
Lugdunensis, 306.
Luna, 58, 126.
Lupercalia, 19, 278.
Lupercus, 26.
Lusitani, 137, 197, 198.
Lutatius Catulus, C., 82.
Lutatius Catulus, Q., 159, 171.
Lutatius Catulus, Q. (Cos. B.C. 78), 197, 220.
Lycaonia and Galatia, province of, 306.

Macedonia, first war with, 113-115; second war with, 119-124; third war with, 128, 129; division of, into four districts, 120; province of, 132, 133, 193, 285.
Machares, 207.
Macra, R., 2.
Maelius, Spurius, 40.
Magna Graecia, 5, 59, 117.
Magnesia ad Sipylum, battle of, 124.
Mago, brother of Hannibal, 110, 112.
Maharbal, his advice to Hannibal, 104.
Mamertine Prison, the, 158, 227.
Mamertines, the, 64, 65, 77, 78.
Manilius, C., 207.
Manlius, C., his camp at Faesulae, 224-228.
Manlius, M., defends the Capitol, 41; put to death, 53.
Manlius, T., 47.
Manlius Vulso, Cn., 125.
Marcella, 315.
Marcellus, *see* Claudius.
Marius, C., 138, 157, 160-163, 167-172.
Marius, C. (the younger), 184.
Marius, the One-eyed, M., 203.
Marrucini, 66, 165.
Mars, temple of, 31.
Marsi, the, 9, 66.

Masannasa, 110-113, 134, 135, 138, 156.
Massilia, 155, 225, 259, 260, 261.
Massiva, 157.
Mastanabal, 156.
Mathos, 84.
Mauretania, 271, 306.
Mausoleum at Alexandria, 301.
Mavers, 26.
Memmius, C., 163.
Mesopotamia, 204, 309.
Metapontum, 4.
Metaurus, R., battle of the, 106, 107.
Metellus Scipio Pius (Q. Caecilius), father-in-law of Pompey, 251, 257, 264, 271.
Mevania, 50.
Micipsa, 156.
Milo, *see* Annius.
Milvian Bridge, the, 197.
Minerva, 26.
Minervia, 58.
Minturnae, 57, 168.
Minucius, 102.
Misenum, peace of, 293, 294; fleet at, 312.
Mithridates, 167, 176-182, 201-205, 207; death of, 208.
Mitylene, 201, 209.
Moesia, 306.
Mons sacer, 37.
Morini, 243.
Mucius, Caius, 30.
Mucius Scaevola, Q., 164, 176.
Munatius Plancus, L., 286.
Munda, battle of, 276.
Mundus, 8.
Municipium, 66, 68, 166.
Municius (Tr. Pl.), 152.
Murcia vallis, 9.
Mutina, 58, 87, 126, 197, 284.
Mylae, battle of, 80.

Nabis, tyrant of Sparta, 122.
Naevius, Cn., 89.
Narbo Martius, 155, 156.
Narbonensis, 306.
Narnia, 57.
Neapolis, 49, 78, 104.
Nepete, 55.

INDEX. 335

Neptunia, 58, 151, 153.
Nervii, 242, 244.
Nexum, 36, 53.
Nicomedes, 202.
Nicomedia, 203.
Nola, 50, 104, 166, 168-170.
Nomen Latinum, 10.
Norba, 32, 55.
Noreia, 156.
Numa Pompilius, 11, 275.
Numantia, siege of, 138, 157.
Numidia, 110, 156, 157, 289.
Numitor, 7.
Nursia, 291.

Octavia, sister of Augustus, 293-295, 317.
Octavius M. (Tr. Pl. B.C. 133), 145.
Octavius, Cn. (Cos. B.C. 87), 170.
Octavius, C., *see* Augustus.
Opimius, L., 153.
Oppius, Q., 179.
Optimates, 118, 161, 167, 195, 196, 214.
Orchomenus (in Arcadia), 133; (in Boeotia), 181, 182.
Ordo equester, 148, 149.
Oricum, 262.
Orodes, 266.
Ostia, 12, 17, 55, 171, 277.
Ovidius Naso, P., 322.

Paestum, 4, 57, 65.
Palaepolis, 49.
Palatine, the, 7, 8.
Palestine, 295.
Palilia, 10, 19.
Palladium, 27, 41.
Pamphylia, 201.
Panormus, 81.
Paphlagonia, 179.
Papirius Carbo, C. (land commissioner), 147.
Papirius Carbo, C., 166.
Papirius Carbo, Cn., 156, 170, 172, 183.
Papirius Cursor, L., 50, 65.
Paraetonium, 301.
Parma, 58, 87.

Parthians, the, 207, 250, 252, 265, 293, 295, 308.
Parthini, the, 293.
Patria potestas, 238.
Patricians, 23, 36, 37, 53, 54, 304.
Pedius, Q., 285.
Pedum, 46.
Peligni, 66, 165.
Pelusium, 266, 268, 269, 301.
Perduellio, 21.
Pergamos, 14, 148, 201.
Perpenna, M., 198.
Perseus, 129.
Perusia, 100; siege of, 292, 315.
Petilia, 201.
Petreius, M., 260, 273.
Petronius, 309.
Phanagoria, 209.
Pharnaces, son of Mithridates, 209, 270.
Pharos, 269.
Pharsalia, battle of, 264, 265.
Phasis, R., 207.
Philip V., king of Macedonia, first war with, 113-115; second war with, 119-121; death of, 129.
Philippi, battles of, 287-289.
Phoenice, peace of, 114, 119.
Phoenicians, 207.
Picentes, 66.
Pinarius Scarpus, Q., 301.
Pirates, 175, 183.
Pisae, 58, 126, 127.
Pisaurum, 57, 255.
Pisidians, 125, 201.
Pistoria, 228.
Placentia, 57, 86, 87, 98.
Plautius Silvanus, M., 166.
Plautus, T. Maccius, 119.
Plebs, 21, 22; struggles for equality, 35-40, 53-55, 139; *plebiscita*, 40, 54.
Po (Padanus), R., 4, 117.
Pompaedius, Silo, 295.
Pompeius Strabo, C., 166, 170.
Pompeius Rufus, Q., 168, 170.
Pompeius Magnus, Cn., 184, 190, 197, 198, 205-210, 214, 215; supported by Caesar, 217; character of, 218; his position after his

INDEX

return from the East, 231, 232; *praefectus annonae*, 248; at Lucca, 249; sole consul, 250, 251; his provinces in Spain, 249, 250, 252; quits Italy, 257; defeats Caesar near Apollonia, 264; defeated at Pharsalia, 265; his death, 266, 267.
Pompeius, Cn., at Munda, 276, 277.
Pompeius Sextus, 276 283, 285, 289, 293-295.
Pomptine Marshes, 16, 277.
Pons Sublicius, 12, 29.
Pontifex maximus, 26.
Pontiae, 55, 70.
Pontius, Caius, 49.
Pontus, kingdom of, 176, 271, 274.
Pontus, the, 176, 177, 202, 208
Popilius Laenas, C., 130.
Populares, 118, 161, 167, 215.
Populi fundi, 166.
Porcius Laeca, M., 224.
Porcius Cato, M. (the Censor), 128, 135.
Porcius Cato, M. (Uticensis), 221, 240, 259, 271-273.
Porsena, 29.
Postumius Albus, A., 31.
Postumius, Sp., 49.
Potentia, 57, 126.
Pothinus, 267-269.
Praeneste, 61, 184.
Praetorship, the, 54, 71; *praetor peregrinus*, 88.
Princeps, 305, 316, 317.
Princeps Senatus, 304.
Principes, 68.
Proconsulare imperium, 305.
Procurator, 305.
Proscriptions, 184, 287.
Province, first, 83; spoliation of the provinces, 131; numbers and government of, 191-193; grievances in, 214; division between the Emperor and Senate, 304, 305.
Ptolemy Epiphanes, king of Egypt, 120.
Ptolemy Auletes, 248.
Ptolemy XII., 266, 268, 269, 274.

Ptolemy XIII., 269.
Publicani, 150, 175, 232.
Punic Wars, I., 76-83; II., 92-115; III., 134-137.
Puteoli, 57.
Pydna, battle of, 129.
Pyrgi, 57.
Pyrrhus, king of Epirus, invades Italy, 60-63; goes to Sicily, 63, 64; defeated at Beneventum, 64, 65; his capital, 125.

Quaestiones perpetuae, 131, 149, 189, 215.
Quaestors, 72.
Quintius Flamininus, T., 120-122.
Quirinal, the, 11.
Quirites, 11; *fossa Quiritium*, 12.

Ramnes, Titii, and Luceres, 20.
Raudian plains, the, 160.
Ravenna, 253, 255; fleet at, 312.
Regillus, Lake, battle of, 31.
Regulus, *see* Atilius.
Religion of Rome, 25-27; affected by Greek theology, 26.
Rhegium, capture of, 65.
Rhine, Caesar crosses the, 243; 308.
Rhodes, 120, 124, 180, 203, 217, 265.
Rhone, R., 97, 98, 241, 309.
Robigus, 2.
Roma quadrata, 8.
Roman history, importance of, 1, 2; government, 70, 71; magistrates, 71-73; Senate, 73, 74; navy, 70, 79; growth of empire, 138, 139; supremacy in Mediterranean, 113; *ager Romanus*, 10.
Rome, site of, 7; date of foundation, 10; origin of name, 18; walls of, 13.
Romulus, reign of, 10; Romulus and Remus, legend of, 7, 20.
Rorarii, 68.
Rubicon, R., 2, 255.
Rupilius, P., 143.
Rutilius Lupus, P., 166.
Rutilius Rufus, P., 176.

INDEX.

Sabellians, the, 4.
Sabine women, seizure of, 11; Sabines, 5; joint occupation of Rome, 11; wars with, 12.
Saguntum, 95, 96.
Salassi, 295.
Salernum, 57.
Saltus Castulonensis, 95, 108.
Salvidienus Rufus, 291, 316.
Salvius, 266.
Samnites, the, 5, 13, 45; first war with, 46; second war with, 48-50; third war with, 50-53; in the Social war, 165, 166; Sulla's severities to, 186; Samnium, 7.
Samos, 298, 301.
Sardinia, 79; made a Roman province, 84, 112, 193, 261, 291.
Saticula, 46, 55.
Satricum, 55.
Saturnia, 9, (Etruria) 58.
Saturninus, *see* Appuleius.
Scipio, *see* Cornelius.
Scotussa, 264.
Scribonia, wife of Augustus, 292, 294.
Secession of Plebs, 37.
Sempronius Gracchus, Tib. (the elder), 128, 138.
Sempronius Gracchus, Tib. (Tr. Pl. B.C. 133), 144-146.
Sempronius Gracchus, C., 148-152.
Sempronius Longus, Tib., 98.
Sena Gallica, 57.
Sena, R., 106.
Senate, the, 20, 73, 74, 90, 118; Sulla's reform of, 186; hostility of Equites to, 215; treatment of, by Iulius Caesar, 278; relations with Augustus, 313.
Senatus consultum ultimum, 146, 151, 224, 228, 254, 255.
Senones, 40, 41, 52, 59.
Sentinum, 291.
Septimius, 266.
Septimontium, 10.
Sergius Catilina, L., 185, 222-228.
Sertorius, Q., 170, 197-199, 203.
Servilius Caepio, Q., 137.
Servilius Glaucia, C., 163.

Servilius Vatia Isauricus, P., 201, 206.
Servius Tullius, 13, 14; his reforms, 22, 23; his wall, 14.
Setia, 55.
Sextius Calvinus, C., 155.
Sibyl, the, 27.
Sicambri, 243, 310.
Sicily, Pyrrhus in, 63; war in, 79-82, 107, 108; made a province, 83; Marcellus in, 107, 108; slave war in, 142, 143; abandoned by Cato, 261; held by Sext. Pompeius, 291.
Sicoris, R., 260, 261.
Sicyon, 134.
Sidon, 209.
Signia, 16, 31, 55.
Sinope, 202.
Sinuessa, 57.
Sipontum, 57.
Slaves, 141, 142.
Social war, 64-167.
Socii navales, 80.
Soldiers, pay of, 35.
Sora, 57.
Soracte, Mt., 12.
Sosius, C., 295, 297.
Spain, 92; Carthaginians in, 93-96, 97; the Scipios in, 108-110, 113; organization under Cato and Gracchus, 127, 128; provinces in, 193; Caesar in, 217, 230, 260, 276; Augustus in, 308.
Sparta and the Achaean League, 133; its position under Rome, 134.
Spartacus, 199-201.
Spendius, 84.
Spoletium, 57.
Spolia opima, 34.
Statilius, 226.
Suessa Pometia, 16, 55; Suessa Aurunca, 55.
Suessula, 46.
Sulla, *see* Cornelius.
Sulla, Faustus, 273.
Sulpicius, P., 167-169.
Sumptuary laws, 132.
Sutrium, 55.

Sweet Harbour, the, 299.
Syphax, 110-112.
Syracuse, 63; siege of, by Marcellus, 107, 108; works of art from, 110.
Syria, province of, 207, 208, 249, 252, 285, 306, 308.

Tannetum, 97.
Tarentum, 59-61, 65, 78, 105, 118, 151.
Tarpeian Rock, 53, 168.
Tarquinius Priscus, 12, 13; Superbus, 16.
Tarraco, 93, 95.
Tarsus, 270.
Taurini, the, 98.
Taurus, Mt., 124, 201.
Taxilus, 181.
Teanum Sidicinum, 257.
Tellus, 26.
Tempe, 121, 264.
Tempsa, 57.
Tencteri, 310.
Terentius Varro, C., 102-104.
Terentius Varro, M., 260, 261, 320.
Terracina, 32.
Teuta, Queen, 87, 88.
Teutones, 156, 159, 160.
Thapsus, battle of, 271, 272.
Theodotus, 266.
Theophanes, 165.
Thermopylae, battles near, 124, 133, 181.
Thurii, 57, 60, 200.
Tiber, R., 7; first bridge over, 12; embankment of, 312.
Tiberius (Caesar), 309; his father, Tiberius Nero, 316.
Tibullus, Aulus, 321.
Ticinus, R., battle of the, 98.
Tifata, Mt., 101.
Tifernum, 46.
Tigranes, 203, 204, 207.
Tigranocerta, 204.
Tigurini, 156.
Tillius Cimber, L., 281.
Tolumnius of Veii, 34.
Tomi, 322.

Trasimene Lake, battle of, 100, 101.
Trebia, R., battle on the, 98.
Trebonius, C., 249, 260, 280.
Treveri, 244.
Triarii, 68.
Tribuni aerarii, 205, 216, 275.
Tribunicia potestas, 303, 304.
Tribes, 22; increase of, 44.
Tribuni militares consulari potestate, 39, 53.
Tribuni plebis, 35-37, 91; Sulla's measures against, 188; powers restored by Pompey, 205.
Tributum, 35; abolished for citizens, 131.
Triumph, a, 31.
Triumvirate, first, 219, 232-234; the second, 285, 296.
Trogus, Pompeius, 320.
Tryphon, 143.
Tullius Cicero, M., 190, 221, 222; his contests with Catiline, 223-228; banished, 238, 239; joins Pompey in Epirus, 261; his death, 285; as a writer, 320.
Tullius Cicero, Q., 244.
Tyre, 209.

Umbrians, the, 4, 52.
Usipetes, 310.
Utens, R., 40.
Utica, 111, 135, 271, 273.

Vada Sabbata, 127.
Vadimonian Lake, battle of the, 50.
Valentia, 57.
Valerius, L., at Tarentum, 60.
Valerius Flaccus, L., 172, 182.
Valerius Laevinus, P., 61.
Valerius Corvus, 45.
Valerius, Quintus, 159.
Valerius Messala, M., 295, 320, 322.
Varius, Q., 165.
Varro, *see* Terentius.
Varus, Quintilius, 310.
Vatinius, P., 234.
Vectigal, 134, 213.

INDEX.

Veii, 11, 29, 32-35, 41.
Velitrae, 55.
Veneti of N. Italy, 41, 126; in Gaul, 243.
Ventidius Bassus, P., 285, 293, 295.
Venusia, 57, 104, 105.
Vercellae, 160.
Vercingetorix, 245.
Vergilius Maro, P., 321.
Verres, C., 195.
Veseris, 46.
Vesontio, 242.
Vesta and Vestal Virgins, 27, 41, 319.
Vestini, 165.
Via Flaminia, 87, 312; Aemilia, 26, 126; Aemilia Scauri, 127; Aemilia Lepidi, 127; Egnatia, 133, 264, 288. *See* Appian Way.
Vibius Pansa, C., 284.
Vipsanius Agrippa, M., 292, 293, 308, 315.
Viriathus, 137.
Volscians, the, 5, 16, 31, 32, 42-44.
Volternum, 57.
Volturnus, R., 101.

Xanthippus, 81.

Zama, battle of, 112, 120.
Zela, battle of, 271.

GLASGOW: PRINTED AT THE UNIVERSITY PRESS BY ROBERT MACLEHOSE AND CO.

www.ingramcontent.com/pod-product-compliance
Lightning Source LLC
Chambersburg PA
CBHW020230240426
43672CB00006B/475